Reading the Church Fathers

Reading the Church Fathers

Edited by
Morwenna Ludlow
and
Scot Douglass

t & t clark

Published by T&T Clark
A Continuum imprint
The Tower Building   80 Maiden Lane
11 York Road   Suite 704
London SE1 7NX   New York, NY 10038

www.continuumbooks.com

British Library Cataloguing-in-Publication Data
A catalogue record for this book is available from the British Library.

ISBN: HB: 978-0-567-53803-1
       PB: 978-0-567-60762-1

Typeset by Newgen Imaging Systems Pvt Ltd, Chennai, India
Printed and bound in Great Britain

CONTENTS

PART III: READING THE FATHERS READING THEMSELVES

ACKNOWLEDGEMENTS

Interdisciplinary dialogue demands of its participants not only patience and intellectual flexibility, but also a willingness to have one's own methodology exposed to scrutiny. Particularly in a small group and when a considerable amount of time is spent on each paper, each participant allows his or her work to be exposed and vulnerable. We would like to acknowledge here with gratitude the generosity, enthusiasm and good humour with which our contributors engaged in this task (not least because it was not made easier by the combined effects of altitude and jet lag).

For the funding of the symposium from which this book developed, we would like to extend our thanks to the University of Colorado at Boulder, specifically to the Center for Humanities and the Arts, The Herbst Program of Humanities and the Engineering Honors Program. For the opportunity to spend six months in the United States, Morwenna would like to thank Princeton Theological Seminary, at which she was a visiting scholar, and her home department of theology and religion at the University of Exeter. Many thanks to the students of the University of Colorado at Boulder/ the Engineering Honors Program for their help with the symposium (Takako Hirokawa and Erik Bergal, in particular, for their French translation work), and to Jon Roberts (University of Exeter) for his editorial work on the final text.

Finally, to our families: thank you for climbing this mountain with us.

Participants in the Conversation

Virginia Burrus is Professor of Early Church History and Chair of the Graduate Division of Religion at Drew University. She has published, most recently, *Saving Shame: Martyrs, Saints, and Other Abject Subjects* (University of Pennsylvania Press, 2008) and *Seducing Augustine: Bodies, Desires, Confessions* (Fordham, 2010), the latter was co-authored with Mark Jordan and Karmen MacKendrick.

Matthieu Cassin is post-doctoral fellow of the Fondation Thiers and associate researcher of the Institut de recherche et d'histoire des textes (CNRS, Paris). He is currently working on the transmission and reception of Gregory of Nyssa's works and on the history of manuscripts and libraries.

Scot Douglass is Professor in the Herbst Program of Humanities, Faculty Director of the Engineering Honors Program, Faculty-in-Residence and Director of the Andrews Hall Residential College at the University of Colorado, Boulder.

Tamsin Jones is Lecturer on Religion and Director of Undergraduate Studies for the Committee on the Study of Religion at Harvard University. Her recent book, *A Genealogy of Marion's Philosophy of Religion: Apparent Darkness* (Indiana University Press, 2011) probes the coherence of Marion's phenomenological project through an analysis of his use of early Christian sources.

Morwenna Ludlow is Lecturer in Patristics at the University of Exeter. She is interested in the reception of the Church Fathers by modern theologians and philosophers and on this theme has published *Gregory of Nyssa, Ancient and (Post)modern* (Oxford University Press, 2007). She has also published an introduction to Christianity in late antiquity: *The Early Church* (I. B. Tauris, 2009).

David Newheiser is a Ph.D. student in Theology at the University of Chicago. His recent research aims to illuminate the character of hope, love and theological discourse through readings that carefully attend to the rich ambivalence of Christian tradition.

Johannes Zachhuber is Reader of Theology in the University of Oxford. He works on Christian theology in late antiquity and in the nineteenth and twentieth centuries.

FOREWORD

In May 2009, a group of scholars met high in the Rocky Mountains above Boulder, Colorado to present, discuss and argue about their various ways of 'reading the fathers'. In choosing our protagonists for that colloquium – now the contributors to this book – we had in mind no plan to come up with an agreed formula for the best way to read these texts, nor any inclination towards forming a new movement or sensibility whose key focus would be the reading of these texts. Rather, our aim was to bring together a rather diverse collection of scholars who, while having different methodological approaches, would be willing both to offer an example of their own practice and to engage in constructive debate of their own and others' ways of reading early Christian texts.

This book, then, is neither a sure-footed defence of 'postmodern' readings of the fathers, nor a plaidoyer for methods based on modern philological and historico-critical tools. Nor, finally, does it attempt to recover the fathers' hermeneutical methods as *the* means towards a good reading of their own works. Rather than advocate any particular method, this book seeks to ask what exactly is meant by 'a good reading'. More precisely, through constructive engagement with various answers to that question, it seeks to interrogate the assumptions which underlie contemporary readings of the fathers.

One of the starting points of this book is that these assumptions often remain unquestioned. Frequently, indeed, groups of scholars who read the fathers are bound together by common notions about what makes a 'good' reading and – perhaps even more strongly – what makes a 'bad' reading. Far from being subjected to scrutiny, these assumptions form the basis for tribal loyalties in such a way that an attempt to critique them can be perceived as an attack on one's own tribe or even as the announcement of one's own departure. Conversely, it is a given that the methods of other tribes must necessarily be subject to criticism, even though attacks on rival methods frequently have a kind of ritual or game-like quality, which suggests that the attacks have as much to do with the reinforcement of the attackers' own identity as they do with a profound engagement with rival methods. In this way, readers of the church fathers sometimes seem to re-enact the characteristics of the literature they are reading: the 'ortho-dox' are pitted against 'heretics', united in the texts they are reading and in their confidence in the self-evidence of their own position, though divided by their respective hermeneutical approaches. There are, of course, scholars who have challenged such tribalism, but nevertheless, the phenomenon of those united in their reading matter, but divided by method, will be familiar to those attending international conferences on the fathers. Scholars are even divided by the way in which we label ourselves: Patristics scholar or scholar of late antiquity? Church history or early Christian studies? Historian, philosopher or theologian?

With these issues in mind, we invited a group of scholars who could not easily be grouped together under any common banner, save for their inter-est in the Christian texts of late antiquity. Some were already known to each other through their common interest in Gregory of Nyssa – but this volume is no more intended to be a book 'about' readings of Gregory than it is a book on the fathers and postmodernism. Our group included scholars who could identify themselves with one or more of the disciplines of church history, classical philology, comparative literature, Patristics, philosophy and systematic theology. In recognition that different national intellectual cultures often reinforce the tribalism described above the group comprised scholars who were variously formed in British, French, German and North American scholarly traditions. Having said all this, however, we are not saying that the members of our group can claim to be repres-entative of all possible ways of reading the fathers: inevitably in an exercise like this the choice falls short of being comprehensive, and it is well to acknowledge that from the start. One obvious criterion for inclusion, for instance, was a readiness to join in the conversation, which inevitably ruled out some of the more polarized views. We acknowledge that there is a degree to which we have, by our enthusiasm for this kind of interdisciplinary exercise, constituted our own tribe.

Our contributors were asked to submit papers which were read in advance of the colloquium in the Rockies and then, in the light of our discussions, rewritten for this volume. Each was asked to write something which broadly addressed the question 'how can/should one read the fathers?' What was interesting and most rewarding about the resultant papers was the way in which each not only was a paper about a certain kind of reading, but also enacted or put that kind of reading into practice. This is, perhaps most evident in **Virginia Burrus**'s paper, for, as she writes, 'I am not *merely* searching for a performative practice of writing that does justice to the complex temporality of reading and thus of historiography (though that too!). I am also anticipating some quite specific interpretive pay-offs' (p. 44). In her chapter, Burrus reads Augustine, Franz Rosenzweig and Elliot Wolfson – but much more. For the dynamics of her reading strategy move backwards from Rosenzweig's reading of Augustine to Augustine himself and thence forwards to Wolfson's reading of Rosenzweig. Wolfson's interpretation of Rosenzweig's musings on time and eternity reflects Wolfson's own concerns with mysticism (especially Kabbalah) and with philosophical postmodernism: 'To read Rosenzweig postmodernly', Burrus writes of Wolfson's approach, 'is to read directly into some of the greatest tensions in his text' (p. 51). The exposing of these tensions, however, reflects light back not only on Rosenzweig, but on Augustine himself. Indeed, Burrus concludes that from the perspective of Wolfson's reading, neither writer 'has pushed the theory of time and eternity to its logical conclusion' (p. 54). Wolfson's reading therefore leads Burrus to the discovery of some surprising affinities not only in Augustine's and Rosenzweig's respective 'readings' of time and eternity, but also in their readings of their own religious traditions. It is precisely these affinities which, Burrus suggests, have the potential radically to undermine the very differences which Augustine's and Rosenzweig's own reading practices presuppose.

Burrus seems herself to be following Wolfson's advice on reading Rosenzweig: 'to think in his footsteps – the thinking that is the highest mode of thanking', although her 'thinking in the footsteps' also involves a certain amount of scholarly 'tracking' of Augustine's trail.[1] This scholarly tracking has often been done in the academy through the discipline of reception history, and both Johannes Zachhuber and David Newheiser draw on this method in their analyses of two different postmodern readers of Pseudo-Dionysius. For **David Newheiser**, the reception history of Pseudo-Dionysius reveals that some scholars flatten the significance of the Dionysian corpus by demanding that he be read in light of a particular hypothesized historical context. By contrast, Newheiser argues, Jacques Derrida's recognition that no univocal reading is adequate not only allows him to attend to the ambivalence of Dionysius's texts but also resonates with Dionysius's own reading practices. In both cases, these reading practices are conditioned by the complex relationship in their thought between the present and what is to come, for both argue that the silence required by the future calls for responsible speech in the present. Newheiser applies this insight to the problem of reading texts from the past by suggesting that while the distance between the interpreter's present and the text's past means that no interpretation is adequate, this apparent failure opens up a perpetual re-reading in the spirit of an eschatological responsibility.

In Newheiser's chapter, then, the 'tracing of the tracks' of Dionysius in his later readers makes possible Newheiser's main task of 'thinking in the footsteps' of both Dionysius and Derrida. **Johannes Zachhuber** also writes about Dionysius, but this time as read by Jean-Luc Marion. For Zachhuber, more than for Newheiser, the project of 'tracing the tracks' is the main focus, since Zachhuber contends that only in the light of the reception history of Dionysius does Marion's reading makes sense: '[Marion's] "reading" of Dionysius . . . presupposes an advanced stage of the Areopagite's reception history' (p. 18). But Zachhuber's project here is not simply to elucidate Marion's reading – rather it interrogates the very nature of reading (and of reception history) itself. In particular he suggests that attention to the complexities of the reception history of a text explodes what might be called the myth of the individual reader: the myth, that is, that reading Dionysius (for example) consists in the 'ahistorical encounter between a contemporary reader and a 1500-year-old text' (p. 3). While modernity has found it very tempting to assume an intimacy between a reader and a text, in fact, Zachhuber argues, this intimacy is always disrupted by the history of the reading of the text and the culture in which it is read – that is, its reception history. The recognition of this disruption is as necessary as was the modern scholarly disruption of the premodern assumption of a different kind of intimacy, 'not that of an individual encounter, but that of communal possession on account of seemingly unbroken tradition' (p. 5). A more nuanced attention to the history of the text disrupts both kinds of illusory 'intimacy' but does not replace them with an unbridgeable gulf between the text and its the reader, for it is precisely a better understanding of reception history which can reconnect texts with their readers and do justice both to the creative and receptive aspects of reading. Zachhuber examines this in the context of eighteenth-, nineteenth- and twentieth-century thinkers such as Kant, Schelling, Nietzsche, Heidegger, Barth, Derrida, Levinas and Balthasar.

While Burrus, Newheiser and Zachhuber can all be characterized as reading a postmodern reader of the fathers, albeit in three rather different ways, a second method evident in our papers is to read a church father *in parallel with* a postmodern thinker with whom he might be seen to resonate but who had not read the father in question. Thus Tamsin Jones reads Gregory of Nyssa in parallel with Levinas, and Scot Douglass reads him with Heidegger. **Tamsin Jones's** paper proceeds through a comparison of Gregory's and Levinas's understandings of what kind of text Scripture is and, consequently, what kind of reading and reader it calls for. She argues that despite the distinct historical and theological milieus of Gregory and Levinas, there are structural similarities in their thought: both link the hiddenness of Scripture with divine incomprehensibility, and from this they draw the conclusions, first, that revelation requires infinite translation to be completed and, secondly, that subjectivity is cultivated through a particular understanding of reading, that is, one marked by an increasingly expansive desire. Through analysing what Levinas and Gregory both have to say about reading authoritative texts, Jones questions contemporary notions of reading and authority as well. Ancient and modern authors, like Gregory and Levinas (indeed like all the authors examined in this book), are regarded as authorities in their own spheres, with their own devotees who are understandably protective of that interpretative domain. So, Jones challenges us with the question: might not her model of reading Gregory 'with' Levinas break open the way in which we are 'licensed' to read them both?

Scot Douglass reads Gregory 'with' Martin Heidegger, working from a conviction that despite their differences – notably 'a difference regarding the possibility of a revelation of the type claimed within Christianity' (p. 84) – there are significant resonances, both methodological and thematic. With regard to method, Douglass argues that both thinkers share a concern to clarify (or at least to sound caution about) the 'inner possibility' of pure knowledge. He suggests that Heidegger's interrogation of metaphysics might provide a useful frame for thinking about Gregory's critique of Eunomius's epistemological claims in the *Contra Eunomium* books I–III. But this critical mode is complemented in each thinker by what one might call a constructive mode, in which each reflects on the consequent possibilities for doing philosophy/theology, the consequent possibilities of the appearance of truth. Through an analysis of Heidegger's essay 'On the Origin of the Work of Art', Douglass suggests that Heidegger's reflections on materiality and truth resonate with Gregory's thought about doing theology. For Heidegger, 'the truth of art cannot be separated from its thingly manifestation' (p. 89); for Gregory, theology cannot be done except with the *diastema* of God's creation. One might say, then, that this reading 'with' Heidegger reveals Gregory not as concerned with theology as a pure science of knowing, but as an art: 'As a result, the question of Art in its widest sense – the visual arts, poetry, literature and music – is first and foremost a question for the Christian theologian' (p. 88). Douglass suggests that such a reading of Gregory with a thinker like Heidegger, is not eisegesis, but re-opens possibilities in his texts which have become obscured in their later reception history.

While the chapters mentioned so far all focus explicitly on the intersection between a reading of a postmodern writer and a reading of one of the fathers, our final two papers look more intently at the fathers themselves and, specifically, how those fathers viewed themselves as readers and writers. These papers ask whether more might still be learnt from the reading (and writing) strategies of the fathers themselves: thus, for example, **Matthieu Cassin** argues, on philological grounds, that a scholarly reading of the fathers should be more open to the literary qualities of patristic theological writing. He begins by noting that this text was 'most often read . . . through a single frame: research on the history of Christian doctrine' (p. 110). Through a careful study of Gregory's *Contra Eunomium* III, its context and paratext, Cassin suggests that an exclusively doctrinal frame is too narrow and that a broader – but still historical – method can 'unfold more readings' of this rich text (p. 110). He claims neither that his new reading is neutral nor that it is exhaustive, and he is well aware of the impossibility of freeing the text from the layers of its successive interpretations. Nevertheless, he challenges the implicit claim of some interpreters of the fathers that it is only contemporary philosophy that can shed new light on a text. Rather, Cassin defends the use of the philological method: the problem is not that philology *necessarily* 'closes down' the text, but that it has often been put to the service of particular kinds of narrow textual reading. In particular, Cassin suggests that the usual 'dogmatic' reading of the *Contra Eunomium* needs to be complemented by a reading which takes into account Gregory's self-confessed literary ambitions. A deeper understanding of Gregory's employment of polemic, for example, highlights the literary qualities of the text – not least the fact that one of the aims of the text was to give its readers pleasure.

While Cassin works from 'Nyssen's hints about how to read Nyssen's text' (p. 111), **Morwenna Ludlow** asks what it would look like if one attempted to read the fathers using the guidelines that they set down for their own reading of Scripture. While this method might seem anachronistic, she suggests that it might be fruitful because a writer like Origen was, after all, wrestling with the same kind of problem as a twenty-first-century reader of the fathers: how should one read a text which comes from a context so different from one's own? Origen's method of interpreting the Bible rested on the principle that 'just as a person consists of body, mind/soul and spirit, so in the same way does the scripture': it is the exegete's role to investigate all the meanings of Scripture – bodily, soulish and spiritual (Origen, *On First Principles* IV.2.4). Ludlow suggests that one does not have to read this method as a transition from the material to the immaterial/spiritual (as many earlier commentators have done). Rather, one can read it as possessing a dynamic movement from the past (the 'bodily' meaning) to the present circumstances of the reader (the 'mind' or 'soul-ish' meaning) and beyond (the 'spiritual' meaning). In particular, the spiritual meaning of the text seems to suggest to Origen the possibility of future, even eschatological, meanings which lie beyond present readers' knowledge and which preclude them from regarding their own interpretations as totalizing or absolute. A key feature of Origen's method in theory (which he does not always pursue in practice) is that the present and future meanings should not undermine the validity of the way in which the text has been read in the past. Ludlow suggests that this dynamic reading of Origen's hermeneutics might serve as the basis for a model of reading the fathers today, while avoiding any suggestion that the three kinds of meaning are discrete or can be practiced sequentially in isolation. Her thesis is quite the opposite and demands a recognition of the complexity of the relationships between different kinds of meaning (and, indeed, between different *ways* of reading). Using Gregory of Nyssa and Origen as foils for each other, Ludlow examines the degree to which each writer acknowledges both a fluidity between the different meanings of a text and the text's own resistance to the complete absorption of one meaning into the other – a sense of *relative* permeability which, she suggests, resonates with the contemporary recognition of the way in which each reader's interpretation is distinct, yet not absolutely discrete from a text's reception history.

Given the very general rubric our contributors received, as well as their own widely divergent research interests and academic contexts, we were all struck by the remarkable lines of convergence which emerged from the papers and from the discussions at the colloquium – convergences which went well beyond the fact that three of us chose to write on Gregory of Nyssa and two on Pseudo-Dionysius. The choice to focus on these writers, together with Origen and Augustine, was not in itself surprising, given those fathers' interest in hermeneutical questions. Nor was it surprising that for the fathers the key hermeneutical question was 'how should one read Scripture?', while the question for later thinkers is much broader (although not excluding the question of Scripture, as the studies of Rosenzweig and Levinas show).

One striking theme was the importance in the twentieth and twenty-first century of reading the early church fathers through, or with, writers who came from a Jewish tradition. Since the reading of the fathers within Christianity is often complexified by overt or covert confessional loyalties, the insights of writers like Derrida, Levinas, Rosenzweig and Wolfson shed interesting new light on certain aspects of Christian reading strategies which are perhaps less examined within Christianity itself. As Tamsin Jones notes, some Jewish thinkers have accused Christian hermeneutics of 'logocentrism' (a reading practice especially associated with allegory, in which 'every text contains a single meaning, and behind one signifier there is always one single intended "true" signified' (p. 65)), contrasting this with, for example, the polyvalence of Midrash. While not denying the usefulness of this contrast as a critique of many Christian reading practices, Jones shows that it need not describe all Christian hermeneutics. In particular, she argues that allegorical interpretation as practised by Gregory of Nyssa seems precisely to steer away from univocal readings. The question then becomes not why Christians did not pursue polyvalent reading strategies, but why those strategies were not (or did not remain) more dominant. Another accusation is that Christian allegorical hermeneutics as practised by Origen, for example, led to abstract and de-historicizing readings which had the effect of 'writing out' Jews from the biblical text. Though one must acknowledge that this was the effect of much Christian interpretation of the Hebrew Bible, Ludlow's paper suggests that abstraction and de-historicization is not a necessary consequence of the idea that there are multiple levels of meaning in a text. Jones and Ludlow thus both remind one of the importance of understanding how one hermeneutical method (such as allegorical interpretation) might be applied in different ways in various historical/religious/cultural contexts, challenging analyses that define any particular hermeneutical method too narrowly.

More broadly, the practice of reading the fathers with or through writers like Rosenzweig and Derrida raises the question of reading and responsibility in a provocative way. As Burrus and Newheiser discuss, the intellectual and/or spiritual commitments of Rosenzweig and Derrida are very complex, too complex certainly for one to be able to label their interpretations of Augustine or Dionysius as in any way definitively 'Jewish'. Yet to write out that dimension of their background would also be to miss something. Reading the fathers with such writers, then, perhaps forces us to grapple with the *particularity* both of the reader and the author being read: the question is not the facile '*can* a "Jewish" reading of a "Christian" text be a good one?', but 'what is it that make *this* reading of *that* text a good one?' Finally, reading the fathers through Jewish readers disrupts any assumption that it is a homogenous community which is reading these texts. That the reception history of the fathers is a good deal more complex than a question of 'Christian tradition' is revealed by, for example, the particular chains of reception created by Burrus-reading-Rosenzweig-reading-Augustine-reading-Genesis, or Ludlow-reading-Boyarin-reading-Origen-reading-Exodus.

Reading the fathers with these writers also reminds one that the assumption that a 'good' reading is a responsible reading merely raises further

questions: Responsible to what – or to whom? Which community of
readers? Which authority? Several of our papers highlighted the point that
readers are readers-in-communities, whether those communities are faith
communities who feel that they have a particular stake in the interpretation of a particular thinker (see, for example, Newheiser's discussion of
Eastern Orthodox interpretations of Pseudo-Dionsyius) or communities of
scholars in today's universities who feel that they have a stake in defending
a particular method (such as historical criticism). In each case a particular
community identifies itself implicitly or explicitly with a particular kind
of authority against which its reading practices are judged. A reading
community is perhaps usually assumed to be synchronic, but Zachhuber's
paper reminds us of the (illusory) intimacy between a text and a reader in
a community whose members assume themselves to be connected to the
author by an unbroken chain of tradition (another form of authority).
That is not to say there is no such thing as a diachronic reading community, however: Zachhuber's paper encourages us to think more deeply
about the complex character of a community of readers, who are each
receptive and creative, over time. This analysis is echoed in Jones's reading
of Levinas's understanding of revelation: 'The fact that it is the reader who,
in part, writes revelation presupposes that what "I" as the reader write is
only partial; there are other "I's", other readers, who are in turn scribes,
or interpreters of that which they encounter in the revelation of scripture'
(p. 67).

   A third important theme in our papers was that of time. To a greater or
lesser extent, each of our contributors grapples with the question of
what makes a good reading of a text which was written so long ago. Cassin
suggests that although historical methods cannot recover a pristine text
free from later interpretational accretions ('I do not want to bleach the text
of Gregory, as German archaeology did with Greek temples' (p. 111)), it
can tell us *something* about the text. He argues that 'it is first necessary to
use the tools of a historical and literary reading, in order to emphasize the
elements hidden to our modern eyes, so as to display the complexity of the
texts' (p. 111). According to this argument, paradoxically, an understanding of alien features of a text ('elements hidden to our modern eyes',
p. 142) helps readers to come closer to it in a sense, while avoiding the
temptation of assuming a kind of scholarly intimacy with the text. Looking
at what one might call more theological or philosophical readings of the
fathers, Zachhuber argues that our best way of understanding them is to
set the readers (as well as the fathers) in their historical context. However,
he leaves us with the intriguing question of whether some excellent readings
of ancient texts are naïve about or even disavow their own historical con-

text. Picking up the example of Barth from his own paper, Zachhuber admits in the dialogue section at the end of this volume that 'while it is true that Barth was (in a sense) naïve about his reading, this spared him a kind of self-consciousness that might otherwise have prevented him from writing the very book he wrote without necessarily enabling him to write a better one' (p. 169).

Cassin and Zachhuber look back in time, but the focus of Newheiser's and Ludlow's essays is forwards; both argue from their different sources for an eschatological understanding of the future of the text. Ludlow's dynamic reading of Origen's hermeneutics as received by Gregory of Nyssa suggests that the text is in a sense perpetually transformed or transfigured as it is 'worked on' by its readers (a temporal fluidity which is also evident in Jones's reading of Nyssen). This resonates with an idea which recurs in Newheiser's chapter, that is, the text being 'in motion' (p. 37, p. 44). It is in Burrus's essay, however, that the temporality of reading is presented most radically, even as – paradoxically – she reflects perhaps most realistically of all our authors the backwards and forwards nature of any scholar's own reading practices. To those who would regard her approach as 'irre-sponsible', one answer is surely, 'do you not, in fact, do the same?' (even if Burrus's reading yields more radical philosophical results).

The performative quality of Burrus's paper also reminds us that reading is an activity. The complex relationship between reception and activity/creativity is highlighted in Jones's reading of Levinas and Gregory of Nyssa. For both thinkers, revelation elicits a response of desire – 'the reader reacts to revelation by wanting more' (p. 80). Because revelation is excessive, this desire can never be sated and thus continues to form the reader: 'receiving revelation necessitates a response that is both transformative and destabi-lizing' (p. 97). Jones notes that for Levinas the reader of revelation is at once its translator and 'writer' – another way of expressing the nexus between reception and creativity. This nexus lies at the heart of Douglass's paper, as he uses Heidegger's analysis of the work of art as a way of understanding Gregory of Nyssa's theological production. For Gregory, Douglass argues, the impossibility of ever grasping the divine conceptually does not lead the theologian to mute passivity, but rather drives him to an excess of theological language. But theology always takes the form of a 'thinking *with*' (a sensibility Douglass connects with Gregory's passion for the Greek prefix *sun-*). Gregory's use of metaphor and symbol is not a resigned second best, but the result of an active desire to grapple with the question of God in the conditions of creation. Hence, 'Gregory "makes use" of these various images and systems of thought; in the language of Heidegger, he sets them to work. He first delimits their meaning and then makes them mean something new by bringing them together' (p. 118). In Douglass's chapter, Gregory's theologian is not, as it were, a 'failed scientist', but a great artist for whom materiality and temporality are not obstacles but the very (God-given) condition for the possibility of his art.

This sense of impassioned artistry chimes both in and out of harmony with Matthieu Cassin's portrait of Gregory as a writer. Both Douglass and Cassin agree, for example, that the theologian was an artist. Indeed, Cassin draws to our attention the pleasure that could be derived from a theological text (a pleasure which lies surely in Gregory's writing of it as well as in his audience's reception of it). Although this view is derived from a thoroughly historical analysis of Gregory's writings, it recalls – in a Derridean vein – those hermeneutical theories which call for a somewhat playful attitude to the text. (Could historian and theorist perhaps be united in their conviction that one can take joy in early Christian texts and that, to some extent, joy can come from approaching the text – but not oneself as exegete – with utter seriousness?) However, in Douglass's account of Gregory, the art in question seems at its best to rise to great art, while Cassin challenges one to ask to what extent Gregory's verbal fireworks were expended merely for the entertainment of their audience. Entertainment seems to be a cause which is either relatively trivial or – when it is crude polemic at the expense of an opponent – even an abuse of his art.

This raises another theme which crossed several papers, that of seeing some reading as an abuse of or violence to the text. Ludlow suggests that the way in which Origen and Gregory speak of the 'body' or 'bodily meaning' of the text reveals that they were aware of the ambivalence which arose from the material conditions of human speech. For early Church theology asserted that just as human bodies could tend towards or away from a godly aim – though never being able to rise above their bodily condition – so could human language tend towards or away from God. As Scot Douglass shows, Gregory of Nyssa grappled with the question of how human language could dare to talk about God while remaining within the created realm. In particular, Gregory seems to distinguish approaches which work *with* their createdness from those which, in their attempt to rise above the created realm, force or do violence to language about God (p. 118). Douglass's paper reminds us that early Christian reflection on the status of language had a particular character because of the Christian doctrine of creation and (after Gregory of Nyssa) the doctrine of divine infinity. But, in some respects, Christianity was carrying on an ancient debate about rhetoric: given that all rhetoric is creative or artistic (in the sense that it is speech constructed for a particular end), what makes the difference between a good use or an abuse of that art? The awareness among our contributors that a modern reading of a father could be for an apologetic purpose, a purpose that is often ambivalent, is itself an awareness of that same debate about rhetoric and the many modes of persuasive speech. Tamsin Jones raises a related issue with respect to the use of comparisons between fathers and their later readers. As she notes, comparison can be made with the purpose of showing 'the innate superiority' of one over the other, that is for excluding one or the other (p. 82). Or, more insidiously, a comparison can attempt to assimilate or absorb one thought world into another – a danger which, as Jones points out, is particularly acute with comparisons of Jewish and Christian thinkers. The attempt either to dominate one text by another or to absorb one text into another can be seen as a form of violence, especially when viewed against the history of Christian and Jewish relations over the past two thousand years. But there is another kind of 'violence' to the text which preoccupies some readers: the alleged result of readings which seem to take liberties with a text, in the light of its historical, linguistic context. Whether directed against Origenist allegory or postmodern deconstruction, these allegations often seem to stem from a belief that these practices of reading are irresponsible because they undermine accepted ways of reading (whether those are accepted by a scholarly or a faith community). In the light of these concerns, it is helpful to be reminded by David Newheiser that Derrida – whom some would accuse of flagrant irresponsibility to the text – was driven by a profound concern for the ethics and politics of reading. Furthermore, Ludlow and Cassin both argue that there is more to various methods of reading than meets the eye, whether one is dealing with allegory or with historico-critical methods. The result of this is perhaps that the complaint that allegory is irresponsible might rely on too narrow a conception of allegory and of the historico-critical methods against which it is being judged.

In the following chapters, therefore, we hope that we present a more varied and a more nuanced picture of what it means to read the fathers than has previously been the case in much academic discussion. As we noted earlier, we are not hoping to present a programmatic statement about how one *should* read the fathers. On the other hand, in this volume we do attempt more than merely raising a series of rather empty rhetorical questions. To this end, after the individual chapters, we present a dialogue which developed out of those papers. This to a certain extent reflects the conversations at the symposium itself, but it has been drawn together by the editors in the months after the symposium in order to address the question which seemed to rise most insistently out of our discussions: what makes a responsible reading?

Scot Douglass and Morwenna Ludlow

Note

1 Elliot R. Wolfson, 'Light Does not Talk but Shine: Apophasis and Vision in Rosenzweig's Theopoetic Temporality', in *New Directions in Jewish Philosophy* (Elliot R. Wolfson and Aaron W. Hughes (eds); Bloomington: Indiana University Press, 2010), 123. See her use of Ciglia's 'Auf der Spur Augustins' – 'on Augustine's track' (Francesco Paulo Ciglia, 'Auf der Spur Augustins: *Confessiones* und *De Civitate Dei* als Quellen des Stern der Erlösung' in *Rosenzweig als Leser: kontextuelle Kommentare zum "Stern der Erlösung"* (Martine Brasser (ed.); Tübingen: Max Niemeyer Verlag, 2004), 223–44).

ABBREVIATIONS

CE	*Contra Eunomium*
CH	Pseudo-Dionysius the Areopagite, *The Celestial Hierarchy*
Conf.	Augustine, *Confessions*
DN	Pseudo-Dionysius the Areopagite, *The Divine Names*
Ep.	Epistula/Epistulae (Letter/s)
GNO	*Gregorii Nysseni Opera*
L&S	H. G. Liddell and R. S. Scott, *Greek-English Lexicon*
MT	Pseudo-Dionysius the Areopagite, *The Mystical Theology*
SR	Rosenzweig, *The Star of Redemption*
TLG	*Thesaurus Linguae Graecae*

Part I

Reading Postmodern Readings of the Fathers

Jean-Luc Marion's Reading of Dionysius the Areopagite: Hermeneutics and Reception History

Johannes Zachhuber

The aim of this essay is to elucidate Jean-Luc Marion's reading of the fifth-century theologian known as Pseudo-Dionysius the Areopagite.[1] This has been done before,[2] but it seems to me that existing studies leave room for further investigation. Specifically, I contend that Marion's interpretation of Dionysius's thought, in order to be properly understood, needs to be placed within the context of the latter's reception history. I shall argue that such a focus on reception history, which is both the foundation of individual engagements with a text and their product, integrates creative and receptive aspects of reading better than the notion of an ahistorical encounter between a contemporary reader and a 1500-year-old text.

In order to develop this argument, I shall start with some remarks about the ambiguities of the modern idea of reading past texts. From those I shall move on to consider Marion's engagement with the Dionysian corpus and argue in the third and final part of this paper that (and how) a consideration of the historical context of Marion's interpretation can help elucidate his appropriation of those Patristic texts for a remarkable and, for all its internal tensions, immensely fruitful theological project.

Reading – A Modern Ambiguity

Reading has become for us a personal and even intimate experience: when we read we are alone with a book. This, at least, is what we wish to believe. Ever since people became accustomed to silent reading, in the late Middle Ages,[3] much of its fascination appears to have resided in the private world constituted solely by the interaction between the reader and the text. And while it has remained deeply controversial just how much either side contributes to this world, the fact as such of an individual world created in the encounter between reader and text and jointly inhabited by them possesses sufficient intuitive plausibility to make us speak without hesitation of modern or postmodern 'readings' of Patristic texts, thus indicating that the result of the reader–text interaction tells us at least as much about the individuality of the interpreter as it does about the object of their study.

There are, of course, famous intruders into that intimacy, the most notorious perhaps being the author. True, there is a veritable hermeneutical tradition for which the real and ultimate intimacy the reader aims at through their engagement with a text is not at all with the text itself, but with the person who wrote it. Thus Friedrich Schleiermacher's hermeneutics moves from the grammatical to the psychological; for him, understanding a text ultimately means understanding another individual human being.[4] Most twentieth-century commentators, however, have dismissed this as an unduly romantic notion. Hans-Georg Gadamer, for example, in his discussion of Schleiermacher's hermeneutics in *Truth and Method*, categorically stated that his theory of 'psychological understanding' will be left to one side: we seek to understand a text, after all, not a person.[5] One might ask though whether such a protestation is not in a sense even more romantic in that it seeks to exclude a potential invader from the privacy of the reading experience, which thus becomes ever more strictly a matter between just the text and the reader.

Another intruder is the concept of an objective, transtextual content, spirit or mere 'meaning' that reading is supposed to discover. We find this idea in Karl Barth's famous reflections in the preface to his commentary on Romans:

> When an investigation is rightly conducted, boulders composed of fortuitous or incidental or merely historical conceptions ought to disappear almost entirely. The Word ought to be exposed in the words. Intelligent comment means that I am driven on till I stand with nothing before me than the enigma of the matter: till the document seems hardly to exist as a document; till I have almost forgotten that I am not its author; till I know its author so well that I allow him to speak in my name and am even able to speak in his name myself.[6]

The idea of intimacy looms large here – Barth evidently thinks of long and arduous hours spent at his desk in Safenwil trying to penetrate the difficult texture of Paul's most theological letter. And, as in Schleiermacher, the ultimate aim is to create a common universe by destroying the text as such, or at least by making it redundant. The signs of the text point to something else, and it is this 'something' that is of interest: not the letter that killeth, but the spirit that giveth life (2 Cor. 3.6). The spirit for Barth is the divine spirit, which Paul sought to capture in his work and with which every theologian needs to wrestle:

> My whole energy of interpreting has been expended in an endeavour to see through and beyond history into the spirit of the Bible, which is the Eternal Spirit.[7]

Ultimately, both Schleiermacher and Barth presuppose that the process of bringing the reader and the text together is, at least ideally, objective, leading to results that can be either true or false. Yet it is not difficult to see how, following on from ideas such as theirs, this assumption could be exposed as fictitious. Whatever his hermeneutical rhetoric, Barth's reading of Romans unmistakeably expounds European religious concerns in the wake of the Great War and is far removed from those of a renegade Pharisee in the first century. In fact, this may be the major strength of his interpretation, but it indicates also the weakness of his interpretative premise. What his book does represent, in effect, is the creative interaction of reader and text, and the fact that it does this in a uniquely suggestive and evocative way is the secret of its success and its impact on subsequent theological developments.

It seems to be this kind of insight more than any particular hermeneutical theory that has made it so strikingly persuasive for us to see reading as a creative as well as an individual event. The modern world appears as a long chain of such 'readings' beginning perhaps with the iconic moment on 26 April 1336 when Petrarch, standing on Mount Ventoux and reading (albeit not silently!) from Augustine's *Confessions*, thought that 'what I had there read I believed to be addressed to me and to no other'.[8]

Yet if modernity has thus fostered a belief in the privacy and individuality of text worlds emerging from the intimacy between readers and their texts – a notion quite different from the largely public and, as it were, objective traditional practice of commentary or the production of catenae – it has also, in a paradoxical way, concomitantly destroyed another notion of intimacy that used to exist between premodern readers and their texts. This intimacy was not that of an individual encounter, but of communal possession on account of a seemingly unbroken tradition. Into the eighteenth century, European scholars and literati interacted with church fathers, ancient philosophers or other classical authors as though they were quasi-contemporaries. Thus, within a theology course at a German university, Patristics was normally taught after dogmatics and polemics:[9] reading the fathers offered exemplary applications of the principles of theological judgment that were assumed to have been valid then as they were in the present; they were 'fathers' precisely insofar as they provided supreme instances of the defence of Christian doctrine and the rejection of heresy.

Within a few decades all this changed, and at the end of the eighteenth century, reading the church fathers meant an encounter with theological voices from a different world. Like Biblical and, indeed, classical scholarship, Patristics now served primarily a historical purpose; the fathers became important on account of their closeness to the original formation of Christianity. Depending on the scholar's standpoint, the fathers were seen as expertly developing the full system of Christian doctrine or as sullying the purity and simplicity of the original Gospel. However their contribution was assessed, it was undisputed that *reading* them required increasingly complex philological and hermeneutical preparations in order to avoid misunderstanding, and critics and apologists of the church's tradition accused (and continue to accuse!) each other of falling into precisely this trap.

Contemporary 'readings' of church fathers reside in the specific tension created by this ambiguous development. On the one hand, they are supposed to be the expression of an individual and private encounter between a reader and a text; on the other hand, the intimacy and immediacy of any such interaction is interrupted by the awareness of historical difference. The conventional result of this tension is the duality of so-called systematic and historical readings, but while this may work reasonably well pragmatically, there is little theoretical justification for such a divide.

One way of at least easing the tension – and this is what I undertake in the following – may be to question the premises that have led to it. Thus we may ask whether it is in fact correct to see reading as a purely private and intimate affair. Are we really all that alone when we read a text? Are not others present with us, however little noticed, while we engage with a text? The truth is that we are part of a world and do not simply leave it behind when holding a book in our hands. Our reading is inevitably conditioned by the cultural parameters governing our perception – by our national, religious, and generational preconceptions and prejudices. The highly public relevance, for example, of Barth's interpretation of Romans would otherwise be difficult to account for: while this indubitably was *his* reading of this Biblical text, it was also and at the same time an articulation of some concerns, hopes and ideals shared widely in early twentieth-century Germany and beyond.

If our readings, then, are conditioned by the culture within which they occur this implies an influence of the specific histories that have given birth to and shaped the world we inhabit. This further insight serves to mitigate the second premise of my initial argument. We are not totally and entirely cut off from the past; if we were we could no longer interact with its remains and testimonies in any meaningful way. Reading Patristic texts still presupposes a continuum, but this continuum is itself historical in character. It is what we call 'reception history'. This is a history of which readers are a part, but which they also, knowingly or unknowingly, collectively produce. It is in this specific sense of reading the fathers as a continuation of reception history that I wish my subsequent remarks on Marion's reading of Pseudo-Dionysius to be understood.

Jean-Luc Marion and Dionysius the Areopagite

Looking at Jean-Luc Marion's readings of the Pseudo-Dionysian corpus in the light of these considerations makes it clear almost at once how 'modern' his 'postmodern' reading is. Marion seeks to offer *his* interpretation of Pseudo-Dionysius, and I take it that the intuitive meaning we attach to the project of analysing Marion's *reading* of Pseudo-Dionysius can be broken down along the lines of the two major premises of modern reading, which I outlined in the first part of this essay. In other words, the two central questions pertaining to it would appear to be these: To what extent are we confronted with *Marion's* reading, the product of an individual encounter between a reader and a text? Also, does his reading do justice to the alterity presented to us in a writing that originated 1500 years ago in a world which in many ways was extremely different from our own? We can easily imagine not only that replies to these questions will vary greatly but that their underlying normative assumptions might be assessed extremely differently by systematic and historical scholars. These divisive questions cannot be avoided, yet I shall propose that the juxtaposition they produce can be mitigated through the assumption that Marion's 'reading' is part of the reception history of Dionysius and of the history of negative theology more broadly.

Dionysius in Marion's Thought

In order to understand Marion's interpretation of Dionysius as *his* reading of this author, it may be helpful to start from some brief remarks about the broader outlines of his philosophical and theological thought. Jean-Luc Marion's philosophical work is part of what a critic has called the theological turn (*tournant théologique*) of more recent phenomenology in France,[10] and, while I am unable here to give anything like a sufficient sketch of his philosophy,[11] it is important to realize that Marion's more specifically theological interests and ideas have arisen in close connection with an attempt to develop further Edmund Husserl's phenomenology.[12] Marion believes that Husserl's method of phenomenological reduction can be extended to the point where it reveals an unconditioned phenomenon of 'pure givenness' (*étant donné*), and thus the fundamental structure of the world turns out to be based on an excess of self-giving. This, however, becomes manifest only at the end of a reflexive process designed, paradoxically, to recover strict immanence. While Marion has always insisted on a distinction between his philosophy and his theology, the structural parallels between the two are obvious and willingly admitted by the author himself.[13] Just as the positive truth about reality is revealed to phenomenological research only as the result of a process seemingly designed to reduce to immanence all outward layers of transcendence,[14] so the theological truth of God as love becomes manifest only after the complete destruction of his idolatrous representations. This has a number of immediate consequences: First, the radical otherness of God is revealed by careful attention to reality as it is – not by turning away from it. Second, God's commitment to us is recognized alongside his majestic distance from us.[15] Third, there is resistance to both our encounter with the phenomenon as well as our recognition of God, and this resistance needs to be overcome through a critical and, as such, destructive movement. No knowledge of God without critique of the idol; no understanding of reality without phenomenological reduction.

Marion thus integrates into both his philosophical and his theological project the postmodern critique of metaphysics as a necessary liberation of the 'other' from the shackles of visual or conceptual constraints. Only when we have forsaken any such attempt to bring the other under our control are we capable of receiving it in its selfless superabundance. Yet while postmodern critics of metaphysics may have given new testimony to this important insight, they are by no means its originators. Rather, Marion claims, postmodern philosophy is only a late variation, and not an unproblematic one, of the specifically theological tradition of *apophasis* associated initially and most famously with Pseudo-Dionysius the Areopagite. Jacques Derrida's rejection of this parallel,[16] in particular, indicates for Marion that recognizing the potential of negative theology would be extremely risky for the advocate of deconstruction:

> This quasi-deconstruction [sc. in negative theology] cannot be said simply to anticipate, unknowingly, the authentic deconstruction since it claims to reach *in fine* what it deconstructs: It claims to put us in the presence of God in the very degree to which it denies all presence. Negative theology does not furnish deconstruction with new material or new an unconscious forerunner, but with its first serious rival, perhaps the only one possible.[17]

Marion's reception of negative theology, then, has an apologetic interest. Christian theology, rather than being a prominent casualty of deconstruction, has pre-empted its most valuable theoretical insight and can, therefore, self-confidently be maintained in the teeth of postmodern critique. This provocative and far-reaching claim is largely based on Marion's interpretation of the Dionysian corpus. How, then, does he read these texts and how does his reading inform his overall thought?

Perhaps it is not entirely trivial to begin by saying that Marion evidently has carefully studied Dionysius's writings. He certainly is not one of those who make a merely fashionable appeal to a traditional writer. The results of those studies were originally published in his early study *Idole et la Distance* (1977), translated into English as *The Idol and Distance* in 2001. This interpretation in many ways underlies, albeit with modifications, Marion's major theological work, *Dieu sans l'être*, which appeared in 1991 and was translated into English in the same year.[18] Marion expressed it again in his 1997 engagement with Derrida and others at Villanova University, to which I have referred previously.

Underlying Marion's approach to Dionysius is a straightforward question: how can God be spoken? With Étienne Gilson and many others, he started, at least originally, from God's self-revelation in Exod. 3.14: אהיה אשר אהיה.[19] This expression has been translated in two different ways: 'I am who I am' is the rendering often preferred by scholars of Hebrew, whereas the Septuagint, followed by the Vulgate and much of traditional Christian theology, reads, 'I am the one who is' (ἐγώ εἰμι ὁ ὤν). These two translations, Marion urges, should not be seen as contradictory or mutually exclusive, however. Rather, they reflect the fact that this Biblical verse expresses precisely the unity of revelation and concealment, of manifestation and distance:

> The name . . . delivers the unthinkable, as the unthinkable that *gives* itself; this same unthinkable also gives *itself*, and hence withdraws within the anterior distance that governs the gift of the Name. The Name delivers and steals away in one and the same movement.[20]

By not offering a 'real' name, God makes himself known. If this insight is translated into a theological programme, this requires a radical transformation of language, a move, as Marion puts it, 'from a model of language in which the speaker makes an effort to take possession of meaning to a model in which the speaker receives meaning'.[21] Conventional, predicative structures of language have to be denied in order for the revelation of God to be accepted. Speaking of God is speaking without speaking, as much as knowledge of God is *docta ignorantia*. Marion quotes the words of St Paul: 'If someone thinks he knows something, he does not yet know in what way it is suitable to know: but if someone loves God, he is known by God' (1 Cor. 8.2–3).[22]

It is fundamentally as a response to the theological difficulty posed by this Biblical idea of God's revelation-in-concealment that Marion understands the so-called negative theology of Pseudo-Dionysius:

> Language carries out its discourse to the point of negation and silence. But just as the death that is refused according to the love matures into Resurrection, so silence nourishes infinite proclamation.[23]

Precisely this reconfiguration of language, a 'linguistic model of the dispossession of meaning' is, in Marion's view, the essence of Dionysius's 'negative theology'.[24] Therefore, the critique of metaphysics in Nietzsche and Heidegger only serves the ultimately theological purpose of making room for the establishment of a radically different discourse based on the principle of love. The Biblical word that God is love (1 John 4.16), therefore, means that he is *not* a being, nor even is he 'being' and he certainly 'is' not God.[25] The modern and postmodern critique of metaphysical theism, therefore, is correct and appropriate, but ultimately only an extension of the traditional theological critique of 'idols' and does not deny the legitimacy of proper theology, but – rightly understood – enables it.

Consequently, negative theology for Marion is a theological method that is fundamentally *critical*, an exercise intended to escape idolatry. Such idolatry would include, but not be limited to, the naïve visual representations of God. Its more dangerous objects are attributes and concepts applied to God by philosophical or theological language: 'To avoid such an idolatry, one must . . . *deny* attributes as imperfections'.[26]

One must, more specifically, deny every attribute including the loftiest ones, such as One, Unity, Divinity, or Goodness. Yet even this is not all, for it might appear that the negation itself reveals the being of God. If understood in this way, however, negative theology itself would still be, in Marion's words, idolatrous.[27] Negation itself then must be denied and God postulated as being beyond affirmation and negation. And this indeed is what Dionysius urges his reader to do. The apophatic way leads to a point where negation itself has to be negated:

> . . . nor can any affirmation or negation be applied to it, for although we may affirm or deny the things below it, we can neither affirm nor deny it, inasmuch as the all-perfect and unique Cause of all things transcends all affirmation, and the simple pre-eminence of Its absolute nature is outside of every negation – free from every limitation and beyond them all.[28]

At this point, however, Pseudo-Dionysius (at least in Marion's reconstruction) runs into a difficulty. Negative theology thus understood makes any theology impossible. With Claude Bruaire, Marion formulates the proposition that 'negative theology is the negation of all theology. Its truth is atheism'.[29] Its practice, then, takes the theologian to the edge of a precipice or even into the abyss of a godforsaken world, to the point enunciated in the words of Christ on the cross, 'My God, why hast thou forsaken me?'

Yet it also takes him beyond that point, and Marion finds this indicated in Dionysius as well. He observes that the Syrian author is still willing to use one word for God until the end, and this is *cause* (αἰτία). In this notion, he suggests, is contained precisely the unity of distance and intimacy that permits us to move beyond the impasse of pure apophaticism:

> Anterior distance . . . governs positively that which it allows to be received in it. We have not thus distanced ourselves from Denys's position, but we have slowly approached what he indicates under the name of Goodness, when he assigns it to the cause/αἰτία.[30]

At the vantage point of utter negation it becomes possible to relate to God in a new way. Dionysius knows, Marion contends, of a third way beyond affirmation and negation, and this is adumbrated by his mention of 'cause' at the every end of *The Mystical Theology*.[31] Cause, of course, must not here mean the *causa sui* of metaphysics, but it indicates that God is beyond affirmation and negation insofar as he is love, pure giving or, as *The Divine Names* suggest, goodness. Goodness and cause, Marion maintains, are interchangeable; goodness is the first name of God according to *The Divine Names*, thus the upshot of Dionysius's theology is the view that intimacy and distance are but two sides of the same coin. 'Revelation communicates the very intimacy of God – distance itself'.[32]

Marion's Interpretation of the Dionysian Corpus

This then is *Marion's* reading of Dionysius – how plausible is it as a reading of *Dionysius*? It would appear difficult not to express some serious reservations about the latter. Admittedly, the transcendence and nearness of God very often form a closely related pair and should not be juxtaposed as mutually exclusive concepts. In Paul's speech at the Areopagus he reminds the Greeks both of their altar 'to the unknown God' *and* of their poet's word that 'in him we live and move and have our being' (Acts 17.23–28). The 'unknown God' then is 'not far from each of us'. Otherwise it would be difficult even to understand why an author such as Pseudo-Dionysius emphasised kataphatic as well as apophatic discourse about God. Yet the way these two are related in Marion appears to be rather different from what one finds in the Dionysian corpus. While the precise order of writings within that collection is a matter of scholarly debate and while, consequently, readers have disagreed over the centuries on the relationship between the kataphatic and the apophatic, it must surely take a bold person to claim that in Dionysius the apophatic discourse is critical in the way Marion seems to envisage. We must not forget that the denials in *The Mystical Theology* and elsewhere negate positive statements – taken from Scripture and tradition – about the divine, and the kataphatic discourse about those makes up much of Dionysius's treatise *The Divine Names*. These names for God are revealed, and Dionysius surely cannot have thought them idolatrous. The apophatic for Dionysius qualifies in a particular way any discourse about God, but there is little indication that it serves the 'deconstructive' purpose Marion is interested in as a theological equivalent to Husserl's phenomenological reductions.

Dionysius is also, it appears, considerably less concerned than Marion to tell his readers what happens after apophatic theology has completed its business. As far as Dionysius's writing is concerned, Marion's musings about a third way seem rather far-fetched; *The Mystical Theology* ends in silence, and in no other writing does Dionysius refer back to it, nor does he indicate the need to discover a way beyond the impasse created by the radical denial of any theological language. Such a need, of course, exists for Marion, who thinks that Dionysius's advocacy of apophaticism anticipates the philosophical critique of metaphysics and religion. Marion expects Dionysius to provide a solution to the problem posed by Bruaire's equation of negative theology and atheism, but it appears doubtful that Dionysius ever intended to address this question.

It might appear at this point that a discussion of Marion's interpretation of Pseudo-Dionysius reverts precisely to the fault line of historical versus systematic readings, which I sketched earlier in this paper. How important, some might ask, is historical accuracy for a philosophical or theological appropriation of ideas? Should not the intrinsic value of Marion's proposal be assessed whatever the historical circumstances of the original composition of the Dionysian corpus? Yet such a demand might be countered by reference to the apparent apologetic purpose of Marion's appeal to this traditional Christian author. His claim that negative theology provides an early rival to postmodern deconstruction may not rest exclusively on the historical accuracy of his Patristic readings, but it would be difficult to deny that it is affected by doubts about the latter. Yet, as I argued earlier, such a dichotomy seems to oversimplify things. No contemporary reading of Dionysius is *merely* historical, and to the extent that it *is* historical it is still, arguably, mediated by previous readings of the same texts. At the same time, only in the modern myth of individual readings could Marion's interpretation of Dionysius be regarded as merely 'his' reading, a purely personal appropriation of a written document by a theologian. What may take us further, then, is a consideration of contexts for this particular interpretation, and I shall therefore proceed to consider a number of such contexts that will, hopefully, enhance both understanding and appreciation of Marion's reading of Dionysius.

The Modern Context: Negative Theology as Critical Philosophy

It has already become clear how much Marion's reading of Dionysius is conditioned by contemporary theological debate. Marion himself referred to Claude Bruaire and his suspicion that negative theology ultimately *was* atheism, thus hinting at the background of his own work in French post-conciliar theology. Part of this context has been very fruitfully explored by Tamsin Jones. In her work on Marion and Pseudo-Dionysius,[33] she draws attention specifically to the pivotal role that the appropriation of the theology of Hans Urs von Balthasar has played for Marion's reading of the early Byzantine writer. Jones shows how von Balthasar stands behind Marion's interesting combination of what we might call apophatic insights with a radically kataphatic vision of divine presence through icons that make the world, as it were, transparent for God. Von Balthasar seems equally to have inspired Marion's adoption of the Proclean-Dionysian idea[34] of a 'hymnic' response to God as a 'third way' beyond affirmation and negation.[35]

Jones is surely correct in establishing a link that helps explain how Marion reads Dionysius. Yet it seems to me that this explanation reveals at least as much in terms of stark contrast as it does in terms of similarity. After all, Balthasar's fundamental theological intuition, expressed in his project of theological aesthetics, is to start *not* from negation and criticism but from the immediate observation of beauty in God's creation. This overall approach is mirrored perfectly in his reading of Dionysius. Balthasar not surprisingly starts from an appreciation of Dionysius's kataphatic theology, which he sees as a singularly rich development of the figure of *analogia entis*.[36] There is no hint that for him apophatic critique must come before any valid affirmation. Consequently, *The Mystical Theology* is dealt with at the very end of the section on Dionysius,[37] and while von Balthasar emphasises that 'mystical theology . . . is present secretly or openly in all his theological utterances and . . . is systematically necessary to the whole',[38] this systematic necessity does not consist in a preliminary critical destruction of idolatrous belief, but in the awareness that God's transcendence is always concomitant with his immanence in creation:

> God is in all things in his immanence and yet in himself is independent, transcendent over them, and therefore even his immanence is comparable with none other.[39]

Von Balthasar does indeed introduce the notion of icon in a way similar to Marion, but whereas for the latter all depends on the contrast between icon and idol,[40] Balthasar has few qualms about Dionysius's syncretistic use of various religious terminologies:

> If then the concept of image (*eikōn*), in all its forms (as *theāma*, object of contemplation, drama, or, using the language of the mysteries, as *agalma*, sacred idol or image of the gods), is applied to the manifestation, through which, for those who can see, 'the blessed beauty of the archetype shimmers through (*apostilbo*) clearly',[41] then only this qualification is needed, that between manifestation and what is manifest there is no sort of link of natural necessity.[42]

He is, for the same reason, rather undisturbed by the evident borrowings in Dionysius from the Neoplatonists. They indicate for him an awareness of 'what we now call natural theology', the recognition that paganism represents 'the misuse of true religious thought for the purpose of Promethean speculation'.[43]

Marion's use of von Balthasar is thus ambiguous, and the reading of Dionysius as well as the place of negative theology differs considerably between the two. Von Balthasar praises Dionysius as the first Greek theologian who stood apart from the spirit of controversy so characteristic of the early centuries and who was therefore able to use affirmatively Gnostic, Manichaean and Neoplatonic ideas with only 'a few corrections from time to time':[44]

> What was once historical, temporally conditioned reality becomes for Denys a means for expressing an utterly universal theological content. . . . Each thought–form of which he makes use will, at this touch, be liberated from its historical context and exalted into eternity.[45]

Marion, on the other hand, sees Dionysius in the tradition of the prophetic critique of 'idols' and hence as forerunner of the modern and postmodern critique of metaphysics who also offers a way beyond the aporiae of that critique. From a theological starting point, the Areopagite recognized at once the impossibility of speaking of God and the necessity of doing so. He described how:

> . . . the absence of names turns into the name of absence, even the name of the Absent. . . . The name of the Absent gives itself to be believed when the failure of names betrays the distraction of possible meanings, which grows in the measure that they approach the unique pole.[46]

The comparison with von Balthasar is thus helpful, not least in pointing out the starkly divergent ways in which he and Marion read Dionysius. It also illustrates considerable differences between the way both authors understood negative theology. For von Balthasar, negative theology merely illustrates the fact that God's immanence in creation always and inevitably has a transcendent dimension; Bruaire,[47] Marion[48] and Derrida[49] on the other hand – in spite of their substantial disagreements – concur that it is a critical discourse which, potentially or actually, has devastating effects on traditional metaphysics and theology.

This latter interpretation of Dionysius's apophaticism has been attractive ever since the rise of modern, critical philosophy. Friedrich Wilhelm Joseph Schelling claimed the support of Pseudo-Dionysius for his own attempt to overcome the ramifications of what he called 'negative philosophy'[50] – a word intentionally reminiscent of the older 'negative theology'.[51] Negative philosophy for Schelling was, in the first place, Kant's transcendental philosophy, which represented a necessary step in the history of philosophy insofar as it exposed the weakness of classical theism or metaphysics but was unable to offer a sufficient ground for our understanding of reality and, specifically, God.[52] It ends in pure negativity.[53] Hegel's attempt to overcome Kantian criticism did not succeed, Schelling argued, because the 'double-negation' of Hegelian dialectic could never reach 'positive' reality.[54] The right response to Kant's critical destruction of the metaphysical tradition therefore was a new philosophy that started from the notion of God's factual self-unveiling in his revelation. This was possible because God, according to 'the oldest doctrine'[55] was '*ousia huperousios,* supersubstantial being'.[56]

Schelling does not mention Dionysius by name, but the references are clear enough. Like Marion, he read Dionysius as offering a successful blueprint for an integration of philosophical criticism into an ultimately affirmative, 'positive' philosophical theology. Both therefore emphasize in Dionysius a third way beyond affirmation and negation – hence Schelling's reference to *ousia huperousios*. For both this is important because they find themselves confronted with a radical critique of philosophical theology which seemingly disqualified all traditional ways of speaking about God. Ultimately, both Schelling and Marion see that critique as partly valid and for that reason need a model expressing its legitimacy *as well as* its limitations. It is this intellectual need that makes Dionysius attractive, but also determines the reading of his corpus.[57]

Marion is thus part of a specifically post-Kantian approach to 'negative theology'. Its logic is determined by the real possibility that knowledge of God might be impossible and that God might not even exist at all. These concerns are absent from earlier interest in the *via negativa*, which was constructed against the backdrop of a hierarchically structured sacred cosmos, whose existence seemed indubitable to most, however difficult it might be to reach its apex or to say anything about the latter. The 'negative theology' inaugurated by Kant, on the other hand, seeks to re-establish the legitimacy of God as the 'Other' in the face of the irrevocable loss of the ontological and epistemological ladder that used to lead up to him. To this end it offers a philosophical and theological justification for the abolition of the old 'chain of being' as the only way to secure the absolute uniqueness and the pure transcendence of the one God.[58]

It is within this tradition that Marion reads Dionysius – as an early witness to the philosophical and theological possibility of overcoming the ultimate negativity of nihilism and atheism. Marion is not part of the more radical, essentially critical trajectory of 'negative theology' that stretches in modernity from Kant via Nietzsche, the early Barth and Levinas to Derrida, but he follows Schelling and Heidegger in their conviction that negation ultimately reveals true positivity.

In light of this, Marion's claim that his reconstruction of Dionysius's thought is 'negative theology'[59] appears puzzling, however. Does he not, rather, consider 'negative theology' in its post-Kantian version – the destruction of idols, Husserl's phenomenological reduction, Derrida's deconstruction – as a necessary but preliminary operation? Is not his own contribution, then, a conscious move beyond those exercises as much as Schelling's philosophy demanded a move from negative to positive philosophy?

Marion may simply be inconsistent here, but if he is not, the reason must be that the revelation of God as love is, for him, still part of 'negative theology.'; In spite of his speculations about a third way beyond the apophatic and the kataphatic, his would not be a Schellingian move from negative to positive philosophy. Instead, the shift from silence to 'infinite proclamation' would indicate that God is paradoxically revealed at the very moment of his most ostensible absence.[60] This indeed has long been one way of understanding the Incarnation and, in particular, the passion of Christ. It is prefigured in the Gospel of John and finds perhaps its most poignant expression in Martin Luther's theology of the cross with its idea that God's salvific plan required his revelation 'hidden under its opposite' (*abscondita sub contrariis*) namely, the humiliation of suffering and cross. Thus he writes in his *Lectures on Genesis*:

> Thus, when Christ himself is about to enter into glory, he dies and descends into hell. There all glory disappears. He says to his disciples (Jn 14.12): 'I go to the Father', and he goes to the grave. Let us constantly meditate on such examples and place them before our eyes.[61]

The possibility emerges here of a genuinely Christian version of negative theology, one whose antecedents do not lie primarily with Plato and his school.[62] The insight that the Word became flesh tutors believers to see God precisely where, in any obvious sense, he is not, and a particular kind of 'negative theology' is needed to reach that hermeneutical and ultimately ethical goal.

In *God Without Being*, Marion seems to reach out for such a view; he spells 'God' with a crossed-out 'o' to indicate that

> ... we are speaking of the Gød who is crossed by a cross because he reveals himself by his placement on a cross, the Gød revealed by, in, and as the Christ.[63]

It is this understanding of 'God' that underlies his subsequent critique of Aquinas's identification of God with 'being' and his defence of Dionysius's preference for 'goodness' as the supreme divine predicate.[64] Once again, one may wonder whether this rightly captures the intention of Pseudo-Dionysius, but if it does not, this might be more of a problem for Dionysius than for Marion. Von Balthasar may have been right in his *interpretation* of Pseudo-Dionysius's willingness to integrate the wealth of pagan religion and speculation into Christian theology; however, in *commending* it without reservation he removed the critical element from the complex relationship between Biblical monotheism and its pagan environment. The Incarnation may have fulfilled the 'promise of ages', but the 'word of the cross' is also 'foolishness' to the Greeks (1 Cor. 1.18–23). To the extent that the Platonic notion of divinity embraces polytheism (and emphatically so in Proclus!) it must be subject to the 'critique of the idols' that has been such a pervasive concern within the Judaeo-Christian tradition.

Marion rightly points this out, and he is equally right in constructing a trajectory from the Biblical polemic against idol worship to the more recent critiques of ontotheology and metaphysics. It appears less clear that he is justified in claiming historical pre-eminence for 'negative theology' over deconstruction;[65] his reading of Dionysius, as we saw, presupposes an advanced stage of the Areopagite's reception history. Marion's interpretation, then, may be more justified if the Dionysian corpus is seen as the starting point of a history of reading and interpretation leading up to and including the radical forms of religious and theological critique to which Marion seeks to respond. Insofar as the historical Pseudo-Dionysius was by no means aware of all or indeed most of these complications, he can hardly be relied upon to provide the modern reader with ready answers, but the apparent dependence of modern and postmodern developments on the seeds sown in the Patristic age should certainly encourage the theologian to engage seriously with them.

Notes

1 On Pseudo-Dionysius cf. Andrew Louth, *Denys the Areopagite* (Outstanding Christian Thinkers; London: Continuum, 2002); Paul Rorem, *Pseudo-Dionysius: A Commentary on the Texts and an Introduction to Their Influence* (New York: Oxford University Press, 1993); Denys Turner, *The Darkness of God: Negativity in Christian Mysticism* (Cambridge: Cambridge University Press, 1995), 19–49.

2 Tamsin Jones, 'Dionysius in Hans Urs von Balthasar and Jean-Luc Marion' in *Re-thinking Dionysius the Areopagite* (S. Coakley (ed.); Oxford: Wiley-Blackwell, 2009), 213–24. Cf. Tamsin Jones, *A Genealogy of Marion's Philosophy of Religion: Apparent Darkness* (Indiana Series in the Philosophy of Religion; Bloomington: Indiana University Press, 2011).

3 Paul Saenger, *Space Between Words: The Origins of Silent Reading* (Stanford: Stanford University Press, 1997).

4 Friedrich Schleiermacher, *Hermeneutics and Criticism: And Other Writings* (Andrew Bowie (trans. and ed.); Cambridge: Cambridge University Press, 2008).

5 Hans Georg Gadamer, *Truth and Method* (2nd rev. edn; Joel Weinsheimer and Donald G. Marshall (eds); London: Sheed & Ward, 1989).

6 Karl Barth, *The Epistle to the Romans* (Edwyn C. Hoskyns (trans.); London: Oxford University Press, 1933).

7 Ibid., 1.

8 Petrarch, 'To Dionisio da Borgo San Sepolcro' in *Selections from the Canzoniere and Other Works* (Oxford World's Classics; Oxford: Oxford University Press, 1985).

9 Cf. the following: Silke-Petra Bergjan, 'Die Beschäftigung mit der Alten Kirche an deutschen Universitäten in den Umbrüchen der Aufklärung' in *Zwischen Altertumswissenschaft und Theologie: zur Relevanz der Patristik in Geschichte*

und Gegenwart (Christoph Markschies and Johannes van Oort (eds); Leuven: Peeters, 2002).

10 D. Janicaud, 'The Theological Turn of French Phenomenology', in *Phenomenology and the 'Theological Turn'. The French Debate* (id. et al. (eds.); B. G. Prusak (trans.); New York: Fordham University Press, 2000), 16–103. Cf. the very helpful 'Translator's Introduction', 3–15.

11 Cf. for this: Robyn Horner, *Jean-Luc Marion: A Theo-logical Introduction* (Aldershot: Ashgate, 2005).

12 Jean-Luc Marion, *Reduction and Givenness: Investigations of Husserl, Heidegger, and Phenomenology* (Northwestern University Studies in Phenomenology and Existential Philosophy; Evanston, Ill.: Northwestern University Press, 1998), esp. 4–39; cf. T. Mooney, 'Hubris und Humility: Husserl's Reduction and Givenness' in *Givenness and God: Questions of Jean-Luc Marion* (Ian Leask and Eoin Cassidy (eds); New York: Fordham University Press, 2005), 47–68.

13 Marion, *Being Given: Towards a Phenomenology of Givenness* (Jeffrey L. Kosky (trans.); Palo Alto: Stanford University Press, 2002), 71–4 with n. 2 (p. 342) and T. L. Carlson, 'Translator's Introduction' in *The Idol and Distance: Five Studies* (Thomas A. Carlson (trans.); Jean-Luc Marion (ed.); New York: Fordham University Press, 2001), xi–xxxi.

14 The famous 'third reduction': Marion, *Reduction and Givenness*, 192–8.

15 Cf. the title of his early theological work, *Idole et la Distance*!

16 J. Derrida, *Writing and Difference* (A. Bass (trans.); London: Routledge, 1978), 146; idem., 'How to Avoid Speaking: Denials' in *Derrida and Negative Theology* (Harold Coward and Toby Foshay (eds); Albany: State University of New York Press, 1992), 73–142. For an alternative reading, cf. the article by David Newheiser in this volume.

17 Marion, 'In the Name: How to Avoid Speaking of "Negative Theology"', in *God, the Gift, and Postmodernism* (John D. Caputo and M. J. Scanlon (eds); Bloomington: Indiana University Press, 1999), 20–42, here 22.

18 Marion, *God without Being: Hors-texte* (Thomas A. Carlson (trans.); Studies in Religion and Postmodernism; Chicago: University of Chicago Press, 1991).

19 Marion, *Idol and Distance* (Thomas A. Carlson (trans.); New York: Fordham University Press, 2001). Cf. *God Without Being*, xx.

20 Ibid., 142.

21 Ibid., 144.

22 Ibid., 145.

23 Ibid., 144.

24 Ibid., 145.

25 The French title *Dieu sans l'être* can be understood as 'God without being it (i.e. God)'.

26 Marion, *Idol and Distance*, 146.

27 Ibid., 147.

28 Pseudo-Dionysius, *De Mystica Theologia* V in *Corpus Dionysiacum, 2: De Coelesti Hierarchia, De Ecclesiastica Hierarchia, De Mystica Theologia, Epistulae* (Adolf Martin Ritter and Günter Heil (eds); Patristische Texte und Studien; Berlin: Walter de Gruyter, 1991), 150.5–9; English translation,

Pseudo-Dionysius: The Complete Works (The Classics of Western Spirituality; Colm Luibheid and Paul Rorem (trans); Mahwah, N.J.; London: Paulist Press; SPCK, 1987), 141.

29 Marion, *Idol and Distance*, 147. Cf. Claude Bruaire, *Le Droit de Dieu* (Paris: Aubier-Montaigne, 1974), 21. On Bruaire, who had a profound influence on Marion, cf. now: Antonio Lopez, *Spirit's Gift: The Metaphysical Insight of Claude Bruaire* (Washington, D.C.: Catholic University of America Press, 2006).

30 Marion, *Idol and Distance*, 154.

31 Ibid., 151. For Marion's use of the 'third way', cf. Jones, 'Dionysius', 218; in *Idol and Distance* he had explicitly rejected such language (ibid. 150).

32 Marion, *Idol and Distance*, 157.

33 Jones, 'Dionysius'.

34 Cf. Proclus, *In Platonis Parmenidem* in *Procli Philosophi Platonici Opera Inedita* (Victor Cousin (ed.); Frankfurt am Main: Minerva, 1962), 1108, 19–25; 1191, 32–5.

35 Marion, *In Excess: Studies of Saturated Phenomena* (Robyn Horner and Vincent Berraud (trans); Perspectives in Continental Philosophy; New York: Fordham University Press, 2002), 137; quoted in Jones, 'Dionysius', 218.

36 Hans Urs. von Balthasar, *The Glory of the Lord: A Theological Aesthetics, 2: Studies in Theological Style: Clerical Styles* (Andrew Louth, Francis McDonagh and Brian McNeil (trans); John Riches (ed.); Edinburgh: T & T Clark, 1985), 168–9. Cf. Edward T. Oakes, *Pattern of Redemption: The Theology of Hans Urs von Balthasar* (New York: Continuum, 1994), 114. The *analogia entis* for von Balthasar was the 'key for unlocking the treasury of the Fathers'.

37 Balthasar, *Glory of the Lord*, 204–10.

38 Ibid., 204.

39 Ibid., 169.

40 Marion, *God without Being*, 7–24.

41 Pseudo-Dionysius, *De Ecclesiastica Hierarchia* III 3,2 Ritter and Heil (eds.) 82,9.

42 Balthasar, *Glory of the Lord*, 169.

43 Ibid., 208.

44 Ibid., 152.

45 Ibid.

46 Marion, *Idol and Distance*, 185.

47 *Le Droit de Dieu*, 21.

48 Marion occasionally expresses reservations about the term 'negative theology': 'On the Name', 21.

49 See n.16; cf. Marion, *Idol and Distance*, 220–33.

50 On Schelling's late philosophy, cf. Emil L. Fackenheim, 'Schelling's Conception of Positive Philosophy' in *The God Within: Kant, Schelling and Historicity* (Toronto: University of Toronto Press, 1996), ch. 7; H. Fuhrmans, *Schellings letzte Philosophie. Die negative und positive Philosophie im Einsatz des Spätidealismus* (Berlin: Junker und Dünnhaupt, 1940); Klaus Hemmerle, *Gott und das Denken nach Schellings Spätphilosophie* (Freiburg: Herder, 1968).

51 Cf. B. Rensch, 'Theologie, Negative' in *Historisches Wörterbuch der Philosophie* Volume 10 (Joachim Ritter et al. (eds); Basel: Schwabe, 1998), 1102–5.

52 On 'negative philosophy' in Schelling cf. Andrew Bowie, *Schelling and Modern European Philosophy: An Introduction* (London; New York: Routledge, 1993).

53 A similar idea underlies the notion of 'nihilism' in Radical Orthodoxy. Cf. Conor Cunningham, *Genealogy of Nihilism: Philosophies of Nothing and the Difference of Theology* (Radical Orthodoxy Series; London; New York: Routledge, 2002).

54 Manfred Frank, *Der unendliche Mangel an Sein: Schellings Hegelkritik und die Anfänge der Marxschen Dialektik* (Munich: W. Fink, 1992).

55 Friedrich Wilhelm Joseph Schelling, 'Die Weltalter (1814?)' in *Friedrich Wilhelm Joseph von Schellings sämmtliche Werke* Volume 13 (Karl Freidrich August Schelling (ed): Stuttgart: J. G. Cotta, 1856–61), 238.

56 Schelling, 'Philosophie der Mythologie' in *Friedrich Wilhelm Joseph von Schellings sämmtliche Werke* Volume 12, 100.

57 Schelling loomed large in French philosophical and theological discussions of the 60s and 70s. Xavier Tilliette's magisterial two-volume *Schelling: Une Philosophie en Devenir* (Paris: J. Vrij) appeared in 1970. Claude Bruaire published a book about Schelling's philosophy in the same year, *Schelling ou la Quête du Secret de l'Être* (Paris: Seghers, 1970) and, elsewhere, observed in perfectly Schellingian terms that negative theology 'refuses to understand the absolute as subject and freedom while clinging to an objective model of knowledge' (quoted in Lopez, *Spirit's Gift*, 66). Marion himself acknowledged his debt to Schelling in the preface to *Idol and Distance* (p. xxxviii) and, in *God Without Being*, gives pride of place to a quotation from one of Schelling's later works: 'We attempt [sc. in this book] to meditate on what F. W. Schelling called "the freedom of God with regard to his own existence" (*God Without Being*, 2. Quoted from Schelling, 'Vorlesung über die Geschichte der neueren Philosophie' [~ 1833/34] in Schelling, *Sämmtliche Werke*, I/10, 22).

58 Cf. Don Cupitt, 'Kant and the Negative Theology', in *Is Nothing Sacred? The Non-Realist Philosophy of Religion: Selected Essays* (New York: Fordham University Press, 2002), here 6–10.

59 Marion, *Idol and Distance*, 145. While he expresses reservations about the term 'negative theology' later ('In the Name', 21), he upholds the claim that 'negative theology' is the 'first serious rival' of deconstruction, 'perhaps the only one possible' ('In the Name', 22).

60 Cf. the beginning of Dietrich Bonhoeffer's 1933 lectures on Christology: 'The silence of the Church is silence before the Word. In proclaiming Christ, the Church falls on its knees in silence before the inexpressible, the ἄρρητον.' Bonhoeffer, *Works*, vol. 12: *Berlin: 1932–1933* (L. Rasmussen (ed.); Minneapolis: Augsburg Fortress Press, 2009), 300. Generally very helpful is David F. Ford, 'Apophasis and the Shoah: Where was Jesus Christ at Auschwitz?' in *Silence and the Word* (Oliver Davies and Denys Turner (eds); Cambridge: Cambridge University Press, 2002), 185–200.

61 Martin Luther, *Lectures on Genesis* in *Martin Luthers Werke: Kritische Gesamtausgabe* (WA) (Weimar: H. Böhlaus Nachfolger, 1883–), vol. 43, 393.24–7; English Translation: *Luther's Works* (J. Pelikan et al. (eds); St Louis, Mo.: Concordia Publishing House, 1955–86), vol. 4, 357. Cf. Bernard McGinn, 'Vere tu es Deus Absconditus: The Hidden God in Luther and Some Mystics' in *Silence and the Word*, 94–114.

62 Cf. the historical account in Louth, *The Origins of the Christian Mystical Tradition* (Oxford: Oxford University Press, 1981).

63 Marion, *God Without Being*, 71.

64 Marion, *God Without Being*, 73–83. Marion's treatment of Aquinas soon became the object of fierce criticism (cf., for example, Dominique Dubarle (ed.), *Dieu avec l'être: De Parménide à Saint Thomas: essai d'ontologie théologale* (Paris: Beauchesne, 1986). Marion, while defending his position in the preface to the English edition (*God Without Being*, xxii–xxiv), eventually retracted in an article titled 'Saint Thomas d'Aquin et l'onto-théo-logie', first published in 1994 and reprinted in the second edition of *Dieu sans l'être*, Paris 2002, 279–332.

65 Marion, 'In the Name', 22.

CHAPTER 2

TIME AND THE RESPONSIBILITIES OF READING: REVISITING DERRIDA AND DIONYSIUS

David Newheiser

Time poses a particular difficulty for the readers of ancient texts. Because the past is distant, the context of a given work, the significance of its terms and the problems to which it responds can be reconstructed with only relative certainty. For some readers, of course, historical concerns are secondary, but they face a corresponding difficulty: if philological methods cannot determine the meaning of a text, how can a responsible reading be delimited? Both problems are posed by the spacing of time, for readings directed towards history and those motivated by constructive intentions both operate within and from a present that remains distant from the time of the text. These two styles of interpretation frequently seem to be at odds in the debate over 'postmodern' readings of the church fathers; it is my suggestion that their relation may be clarified by revisiting Jacques Derrida's reading of Dionysius the Areopagite.

Derrida discusses 'negative theology'[1] at key points throughout his career, and he shows a particular interest in Dionysius. Some commentators enthusiastically conclude that Derrida is close (though ultimately superior) to classic Christian mysticism, while others object that Derrida's reading imposes an alien agenda upon a text that deserves greater respect. Denys Turner writes, 'It is certainly true that what in Dionysius fascinated Derrida and his followers was entirely dictated by the theoretical agendas of their deconstructionist strategies, and that Derrida's Dionysius amounted to little more than a dismembered torso'.[2] Sarah Coakley similarly responds to 'the post-modern "apophatic rage"' by warning that '"rages" are not always tempered by scholarly caution or philosophical precision'.[3] Turner notes that at least Derrida can 'engage in dialogue with [Dionysius] in terms of . . . twentieth-century problematics and agendas, in a way which can seem to be disabled by our scholars' niceties and methodological correctnesses',[4] but Turner's scholarly scruples appear to preclude the dialogue Derrida attempts.

My own hypothesis is that, if historico-critical and theoretical-constructive readings both operate at a distance from the past, the authority of the former is more limited than its partisans appreciate.[5] Ironically, while some complain that Derrida's reading of Dionysius is filtered through his modern agenda, many influential interpreters superimpose their preconceived opinions onto the Dionysian text. While the eisegesis advanced by these scholars claims to delimit the boundaries of acceptable interpretation, I argue that Derrida's reading is exemplary insofar as it displays considerable care for the ambivalent details of the texts in question and remains open to other interpretations. Once Derrida's engagement with Dionysius is thus recuperated, we may recognize the surprising affinity between the two authors, for, despite their many differences, they may be seen to share a rigorous negativity inflected by the alterity of time. Both authors demand that we take responsibility for continuing speech that remains basically inadequate, thus suggesting that interpretation too should continually pursue ever deeper attention to the text.

Revisiting Dionysius

The earliest extant mention of the *Corpus Areopagiticum* came in 532 at the Council of Constantinople, where 'the Blessed Dionysius the Areopagite' was cited in support of the non-Chalcedonian position,[6] and interpretations of Dionysius have since tended to stigmatize or defend him. John of Scythopolis, Dionysius's first commentator, goes to great lengths to demonstrate that Dionysius is untainted by 'the bastard teachings of the Greek philosophers',[7] a suspicion that culminated in Luther's claim that 'this Dionysius, whoever he may have been . . . is downright dangerous, for he is more of a Platonist than a Christian.'[8] This objection gained greater force in the twentieth century, when it was shown that John of Scythopolis' attempt to explain away the Hellenistic tone of Dionysius's terminology inadvertently demonstrates his dependence upon the fifth-century philosopher Proclus.[9] Once Dionysius's claimed relation to the Apostle Paul was proved false, many came to conclude with Anders Nygren that 'now no one could help seeing that the Christianity of Dionysius was entirely different from that of Paul and of the New Testament in general'.[10] Unfortunately, because many assume that Dionysius must either be valorized or rejected, the texts themselves have frequently received a cursory reading.

Jan Vanneste, for one, extends the critical rejection of Dionysius, but his judgement takes little account of the particulars of Dionysius's texts. He complains that 'there is no authentic supernatural mysticism expressed in the text of Pseudo-Dionysius if we interpret it in a strictly objective way',[11] but this conclusion depends upon a set of assumptions concerning the character of 'authentic' mysticism that are foreign to the texts in question. Vanneste claims that 'the expression, *mustikos*, which is used in [*The Mystical Theology*], would indicate only a stylistic procedure that allowed

Dionysius to use the terminology of the mystery cults',[12] but this ignores the possibility that the *mustikos* (a term that occurs thirty-some times in the *Corpus*) has a significance for Dionysius that does not conform to Vanneste's preconceived notion. Because he supposes that Christian mysticism concerns 'the unpredictable details of a vital experience',[13] Vanneste concludes that 'there is, then, no trace in [*The Mystical Theology*] of the reality which is covered by this word in Christian theology'.[14] Surprisingly, though, he fails to consider whether Dionysius suggests an alternative to this tendentious account of mysticism. Although it may be true, as Vanneste suggests, that Dionysius 'is more interested in maintaining the exact and tight articulations of this conceptual structure than in describing the unpredictable details of a vital experience',[15] he fails to appreciate this structure on its own terms, for he hastily applies an alien standard. Vanneste concludes that, 'embedded in a Neoplatonic theory of knowledge, the data of revelation as used by Dionysius can hardly be considered as part of a successful theological synthesis or even as Christian theology'.[16] Although this is a strong claim, it is based on a weak reading of the texts.

In response to accusations like the one leveled by Vanneste, Andrew Louth has shown that *The Mystical Theology* sometimes echoes the language of Christian liturgy; indeed, since *The Ecclesiastical Hierarchy* examines the elements of Christian liturgy with such care, it would be obtuse to ignore this dimension of the *Corpus*. Nevertheless, the liturgical resonances Louth identifies in *The Mystical Theology* are insufficient to justify his claim that 'the context of the *Mystical Theology* is not the individual "mystic's" solitary ascent to God, but the priest's (or rather the bishop's) ascent to the altar'.[17] Although Louth does show that *The Mystical Theology* allows a liturgical reading, other interpretations remain possible, especially since the liturgical dimension remains implicit in this text; after all, reading the work in light of liturgy need not preclude interpretations in relation to other terms and problematics. Louth assumes that 'it is the liturgy . . . that is the fundamental context for Dionysius',[18] but (apart from the fact that complex individuals bear the mark of various contexts, as Dionysius clearly does) Louth is unable to demonstrate that this is so on the basis of the text itself. Much as Vanneste never shows the relation between his broad assumptions about the true content of mysticism and the terms of Dionysius's texts, Louth superimposes constraints upon the text that cannot be internally justified. Although the details of Louth's interpretation offer much to recommend it, his failure to appreciate the distance between his analysis and Dionysius himself obscures dimensions of the texts in question.

Like Louth, Alexander Golitzin attends to the liturgical dimension of the *Corpus*, but he too overstates his case. In response to objections directed at Dionysius's apparent Platonism he writes, 'I came to feel that the portrayal of Dionysius as a villain . . . raised disturbing questions about the trustworthiness of the tradition that I had been led to believe constituted the living esse of the Church and her gospel'.[19] Because Golitzin assumes that the Orthodox tradition is harmonious and authoritative, Dionysius's reception into that tradition requires Golitzin to defend his untainted Christianity or risk jeopardizing his faith. Ironically, although he notes that 'confessional attitudes . . . have in their turn as often obscured the picture as they have illumined it',[20] he affirms an expressly sectarian stance, defending 'a generally Christian, specifically Eastern Orthodox, reading of the Areopagite'.[21] In order to protect Dionysius from Western misreadings, Golitzin claims that Dionysius is 'an Eastern Christian writer and, more-over, a monastic one',[22] but these broad claims are supported by tenuous evidence. By virtue of his use of a pseudonym, we do not know where Dionysius lived, whether he was a monk or (for the most part) what he read. But the point applies more broadly: it is unjustifiable to demand that any author be read in conformity with one's predetermined expectations. Golitzin claims that '"mystical" for our writer carries essentially its general, patristic meaning',[23] but this flattens the significance of the *Corpus* by restricting its meaning with reference to assumptions that are foreign to the text. Like Vanneste, Golitzin assumes that Dionysius must be read against an ostensibly univocal Christian tradition, but in so doing he loses sight of the particular complexity of the texts in question.

Whereas scholars like Vanneste, Louth and Golitzin impose a univocal reading on the *Corpus Areopagiticum*, Dionysius displays an ambivalence that undercuts such simplifications. Since our language operates in the realm of what is immanent to us, and insofar as God 'transcends mind and being'[24] as the creator of both, Dionysius argues that God is wholly beyond the scope of language. He writes, 'If all knowledge . . . is limited to the realm of the existent, then whatever transcends being must also transcend knowledge'.[25] Nor is this the weaker claim that affirmative theology is subject to a negative corrective: Dionysius is clear that every conceptual and linguistic category for God fails completely.[26] For this reason, the required negativity is relentless. He writes, '[God] has no power, it is not power, nor is it light. It does not live nor is it life. . . . It is not wisdom. It is neither one nor oneness, divinity nor goodness'.[27] The remarkable rigour of this passage disrupts the simplifying confidence of his interpreters, for although some assume that Dionysius must either be assimilated with a preconceived account of Christian orthodoxy or rejected as beyond redemption, the negativity Dionysius demands leaves no context undisturbed.

As has often been remarked, the serial negation Dionysius describes resembles Derrida's comment that '*différance* is not, does not exist, is not a present-being in any form; and we will be led to delineate also everything that it is not, that is, everything; and consequently that it has neither existence nor essence. It derives from no category of being, whether present or absent'.[28] Derrida continues, however, 'And yet those aspects of *différance* which are thereby delineated are not theological, not even in the order of the most negative of negative theologies, which are always concerned with disengaging a superessentiality beyond the finite categories of essence and existence, only in order to acknowledge his superior, inconceivable, and ineffable mode of being'.[29] His concern is that Dionysius, despite his denials, still refers to God as superessential, beyond being (that is, ὑπερούσιος), which seems to allow the predicate 'being' to remain in place, though in an elevated sense. Indeed, there is a paradox in Dionysius's claim that mystical negativity serves a positive function. Dionysius writes, 'By an undivided and absolute abandonment of yourself and everything, shedding all and freed from all, you will be uplifted to the ray of the divine darkness beyond being [τὸν ὑπερούσιον τοῦ θείου σκότους ἀκτῖνα]'.[30] There is an epistemological problem here (How can one determine the destination without depending on one's understanding?) which hints at a disingenuous doubledealing. To seek to get to God in this roundabout way suggests that not everything has been abandoned, that some understanding still operates undisturbed and that one still seeks self-fulfilment, at least the fulfilment of the understanding in question and its projected achievement (of God).

This tension is intensified by the fact that, as Derrida notes,[31] this predication 'beyond' institutes a hierarchy that appears to be at odds with the resolute negativity Dionysius elsewhere displays. Dionysius writes that 'the sacred institution and source of perfection established our most pious hierarchy. [God] modeled it on the hierarchies of heaven . . . so that, in a way appropriate to our nature, we might be uplifted from these most venerable images to interpretations and assimilations which are simple and inexpressible'.[32] On this account, God has instituted a gradation descending from God through the angels, then through the church, ultimately including every intelligent being, with stratified divisions at every level. Although Dionysius writes that 'we deny all things so that we may unhiddenly know that unknowing which itself is hidden from all those possessed of knowing amid all beings',[33] he suggests elsewhere that this cosmic structure enables ascent towards God as the medium of divine grace. He explains that 'the Deity first emerges from secrecy to revelation by way of mediation by those first powers',[34] and he describes how enlightenment is passed from God to the highest angels down through 'the lower ranks of heavenly beings'.[35] Since 'this arrangement is copied by our own hierarchy',[36] the mediation is unbroken, and this system acts as the medium whereby secrecy becomes revelation as the inexpressible God is made known.

Derrida's reading raises a question, then, about the relation between Dionysius's resolute negativity and his affirmation of ecclesial life. Dionysius claims that, since God himself modeled the structure of the church ('our hierarchy'[37]) on the angelic order ('the hierarchies of heaven'[38]), one may grasp the inexpressible within the church, but if God is truly inaccessible to knowledge, it would be impossible to know that continuity with God is established in this way. Similarly, Dionysius writes that 'divine scripture teaches us that we will only obtain [union with God] through the most loving observance of the august commandments and by the doing of sacred acts',[39] but this circumscription of our contact with God conflicts with his claim elsewhere that 'everything in some way partakes of the providence flowing out of this transcendent deity which is the originator of all that is'.[40] If it is true that 'we know [God] from the arrangement of everything',[41] it would seem that access to God cannot be limited to the church; conversely, if God 'is beyond assertion and denial',[42] then we cannot know whether God's presence is hierarchically mediated. Dionysius asserts ecclesial privilege while undercutting it at the same time, proliferating assertions even as he demands denial – this is the tension to which Derrida's reading attends.

Denys Turner complains that 'in Derrida's hands Dionysius' theology is cut down to fragments . . . torn from the body of liturgical practice in connection with which, if Andrew Louth is right, [*The Mystical Theology* and *The Divine Names*] alone can be understood with any degree of adequacy'.[43] But, in fact, Derrida is unusually attentive to the significance of prayer and praise in Dionysius. In fact, these liturgical elements simply heighten the tension that Derrida identifies. He writes, 'An experience must yet guide the apophasis toward excellence, not allow it to say just anything, and prevent it from manipulating its negations like empty and purely mechanical phrases. This experience is that of prayer'.[44] Derrida neither rejects Dionysius in the manner of Vanneste, nor does he seek to find confirmation of his own opinions; instead, he reflects upon the paradox implicit in Dionysius's use of the verb ὑμνεῖν, which appears to replace predication with hymnic praise but (as Derrida notes) continues to qualify God and determine the supposedly unknowable object of address.[45] For this reason, Derrida may respond to objections like Turner's: 'When

I read Pseudo-Dionysius, I paid a lot of attention, precisely to the liturgical, to prayer, to the non-predicative form of discourse'.[46] Unlike many of Dionysius's detractors, Derrida recognizes that the appeal to pragmatics only intensifies the problem, for Dionysius demands 'the absolute abandonment of yourself and everything',[47] including (it would seem) ecclesial practice itself.

It is this radical moment in Dionysius that Louth and Golitzin fail to appreciate; indeed, by their interpretation, it makes no sense for him to deny the ecclesial mediation which for them is insuperable. Golitzin claims that 'it is the Church, the body of Christ, which is for Dionysius . . . the "place" of encounter with God . . . and therefore also the place for our considerations of the following treatises'.[48] However, although Dionysius identifies Christ and his church as the means to union with God, Golitzin is wrong to say that 'nothing of any validity or truth may be accomplished outside of our hierarchy'.[49] On the contrary, far from limiting knowledge of God to an ecclesial context, Dionysius writes that 'God is therefore known in all things and as distinct from all things. . . . He is all things in all things and he is no thing among things'.[50] By claiming that the church provides exclusive access to God, Golitzin neglects both the fact that God is 'known in all things' without qualification and that God remains 'distinct from all things', including the church itself. In an attempt to make Dionysius into a good churchman, Golitzin writes that 'neither [Symeon] the New Theologian, nor his disciple, nor Dionysius do push their logic to the limits. They are content with ambiguity, and they are thus very wise'.[51] But the decision not to follow the logic of the *Corpus Areopagiticum* all the way is Golitzin's own, for Dionysius himself is unstinting.[52]

In contrast to interpretations that force Dionysius to fit a predetermined schema, either revering or rejecting him, Derrida highlights a tension present in the texts that remains unabated. Although, as Golitzin suggests,[53] Dionysius does believe that ecclesial life is the means of our union with God, every existing arrangement is relativized in light of the eschatological future. Dionysius writes,

> We now grasp these things in the best way we can, and as they come to us, wrapped in the sacred veils of that love toward humanity with which scripture and hierarchical traditions cover the truths of the mind with things derived from the realm of the senses. . . . But in time to come, when we are incorruptible and immortal, when we have come at last to the blessed inheritance of being like Christ, then, as scripture says, 'we shall always be with the Lord'. In most holy contemplation we shall be ever filled with the sight of God shining gloriously around us . . . and, somehow, in a way we

cannot know, we shall be united with him and, our understanding carried
away, blessedly happy, we shall be struck by his blazing light.[54]

Dionysius's basic ambivalence is encapsulated in the suspension between
the claim that 'we now grasp these things' and his admission that the sight
of God is deferred to some 'time to come'. Since the affirmation that our
union with God will take place 'in a way we cannot know' entails that the
expectation that 'we shall be struck by his blazing light' is an uncertain
hope, we can only speak 'in the best way we can', oriented towards
the future without grasping what is to come. Far from representing his
final word, Dionysius's claim that the church is our means to union with
God may thus be seen as a prudential judgement that remains radically
unsettled by the unknowable future.[55] Indeed, as Derrida helps us to
see, the tension Dionysius describes requires imperfect speech to continue
without settling into an ultimate affirmation.[56] By the same token, though,
it is perverse to constrain the process of interpretation by asserting preconceived opinions; on the contrary, Dionysius suggests that our reading
must remain in motion.

Revisiting Derrida

At this point, we may advance a provisional hypothesis: just as Dionysius
suggests that the gap between our present and future union with God
allows speech to continue, albeit imperfectly, the gap between our present
and ancient texts might likewise be impossible to bridge, thus requiring
interpretations to proliferate without any one possessing total authority.
This suggestion is confirmed by the fact that, whereas some scholars
attempt to limit the significance of the *Corpus Areopagiticum* by assimilating Dionysius to a particular context, Derrida's sensitivity to the tensions
present in the text both encourages and exemplifies an attentive practice
of reading. In this case, a provisional reading characterized by care yields
richer results than those constrained by interpretative prejudice; what is
more, such an interpretation helps to clarify the surprising affinity between
Derrida and Dionysius. Much as Dionysius argues that we must act and
speak as best we can while remaining open to the unforeseeable future,
Derrida develops an ethics of responsibility that is continually disrupted
by what is to come.

Derrida distinguishes a future that remains irreducible to presence,
the arrival of a surprising event: 'what *comes*, what there is and which is
always singular'.[57] Although systems neutralize the unexpected by subjecting

everything to calculation on the basis of present knowledge, the event exceeds presence from within. Derrida writes, 'There is *some* machine everywhere, and notably in language. . . . As soon as there is any calculation, calculability, and repetition, there is something of a machine. . . . But in the machine there is an excess in relation to the machine itself'.[58] Since the certainty that one had finally eluded mechanical calculation would itself remain calculated, one cannot simply sidestep the problem; rather, in the context of calculation and mechanical synchronicity, something other – the future – may come. Derrida explains, 'The coming of the other, *l'arrivance de l'arrivant* – the "arriving-ness" of the arrival – this is *what happens*, this is the one *who or which arrives* as an unforeseeable event'.[59] Whereas the realization of a preordained program would mechanically reaffirm the present order, the event is unprogrammatic and unknowable. In this way, Derrida distinguishes between a future continuous with the present and a 'future to come', a future (in French, *avenir*) that has the character of being yet to come (that is, *à-venir*).

In this way, Derrida, like Dionysius, links a rigorous awareness of the limits of language to a certain account of futurity. In Derrida's view, knowledge remains the domain of presence, for it partakes of the calculation of synchronic systems. For this reason, the future cannot be grasped; that is, it cannot be captured in predicative speech. Nevertheless, he writes, 'The event remains at once *in* and *on* language, then, within and at the surface (a surface open, exposed, immediately overflowed, outside of itself)'.[60] Although the event is *on* language since it is separate from language, it may arrive *in* language because language overflows its own surface. As Derrida argues elsewhere, linguistic systems are necessarily open to that which exceeds them, what he here refers to as the impossible event. Although discourse cannot capture the event, the future may erupt within presence itself. For this reason, expectation is necessarily uncertain, but this deferral of satisfaction does not entail hopeless futility, for the impossible cannot be excluded.

Derrida argues that the negativity required by the unknowable is inseparable from affirmative discourse, which strongly resembles the tension in Dionysius between speech and silence. As we have seen, Dionysius says that it is 'in time to come' that 'we shall be ever filled with the sight of God shining gloriously around us', and he affirms that this event will take place 'in a way we cannot know'.[61] Elsewhere Dionysius is clear that 'these promises exceed all understanding and the words naming them fall far short of the truth they contain',[62] which indicates (once again) that he rigorously distinguishes present discourse from the unknowable future. In a phrase that echoes Derrida's account of the unforeseeable event,

Dionysius writes, 'What comes into view, contrary to hope, from previous obscurity, is described as "sudden"'.[63] He explains that Christ's Incarnation is an example of such suddenness and concludes, 'What is to be said of it remains unsayable; what is to be understood of it remains unknowable'.[64] Because the event of the Incarnation contradicts every expectation and prior possibility, Dionysius affirms that it is unknowable, and yet the unsayable cannot be excluded from 'what is to be said'. Therefore, Dionysius and Derrida both attend to the coming of the impossible through an eschatological orientation that makes space for a silence nonetheless intertwined with speech.

Some argue that, despite their similarity, Derrida does Dionysius one better by dispensing altogether with the affirmative discourse that comprises the bulk of the *Corpus Areopagiticum*. After all, Dionysius writes that 'as Cause of all and as transcending all, [God] is rightly nameless and yet has the names of everything that is',[65] but Derrida names God hardly at all. Yet, although Derrida might seem more stringent, the two are quite close on this point as well, for Derrida too distinguishes the silence required by the unforeseeable future from both language and its absence. He writes, 'Heterogeneous to the hidden, to the obscure, to the nocturnal, to the invisible, to what can be dissimulated and indeed to what is non-manifest in general, [the secret] cannot be unveiled'.[66] The silence required by the future is not something secreted away for safekeeping, nor is it potentially present, for it eludes presence and the machine, and there is no way to ensure that it is safely contained. Thus, he continues, 'It remains silent, not to keep a word in reserve or withdrawn, but because it remains foreign to speech'.[67] It is precisely because the event of this silence is irreducible to speech that it may come within linguistic structures; it can thus be identified neither with discourse nor with its exclusion. For this reason, Derrida says, 'The secret as such, *as secret*, separates and already institutes a negativity; it is a negation that denies itself. It de-negates itself'.[68] Since the secret cannot be grasped even by denying it, it can only deny itself in a reduplicated negation, denying its denial such that its identity is endangered, unsettled by the impossible once again.

Derrida contrasts his denegative secrecy with the calculated secrecy of a secret society, which hides its knowledge from outsiders. He writes, 'The mystagogues claim to possess as if in private the privilege of a mysterious secret . . . The revelation or unveiling of the secret is reserved to them; they jealously protect it'.[69] This strategic secrecy violates the future by claiming the presence of a revelatory *apocalypsis* (an unveiling). Derrida explains that 'they say they are in immediate and intuitive relation with a mystery. And they wish to attract, seduce, lead toward the mystery and by the mystery'.[70] But this might also describe Dionysius's approach, for he envisions a stratified society in which some 'have with perfect understanding learned the divine secret'.[71] Because 'every order in the hierarchical rank is uplifted as best it can toward cooperation with God',[72] Dionysius instructs that 'you must never speak nor divulge divine things to the uninitiated'[73] since 'it is most fitting . . . that the sacred and hidden truth about the celestial intelligences be concealed through the inexpressible and the sacred and be inaccessible to the *hoi polloi*'.[74] Although he elsewhere requires a more radical silence, Dionysius sometimes implies that the sacred is inaccessible only to some and that the mysterious secret may in fact be possessed and protected.

However, far from representing their incompatibility, this ambivalent secrecy brings Dionysius and Derrida still closer. For, although Derrida rejects any claim to grasp the future, he argues that apocalypticism is unavoidable since even an enlightened critique 'keeps within itself some apocalyptic desire, this time as desire for clarity and revelation, in order to demystify or, if you prefer, to deconstruct apocalyptic discourse itself'.[75] Because mystagogic secrecy could only be opposed with reference to a superior unveiling, Derrida concludes that 'all language on apocalypse is also apocalyptic'.[76] Any judgement must appeal to a privileged knowledge, and all predication is apocalyptic insofar as it claims knowledge of the truth: Derrida comments on the Apocalypse of John, 'Truth is the end and the instance of the last judgment. The structure of truth here would be apocalyptic'.[77] Since every claim excludes other possibilities by asserting the presence of truth, apocalyptic mystification is unavoidable. Thus, although Dionysius's appeal to secrecy is problematic, Derrida's is as well, for the secret eludes every discourse, including his own. Ironically, much as some scholars exaggerate Dionysius's identity by overlooking the rigor of the *Corpus Areopagiticum*, many commentators similarly neglect Derrida's reflexive negativity.

John Caputo, for instance, contends that 'deconstruction differs from the Christian mystical theology of Pseudo-Dionysius or of Meister Eckhart as an indeterminate differs from a determinate affirmation of the impossible'.[78] Although Caputo admits that 'the desire of deconstruction for the more-than-possible impossible is a passion that it shares with apophatic theology',[79] he repeatedly claims that apophatic theology betrays the impossible by giving it determinate content. He writes, 'The secret has an apophatic quality, *not* in the sense of negative theology, which is a hyperousiological high to which certain select initiates may be introduced. . . . Rather the "absolute secret" is apophaticism itself, the stuff of . . . a "general apophatics", which is the condition of all these other relative and determinate secrets'.[80] Caputo concludes that, since apophatic theology always asserts a privileged knowledge, it is surpassed by the indeterminate secrecy of deconstruction, whereas '*viens* for Derrida is not the call for a fixed and identifiable other, foreseeable and foregraspable, for that would release the manic aggression of a program, the mania of an all-out rush for a future-present'.[81] Yet this fails to appreciate that for Derrida 'the absolute secret', 'the call "*viens*"' and 'apophaticism itself' (whatever that is) are all unattainable: for Derrida, as for Dionysius, the unforeseeable comes within and despite the relative judgements and inadequate speech that inevitably continue.[82]

Like Caputo, many commentators flatten Derrida's reading of Dionysius in order to stigmatize or defend him, but a closer reading shows that even Derrida's critical reserve concerning Dionysius's supposed superessentialism displays a complex dynamic. Mary-Jane Rubenstein comments that 'Derrida goes on to say – without footnote, qualification, or parenthetical remark – "No, what I write is not negative theology"',[83] but this is patently false. In fact, Derrida continues: 'No, what I write is not "negative theology". First of all, *in the measure* to which this belongs to the predicative or judicative space of discourse . . . Next, in the measure to which "negative theology" seems to reserve, beyond all positive predication, beyond all negation, even beyond Being, some hyperessentiality, a being beyond Being'.[84] Derrida's distance from negative theology is complicated and qualified by these two conditions; it is only insofar as negative theology is hyperessentialist that Derrida differentiates himself. But this suggests that Derrida and Dionysius might be very close '*in the measure* to which' Dionysius differs from the hyperessentialism Derrida describes.

Indeed, Derrida continues by suggesting that Dionysius's texts are not exhausted by a hyperessentialist reading, that perhaps his 'negative theology' pushes discourse beyond predication. He writes, 'Does one have the right to think that, as a pure address, on the edge of silence . . . prayer should never be turned away from its part . . . by a multiplication of addresses? . . . Perhaps there would be no prayer . . . without what we glimpse as a menace or as a contamination; writing, the code, repetition, analogy or the – at least apparent – multiplicity of addresses, initiation.'[85] Derrida's concern is that a prayer that could be expressed in language – in particular, the prayer that opens *The Mystical Theology* – might fall short of pure address, that its intimacy would be lost in (inherently public) speech. As he notes, verbalized praise still 'preserves the style and the structure of a predicative affirmation' insofar as it 'says something about someone'.[86] On the other hand, he suggests that writing and the possibility of repetition might instead condition the possibility of prayer, 'the prayer that apostrophizes, addresses itself to the other and remains . . . absolutely pre-predicative'.[87] Derrida does not decide between these two possibilities, but he does suggest that the relation between secrecy and speech that he sketches elsewhere might apply to a form of prayer intertwined with the discourse of an apophaticism that is now no longer purely negative.[88]

In fact, Derrida was aware all along that what passes as 'negative theology' is complex and variegated. As he comments at one point, 'I . . . am quite convinced of the need for a rigorous and differentiated reading of everything advanced under this title (negative theology)'.[89] Even when expressing his concern about hyperessentialism most sharply, at the outset of his career, his comment that 'negative theologies . . . are always concerned with disengaging a superessentiality . . . only in order to acknowledge his superior . . . mode of being'[90] is complicated by his admission that 'the detours, locutions, and syntax in which I will often have to take recourse will resemble those of negative theology, occasionally even to the point of being indistinguishable from negative theology'.[91] Even at this early stage, he recognizes that deconstruction and negative theology might be indistinguishable, and it remains a constant reference throughout his oeuvre, allowing him to continually refine his reading. Although his interpretation of Dionysius is brief and occasional, he explicitly acknowledges that there is much more to be said; he writes, 'Perhaps there is within it, hidden, restless, diverse, and itself heterogeneous, a voluminous and nebulous multiplicity of potentials to which the single expression "negative theology" yet remains inadequate'.[92] Far from dismissing Dionysius, Derrida recognizes his richness, leaving open the possibility that they are in fact very close.

It is for this reason that Derrida responds with bemusement to Jean-Luc Marion's refutation of four objections supposedly advanced by Derrida in what Marion claims is a 'fundamental and unified argument' designed 'to stigmatize "negative theology's" persistence in making affirmations about God'.[93] Derrida notes, on the contrary, that his comments on negative theology 'are not a thesis on a theme' but instead operate according to 'a performative aspect' that remains sensitive to the 'long displacement of a number of voices' in these texts.[94] Although his initial references to negative theology (from 1964–8) are abrupt enough that they could be seen to imply a polemical stance, a close reading of those texts makes clear that Derrida's stance is complex even at this point. Derrida's views are even more nuanced by the time of 'How to Avoid Speaking' (1986); in 'Sauf le nom' (1992), for instance, the multiple voices of negative theology are represented in the form of Derrida's own text, which constitutes an interchange between interlocutors, a sort of abstracted dialogue. One of these voices goes so far as to say, 'I trust no text that is not in some way contaminated with negative theology, and even among those texts that apparently do not have, want, or believe they have any relation with theology in general'.[95] Far from rejecting negative theology hastily, then, Derrida draws heavily upon it. He acknowledges, for instance, that it plays a crucial role in articulating his eschatological politics,[96] and he goes so far as to suggest that 'this *via negativa* . . . should remain at work (thus give up the work) for the (loved) other to remain the other'.[97] Despite the complaints of some commentators, then, Derrida's reading of Dionysius is circumspect and insightful, thus exemplifying the limitless responsibility required by the eschatological denial of knowledge that he and Dionysius share.

Reading Responsibly

Derrida and Dionysius, for all their differences, display a profound affinity. They have both been subject to interpreters who, in order to attack or defend them, have exaggerated one aspect of their work at the expense of its complexity, but both authors undercut such simplification by attending to a future that keeps their writing always in motion, shot through with a silence that is beyond both speech and its exclusion. Dionysius argues that, because God is 'before time and beyond time',[98] God 'is inexpressible and ineffable',[99] which echoes Derrida's account of the unforeseeable future. Much as Derrida claims that the event is so radically distinguished from the present order that it may intervene at any point, Dionysius explains that God's heterogeneity to time precludes certain knowledge: 'To [God] is properly attributed past, present, and future, came-to-be, coming-to-be, will-come-to-be. All these characteristics, when divinely understood, indicate the complete transcendence of his Being'.[100] Because God is thus 'eternity and is above and prior to eternity',[101] God is entirely beyond the present order; for this reason, just as for Derrida the future requires a secrecy so deep that it cannot be grasped, Dionysius demands 'an undivided and absolute abandonment of yourself and everything'.[102] Because the present is radically distinguished from future union with God, we have no grasp upon what is to come. For both Dionysius and Derrida, however, this rigorous negativity does not preclude the validity of relative judgements; instead, it describes the tense situation of responsible speech.

Derrida's appreciation for negative theology runs so deep that it serves, he says, to describe the condition of responsibility. He writes, 'Without silence . . . we could simply unfold knowledge into a program or course of action. Nothing could make us more irresponsible; nothing could be more totalitarian'.[103] Decision, for Derrida, has the character of an event, rigorously distinguished from knowledge, for as long as decision is sure of itself it mechanically unfolds the program of the present. He explains, 'This terrible law . . . gives responsibility and decision – if there are any – whatever chance they may have, but leaves no chance for a good conscience. No one can ever *know* . . . that a responsible decision was made and that it will have been the best'.[104] Decision thus requires the secrecy described above, a silence so deep that it runs through and alongside speech (like the pure address of prayer). Just as such silence is not the interdiction of language, the denial of knowledge enables activity that strains towards a responsibility that excludes complacent self-satisfaction. Derrida asks, 'Why this language, which does not fortuitously resemble that of negative theology?' and he answers, 'Because one must avoid good conscience at all costs'.[105]

In similar fashion, Dionysius's negativity entails a considerable circumspection. Because 'we shall be united with [God]' only 'in time to come', and since this will happen 'in a way we cannot know' and with 'our understanding carried away',[106] God is not circumscribed by our understanding. As with Derrida, this radical negativity does not entail inaction; on the contrary, because all creation points to God, the proliferation of speech is required. After all, in addition to the 'darkness which is beyond intellect'[107] and absolute, there is a darkness which is corrigible, belonging as it does to error and ignorance.[108] We must 'grasp these things in the best way we can'[109] in order to dispel the darkness of error as far as possible, but such judgements are continually called into question by the fact that 'all human thinking is a sort of error when compared with the solid permanence of the perfect divine thoughts'.[110] Although Dionysius observes that it is better to say that God is goodness than to say that he is stone,[111] elsewhere he notes that the more elevated names 'are actually no less defective than this latter, for the Deity is far beyond every manifestation of being and life'.[112] Relative judgements are necessary, but even our best efforts amount to 'a sort of error'; for this reason, responsible speech must remain insecure and endless.

Ironically, those modern commentators who claim that the significance of the *Corpus Areopagiticum* is limited, for instance, by an ecclesial context are distant from both authors insofar as they lack such circumspection. In fact, Derrida's reading of Dionysius (though brief) is exemplary insofar as it highlights suggestive tensions present in the text without concluding that Dionysius must then be valorized or rejected. This attitude finds support in his crucial recognition that the texts in question are complex, that there is still more to be said, which accords with the account of responsibility that emerges from the surprising affinity between these two authors. Dionysius too is sensitive to the limits of his own interpretation; he writes, 'These, then, are the divine names. . . . But of course I have fallen well short of what they actually mean. . . . In this I have fallen wretchedly short not only of the theologians, their hearers and their followers but even of my own peers'.[113] Such humility suggests that, just as the spacing of time requires continual revision, interpretation itself ought to proceed towards a horizon of significance that is never attained. Because, for both authors, the future cannot be assimilated to present speech, we might surmise that the past likewise remains always beyond us.[114] Such spacing demands circumspect care, for every reading remains ultimately inadequate, but for this reason interpretations ought to proliferate under the demand of a responsibility that is never complete.

Time poses a particular difficulty for the readers of ancient texts, but quantitative differences do nothing to alter the gulf that divides every text from every interpreter – after all, interpretation always follows what it interprets in time. In the case of Dionysius, it is starkly apparent that claims about the texts' 'proper' context are extremely tenuous, for little is known about their author, but every text carries an analogous mystery. Although historico-critical readings may open avenues for interpretation, philological methods offer uncertain results, and their conclusions – even in the case of supposedly contemporary authors – can never determine the meaning of a text. As we have seen, attempts at contextualization often serve to sanctify the interpreter's own prejudice, but because the past is always read in and through a particular present, some distortion is inevitable. For this reason, theoretical-constructive readings should be given free rein within the admission that every interpretation is provisional and imperfect. Although the reading I have developed here is likewise limited, it is meant to model and describe an ethic of ever-deeper attention to the text. The difficulty posed by the distance of time subjects us to a responsibility that is endless, one that offers the joy of perpetual discovery through repeated reading disrupted by the insurmountable distance of time.

Notes

1   This is a contentious term, to be sure, and for Derrida the quotation marks highlight the fact that it oversimplifies. See Jacques Derrida, 'Derrida's Response to Jean-Luc Marion' in *God, the Gift, and Postmodernism* (The Indiana Series in the Philosophy of Religion; Bloomington: Indiana University Press, 1999), 42–53.

2 Denys Turner, 'How to read the Pseudo-Denys today?', *International Journal of Systematic Theology*, 7/4 (2005), 428–40.

3 Sarah Coakley, 'Introduction: re-thinking Dionysius the Areopagite', in *Re-Thinking Dionysius the Areopagite* (Sarah Coakley and Charles M. Stang (eds); Oxford: Wiley-Blackwell, 2009), 1–25.

4 Turner, 'How to read the Pseudo-Denys?', 433.

5 I disagree, then, with John Jones's claim that 'current constructive theologies should be conscious of the difference between how Dionysian theology may be retrieved and how it is to be interpreted in its own right' (John N. Jones, 'Sculpting God: the logic of Dionysian negative theology', *Harvard Theological Review*, 89/4 (1996), 355–71, here 369). Although the difference between different styles of reading should certainly be maintained, it is not located here, for interpreting a text 'in its own right' always takes the form of retrieval insofar as its milieu is not our own.

6 Bishop Hypatius of Ephesus, quoted in Jaroslav Pelikan, 'The Odyssey of Dionysian Spirituality' in *Pseudo-Dionysius: The Complete Works* (The Classics of Western Spirituality; Colm Luibheid and Paul Rorem (eds); Mahwah, N.J.; London: Paulist Press; SPCK, 1987), 11–32, here 14.

7 John of Scythopolis, 'Scholia' in *John of Scythopolis and the Dionysian Corpus: Annotating the Areopagite* (Paul Rorem and John C. Lamoreaux (eds and trans); Oxford Early Christian studies; Oxford: Clarendon Press, 1998), 146.

8 Martin Luther, 'The Babylonian Captivity', in *Luther's Works*, vol.36: *Word and Sacrament II* (Abdel Ross Wentz (ed.); Philadelphia: Fortress Press, 1959–71), 109.

9 See Henri-Dominique Saffrey, 'New Objective Links between the Pseudo-Dionysius and Proclus' in *Neoplatonism and Christian Thought* (Dominic J. O'Meara (ed.); Albany: State University of New York Press, 1982), 64–74, here 67.

10 Anders Nygren, *Agape and Eros* (London: SPCK, 1983), 577.

11 Jan Vanneste, 'Is the mysticism of Pseudo-Dionysius genuine?', *International Philosophical Quarterly*, 3/2 (May 1963), 286–306, here 305.

12 Ibid., 303.

13 Ibid., 290.

14 Ibid., 303.

15 Ibid., 290.

16 Ibid., 303.

17 Andrew Louth, *Denys the Areopagite* (London: Continuum, 2002), 31.

18 Ibid., 30.

19 Alexander Golitzin, 'The mysticism of Dionysius Areopagita: Platonist or Christian?', *Mystics Quarterly*, 19/3 (1993), 98–114, here 107.

20 Golitzin, 'Dionysius Areopagita: a Christian mysticism?', *Pro Ecclesia*, 12/2 (2003), 161–212, here 207.

21 Golitzin, 'mysticism of Dionysius Areopagita'.

22 Golitzin, 'Dionysius Areopagitica', 163.

23 Ibid., 194. Of course, the abrupt claim that 'mysticism' has a 'general, patristic meaning' is itself a violent oversimplification.

24 Pseudo-Dionysius the Areopagite, *Letters* [henceforth *Ep.*] 1.1065A, in *Pseudo-Dionysius: The Complete Works*, 263.

25 Pseudo-Dionysius the Areopagite, *The Divine Names* [henceforth *DN*] (*De Divinis Nominibus*) 593A, Luibheid and Rorem (trans), 53.

26 Pseudo-Dionysius the Areopagite, *Mystical Theology* [henceforth *MT*] (*De Mystica Theologia*) 1048B, Luibheid and Rorem (trans), 141.

27 *MT* 1048A, 141.

28 Jacques Derrida, 'Différance', *Margins of Philosophy* (Alan Bass (trans.); Chicago: University of Chicago Press, 1982), 10.

29 Ibid., 10.

30 *MT* 997B–1000A, 135; translation modified.

31 Derrida, 'How to Avoid Speaking: Denials' in *Derrida and Negative Theology* (Harold Coward and Toby Foshay (eds); Albany: State University of New York Press, 1992), 73–142, here 90.

32 Pseudo-Dionysius the Areopagite, *The Celestial Hierarchy* [henceforth *CH*] (*De Caelesti Hierarchia*) 121C, in *Pseudo-Dionysius: The Complete Works*, 146.

33 *MT* 1025B, 138.

34 Pseudo-Dionysius the Areopagite, *The Ecclesiastical Hierarchy* [henceforth *EH*] (*De Ecclesiastica Hierarchia*) 305B in *Pseudo-Dionysius: The Complete Works*, 180.

35 *CH* 209A, 164.

36 *CH* 241C, 169.

37 *EH* 373C, 197.

38 *EH* 121A, 14.

39 *EH* 392A, 200.

40 *CH* 177C, 156.

41 *DN* 869D, 108.

42 *MT* 1048B, 141.

43 Turner, 'How to read the Pseudo-Denys?', 428–9.

44 Derrida, 'How to Avoid Speaking', 110.

45 Ibid., 111.

46 Derrida, 'Response to Jean-Luc Marion', 43.

47 *MT* 997B–1000A, 135.

48 Golitzin, 'Dionysius Areopagitica', 189.

49 Golitzin, *Et Introibo ad Altare Dei: The Mystagogy of Dionysius Areopagita, With Special Reference to its Predecessors in the Eastern Christian Tradition* (Analekta Vlatadôn, 59; Thessalonike: Patriarchikon Hidryma Paterikôn Meletôn, 1994), 167.

50 *DN* 872A, 108–9.

51 Golitzin, 'Hierarchy versus anarchy: Dionysius Areopagita, Symeon the new theologian, and Nicetas Stethatos' in *St Vladimir's Theological Quarterly*, 38/2 (1996), 175.

52 For a longer response to Golitzin, see David Newheiser, 'Ambivalence in Dionysius the Areopagite: the limitations of a liturgical reading' in *Studia Patristica* XVLIII (Jane Baun, Averil Cameron and Mark Julian Edwards (eds); Leuven: Peeters, 2010), 211–16.

53 Golitzin, 'A contemplative and a liturgist': Father Georges Florovsky on the Corpus Dionysiacum', *St Vladimir's Theological Quarterly*, 43/2 (1999), 131–61, here 148.

54 *DN* 592C, 52–3.
55 Of course, since human lives are finite, this might have represented Dionysius's final word in fact; the point is rather that it cannot represent his final word in principle, for the task that Dionysius describes is endless. Because this latter infinity relativizes the former finality, the fact that Dionysius and Derrida do not share the same ecclesial commitments does not preclude the argument concerning their affinity that I develop below.
56 In this light, as Derrida himself fails to conclude, 'the divine darkness beyond being' may be seen as a placeholder for what cannot be justly described.
57 Jacques Derrida, 'Sauf le nom (Post-Scriptum)' in *On the Name* (Thomas Dutoit (ed.); John Leavey (trans.); Stanford: Stanford University Press, 1995), 35–85, here 56.
58 Jacques Derrida and Elisabeth Roudinesco, *For What Tomorrow: A Dialogue* [De quoi demain] (Jeff Fort (trans.); Stanford: Stanford University Press, 2004), 49.
59 Ibid., 49–50.
60 Derrida, 'Sauf le nom', 58.
61 *DN* 592C, 52–3.
62 *EH* 560B, 253–4.
63 *Ep* 3.1069B, 264.
64 *Ep* 3.1069B, 264.
65 *DN* 596C, 56.
66 Derrida, 'Passions' in *On the Name*, 3–31, here 26.
67 Ibid., 'Passions', 27.
68 Derrida, 'How to Avoid Speaking', 95.
69 Derrida, 'Of an Apocalyptic Tone Newly Adopted in Philosophy' in *Derrida and Negative Theology* (Harold Coward and Toby Foshay (eds); Albany: State University of New York Press, 1992), 25–72, here 33.
70 Derrida, 'Of an Apocalyptic Tone', 33.
71 *EH* 505A, 236.
72 *CH* 168A, 155.
73 *DN* 597C, 58.
74 *CH* 140B, 149.
75 Derrida, 'Of an Apocalyptic Tone', 51.
76 Ibid., 61.
77 Ibid., 53.
78 John D. Caputo, 'Apostles of the Impossible: On God and the Gift in Derrida and Marion' in *God, the Gift, and Postmodernism* (John D. Caputo and Michael J. Scanlon (eds); Bloomington: Indiana University Press, 1999), 185–222, here 198.
79 Caputo, *The Prayers and Tears of Jacques Derrida: Religion Without Religion* (Indiana Series in the Philosophy of Religion; Bloomington: Indiana University Press, 1997), 51.
80 Caputo, *Prayers and Tears*, 106.
81 Ibid., 98–9.
82 Similarly, Mary-Jane Rubenstein is wrong to claim that, for Derrida, 'At the end of the day, even "the most negative of negative theologies" knows where it comes from, where it is going, and how to get there. Différance, by contrast,

neither is nor has any arche-teleological anchor: no being above being, good beyond being, or God without being to govern the play of signs it unleashes' (Mary-Jane Rubenstein, 'Dionysius, Derrida, and the critique of "ontotheology"', in *Re-Thinking Dionysius the Areopagite* (Sarah Coakley and Charles M. Stang (eds); Oxford: Wiley-Blackwell, 2009), 196. For one thing, as we shall see below, Derrida's reading of negative theology is more nuanced; for another thing, Derrida cannot establish his superiority in this way, for, as he is clear to point out, '*différance* remains a metaphysical name' (Derrida, 'Différance', 26).

83 Rubenstein, 'Dionysius, Derrida', 727.

84 Derrida, 'How to Avoid Speaking', 77; *emphasis original.*

85 Ibid., 130–1.

86 Ibid., 137.

87 Ibid.

88 It is for this that John Caputo's valorization of a 'general apophatics' and 'apophaticism itself' is simply absurd, both in light of classic Christian negative theology (in which affirmation and negation always and necessarily accompany each other) and on Derrida's terms (for he recognizes that speech and silence are intertwined).

89 Derrida, 'Letter to John P. Leavey', *Semeia* 23 (1982), 61.

90 Derrida, 'Différance', 10.

91 Ibid. This passage should furthermore be read alongside several references to negative theology from a few years earlier which serve to further complicate his concern with hyperessentialism: see, for instance, Derrida, 'Violence and Metaphysics' in *Writing and Difference* (Alan Bass (trans.); Chicago: University of Chicago Press, 1978), 106, 116, 146 and Jacques Derrida, 'From a Restricted to a General Economy' in *Writing and Difference* (Alan Bass (trans.); Chicago: University of Chicago Press, 1978), 271.

92 Derrida, 'How to Avoid Speaking', 82.

93 Jean-Luc Marion, 'In the Name: How to Avoid Speaking of 'Negative Theology' in *God, the Gift, and Postmodernism* (John D. Caputo and Michael J. Scanlon (eds); Bloomington: Indiana University Press, 1999), 20–53, here 23.

94 Derrida, 'Response to Jean-Luc Marion', 43.

95 Derrida, 'Sauf le Nom', 69.

96 Ibid., 83.

97 Ibid., 74. As I have argued elsewhere, Derrida thus recognizes the rarely noticed relation between apophaticism and love.

98 *DN* 940A, 121.

99 *DN* 648C, 66.

100 *DN* 824A, 101.

101 *DN* 648C, 66.

102 *MT* 997B–1000A, 135.

103 Derrida, *Adieu: To Emmanuel Levinas* (Stanford: Stanford University Press, 1999), 117.

104 Derrida and Roudinesco, *For What Tomorrow,* 132.

105 Derrida, *Aporias: Dying – Awaiting (One Another at) the 'Limits of Truth'* [Mourir – s'attendre aux 'limites de la vérité'] (Thomas Dutoit (trans.); Stanford: Stanford University Press, 1993).

106 *DN* 592C, 52–3.
107 *MT* 139.
108 *DN* 700D, 75.
109 *DN* 592C, 52–3.
110 *DM* 865B, 105.
111 *MT* 1033C, 140.
112 *CH* 140C, 149.
113 *DN* 981C, 130.
114 In Derrida's terms, this would constitute 'a 'past' that has never been present, and which never will be, whose future to come will never be a production or a reproduction in the form of presence' (Derrida, 'Différance', 21).

CHAPTER 3

SEEING GOD IN BODIES:
WOLFSON, ROSENZWEIG, AUGUSTINE

Virginia Burrus

> *For most, I suppose, chronology – and the historical narrative we construct on its basis – extends orderly, even if impenetrably, from beginning to end, but for some doubtless it proceeds from end to beginning, and for still others, probably fewer, it rebounds like a boomerang from middle to middle, starting and finishing always in between. . . . I pose the rhetorical question: What would be the consequences if a historian were to take seriously the conclusion reached on the basis of Einstein's General Theory of Relativity that spacetime . . . is to be regarded as a curve? Does this not at least entail the possibility that the past is as much determined by the present as the present by the past?*
>
> *Elliot R. Wolfson*[1]

I shall begin in the middle – by beginning not with the late ancient theologian Aurelius Augustine but with the precociously postmodern philosopher Franz Rosenzweig. Indeed, I shall begin from the middle of this middle, namely, from part II of Rosenzweig's tripartite *The Star of Redemption*, which is where Augustine makes his first appearance in that text. This beginning is a middle because it is also an *end*; that is to say, it is where I have ended up, having started out from the middle of Augustine's *Confessions* – those famous discussions of love, beauty and time. This end is a middle because it is also a *beginning*, for if Augustine has sent me to Rosenzweig, Rosenzweig will send me back to Augustine, yet the reading will not be the same on the rebound. Nor, as we shall see, will the rebounding stop there, for Rosenzweig's *Star* awaits a future as much as it evokes a past. To move 'from middle to middle' is not, then, to proceed straightforwardly from the present of one historical moment to that of another but rather to trace a curved path of open-ended reversibility that, paradoxically, 'seems always to lead one back to where one has not been'.[2]

Reading backwards from Rosenzweig to Augustine, I am not *merely* searching for a performative practice of writing that does justice to the complex temporality of reading and thus of historiography (though that too!). I am also anticipating some quite specific interpretative pay-offs. These have to do with the intersections of theories of time and eternity with those of beauty, sensation and divine incarnation, as read across (and beyond) the texts of Augustine and Rosenzweig. By the end I hope to have begun to suggest that Augustine's two major narrative works – *Confessions* and *City of God* – radically revise Platonic understandings of contemplative vision and eternal life, not as intellectual transcendence of the bodily but as imaginative transformation of the sensory, blurring boundaries between spirit and matter and ultimately between God and cosmos. In this reading, Augustine's theology is (paradoxically) both more apophatic and more incarnational, his thought both more philosophical and more mystical, than is usually imagined. If this is in part because it is (or will have become) more Rosenzweigian, it must also be said that Rosenzweig will himself have been transformed: the path back to the future will traverse the thought of contemporary mystical philosopher Elliot Wolfson, whose Kabbalistic reinscription of Rosenzweig's 'speech-thinking' will finally usher Augustine into postmodernity.

Back to Augustine: Rosenzweig

Francesco Paolo Ciglia has already blazed a backtracking trail for us, in an essay entitled 'Auf der Spur Augustins: *Confessiones* und *De civitate Dei* als Quellen des *Stern der Erlösung*'.[3] As the title announces, Ciglia is *auf der Spur Augustins*, seeking the trace of an ancient church father in the *opus magnum* of an early twentieth-century Jewish philosopher. Rosenzweig has complicated the search by producing a work initially conceived 'in the form of a biblical commentary' yet finally written 'under erasure of the text' (*unter Weglassung des Texts*).[4] Having edited out his sources, he hopes to renew them as living speech.[5] Interpretation thus becomes a dialogical (re)voicing of what is latent in writing's silent repose: 'What was mute becomes audible, the secret manifest, what was closed opens up, that which as thought had been complete inverts as word into a new beginning' (*SR*, 119).[6]

The introduction to part 2 of *The Star of Redemption* contains two of the very few *explicit* references to Augustine in the work. Here Rosenzweig begins his account of the temporal or 'ever-renewed' world, as distinguished from the 'everlasting primordial world' dealt with in part 1 and the 'eternal supra-world' to be encountered in part 3. He does so by opening a discussion of 'the possibility of experiencing miracle'. His initial mention of Augustine is brief and almost breezy: 'When Augustine, or some other church father, had to defend the divinity and truth of revealed religion against pagan attacks and doubts, he rarely neglected to point to miracles'

(*SR*, 104). A few pages later, Augustine is again named, this time in invocation of his argument for the importance of personal testimony in the validation of miracles (*SR*, 107). However seemingly fleeting, these two references themselves carry the weight of testimony in Rosenzweig's incipiently postmodern retrieval of a premodern theory of miracle – a theory that will ground his understanding not only of revelation as such but also of the irreducible relationality, and thus temporality, of divinity, cosmos and humanity, for which he argues throughout part 2. Other sources for his understanding of miracle might have been named – most notably, the medieval Jewish philosopher and poet Yehuda Halevi[7] – but it suits Rosenzweig's broader scheme that it should be a Patristic figure who aids in 'the transition from the mystery to the miracle' (*SR*, 100), that is, from paganism to revelation.[8]

To designate Rosenzweig's theory of miracle as incipiently postmodern is not much of a stretch – though eventually I will need to stretch the definition a bit further.[9] If the Enlightenment left miracles positioned as a supernatural excess with respect to natural law, the subsequent rise of historical criticism circa 1800 wrote them off as simply unbelievable, Rosenzweig argues. He thus intends that his own discourse move *beyond* modern historicism's flattening linearity by curving *back* to antiquity, when it was widely acknowledged (or so he avers) that 'miracle is essentially "sign"' (*SR*, 104). Rosenzweig summons Augustine as witness to the insight that miracle is distinguished not by its strangeness or improbability – attributes that are merely 'decorative' and thus dispensable (*SR*, 107) – but, paradoxically, by its having been *predicted*. 'Miracle and prophecy go together,' as he puts it succinctly (*SR*, 105): prophecy awaits its fulfillment in miracle, and miracle recalls its origin in prophecy. Miracle thus reveals, through hindsight, the inherently providential character of life experienced in time. Although positioned as an end in relation to prophecy's beginning, it does not inscribe closure but rather marks the openness of time's flow – in which events are predicted only after the fact and thus are never really predictable. If the present is opened and not closed by miracle, this is due not only to the infinite semiotic potentiality secreted in the abyss of 'creation before creation' (*SR*, 119)[10] but also to the infinite inpouring of love that saturates the moment, marking humanity, and thus the cosmos, as inescapably relational.[11] If time is opened and not closed by miracle, it is because its finitude is riven by infinitude, its temporality by eternity. *This* is the site of revelation – eternity irrupting within time's ever-becoming.

One already begins to suspect that Rosenzweig has drawn deeply not only from books 10 and 22 of Augustine's *City of God* but also from the later books of his *Confessions*.[12] Explicitly citing the former (by author, if not title), he uses its discussion of miracle to open up an exploration of time and eternity from the perspective of creation, love and praise in which the Augustine of the *Confessions* might be imagined to be ever present though almost never mentioned. Indeed, Rosenzweig, when read as a reader of Augustine, proves to be an extraordinarily perceptive one; taken as an elusive and creative interpretation of Augustine's theory of time and eternity, the *Star* is perhaps unsurpassed. That is a large claim and an idiosyncratic one, inherently unprovable and certainly not likely to be rendered fully persuasive in the space available here. For now I will confine myself to a brief, but hopefully suggestive, discussion of just one set of passages from the *Star*, those dealing with the exegesis of Gen. 1.2, which I will place in conversation with Augustine's own discussion of that verse in the *Confessions*.[13]

With regard to the crucial second verse of the Bible, Rosenzweig comments as follows: 'There, the darkness of the waste-and-void, here the obscurity of brooding; both thing (*Ding*) and act (*Tat*) appear in the form of attributes, and of attributes situated at the lowest limit, where thing and act constantly emerge out of that which is not yet in any manner thing nor in any manner act' (*SR*, 165–6). He is struck by the ambiguity not only of the figure of chaos but also of the figure of brooding, as these seem to emerge – just barely – from 'that which is not in any manner thing nor in any manner act'. This imagery recalls a passage at the beginning of the *Star* in which Rosenzweig refers to Hermann Cohen's philosophical application of the concept of the differential, drawn from the mathematics of calculus. Contrasting the particularity of the differential with the universality of the zero, he notes: 'It is a nothing that refers to a something, to its something, and at the same time a something that still slumbers in the womb of the nothing' (*SR*, 28). Walking the fine line of an infinitesimal that is neither nothing nor something, Rosenzweig discovers a fork in the *via negativa*: 'It [the differential] thus determines two paths that go from the nothing to the something, the path of the affirmation of that which is not nothing, and the path of the negation of the nothing' (*SR*, 28). Subsequently he elaborates: 'From the nothing to the something, or, more strictly: from the nothing to what is not nothing – for we are not seeking a something – there are two ways, the way of affirmation and the way of negation. . . . To affirm the not-nothing (*Nichtnichts*) is to posit an infinite . . . to negate the nothing is to posit . . . something limited, finite, determinate'. In the case of the divine, affirmation via double negation yields 'the entire plenitude of all that is – not nothing' while negation is 'entirely and only act (*Tat*)' (*SR*, 31–2). 'Opposite the infinite divine essence, the divine freedom rises up, the finite configuration of action' (*SR*, 38).

For the world, it is not essence, but potentiality that is asserted: 'The infinitude of the affirmed *Nichtnichts* appears as infinite possibility of application of the worldly logos'. The world's plenitude of ever-emerging particularity opposes the universal and everlasting logos that lends it 'its thinkable character' (*SR*, 25); irrepressibly, 'each renewed thing is a renewed negation of the nothing' (*SR*, 53). 'Its womb is insatiable in conceiving, it is inexhaustible in giving birth', argues Rosenzweig, 'Or better – for both masculine and feminine are in it – it is, as "nature", as much the mother who endlessly gives birth to its figures as it is the indefatigable procreative force of the "spirit" that is at home in it' (*SR*, 52–3). Returning to Rosenzweig's reading of the Genesis text in part 2 of the *Star*, it might not be far off the mark to suggest that the 'waste-and-void' is the infinite 'not-nothing' of potential intelligibility, doubled by the negation of the particular 'nothing' of the world – the world barely emergent as 'thing-ness'. Correspondingly, 'brooding' is the 'not-nothing' of divine essence, doubled by the negation of the particular 'nothing' of God – the divine barely emergent as creative activity. Rosenzweig's is a doubly doubled account of creation *ex nihilo*.[14]

God's nothing may be '*his* nothing', but the action is still perhaps a bit too broodingly maternal for Rosenzweig's taste.[15] It is in the personification not as mother but as father,[16] not as invisible creator but as self-revealing lover, that the divine self-negation manifests itself as we proceed from book 1 to book 2 of part 2 – what Rosenzweig himself describes as the 'heart' of the *Star*. There, the God who commands by loving, and loves by commanding, cuts across time, opening up presence within the ongoing flow of endings and beginnings. Love arrives always, and ever again, in 'a blink of the eye' (*SR*, 174); indeed, it defines the 'eye-blink' or 'moment' (*Augenblick*) by its significance: 'From now on God is present, present like the moment, like every moment', writes Rosenzweig, 'every moment must become the first glance of love' (*SR*, 176, 174). The play of plenitudinous essence and delimiting action within beginnings always anticipating endings is now recast as the kenotic movement of love at the heart of time. And yet, as book 3 will reveal, the futurity of eternity still tugs at the heart of even a love that 'is always in the today and entirely in the today'. 'God always loves only whom and what he loves', writes Rosenzweig, 'but what separates his love from an "all love" is only a "not-yet"; it is only "not yet" that God loves everything besides what he already loves' (*SR*, 178). Poured into time, eternal love overflows the human soul, opening it to 'the infinite chaos of the world' (*SR*, 257), so that the 'I and thou' of the divine–human love affair triangulates and multiplies into a collective 'we'. Redemption's swelling fullness folds ends back on beginnings: whatever the eternally coming kingdom is, writes Rosenzweig, 'it is not the thing (*Sache*), it is not the act (*Tat*)', indeed not any longer the facticity (*Tatsächlichkeit*) of differentiated elements, but it is also *not* (a fall back into) *nothing* (*SR*, 260).[17]

'Not-nothing' (*Nichtnichts*), a compound neologism that is strangely compacted, even for German, is further compounded by its pairing with the negation of *Nichts*. Do we hear echoes of the nothing-something, the *nihil aliquid*, that Augustine sees when, like Rosenzweig, he contemplates the abyss that opens in the first two verses of Genesis? (The 'waste-and-void' and the 'deep' of the second verse is already prefigured, on his reading, in the 'earth' of the first verse.) 'What should it be called?' he asks. Invisible, unformed, bottomless, dark – 'not altogether nothing (*non omnino nihil*)', a 'nothing–something (*nihil aliquid*)' and an 'is/is not (*est non est*)', 'near nothing (*prope nihil*)', 'almost nothing (*paene nihil*)' (*Conf.*, 12.4, 6, 7, 8). When Augustine – a less abstract thinker than Rosenzweig – tries to imagine what this nothing–something might look like, he succeeds only in picturing a monstrous shuffle of 'countless and varied shapes (*species*)': 'My mind turned up forms (*formae*) that were hideous and horrifying, appearing in confused order, but forms none-theless; and I called it formless not because it lacked form but because it had one so bizarre and incongruous that, if it had appeared before me, my senses would have recoiled and I would have been deeply disturbed'.[18] What he sees is almost nothing because it can become absolutely anything. If he could but capture the moment of transition from one form to the next, could perceive that which is 'capable of receiving all the forms into which changeable things are changed' (*Conf.*, 12.6), then he would be able to see through time to eternity, in the fertile betweenness that is the womb of all things. Taken to its limit, the flow of sheer mutability approaches the stasis of perfect immutability: for without form, there is no longer, or not yet, any division of times (*Conf.*, 12.9, 12.11).

In its very disturbing monstrosity, Augustine's *terra infirma*, his *terra informis*, exposes the ambivalence of his love. What is hidden seduces, but in the *nihil aliquid* he apprehends that there is no stable 'whatness' at all, no *thing* to elude him, only an unending flux of becoming emerging from nothing. There is too much (to) desire – and also not enough – as temporality melts into eternity. The timeless depths of sheer transience both draw and overwhelm love, then. But what of the sublime heights of perfect faith? Unlike her more dubious double, the scriptural figure of heavenly devotion – the 'heaven' found alongside the formless 'earth' in the first verse of Genesis – inspires no horror, as Augustine imagines her. 'The heaven of heaven is some intellectual creature, which, although by no means coeternal with you, trinity, participates nonetheless in your eternity by powerfully restraining her own mutability through the sweetness of your most happy contemplation; cleaving to you without any lapse since her making, she exceeds every whirling vicissitude of time' (*Conf.*, 12.9). God is her only delight (*voluptas*), and in this she is, Augustine notes, a model for every soul. Revelling in the divine presence, she neither anticipates nor remembers anything else (*Conf.*, 12.11). While *terra*'s generativity evades time by taking distention to the limit where mutability eclipses form, the heavenly *creatura* extends toward eternity by allowing form to eclipse mutability through the constancy of her love.[19]

Reading Augustine through Rosenzweig's eyes challenges the oppositional dualism between heaven and earth *seemingly* established by his reading of Genesis – a dualism that won't quite hold anyway. Augustine's primordial earth is a nothing–something much like the originary not–nothing that Rosenzweig ascribes to the world, a plenitudinous 'chaos [that] is in creation, not before it' (*SR*, 145) – a figure of creation's temporal *becoming*, mysterious in its mobility, if only because creation *takes time* and its time runs backwards, like the unpacking of an already-packed suitcase (to borrow Rosenzweig's metaphor [*SR*, 123–4]). His 'heaven of heavens' is in turn much like Rosenzweig's beloved human soul – a figure of the love that sustains difference within relationality even as it lends the depth of eternity to every present moment. She – it – is the responsive face of the ever-convertible deep, one might say, the face of the multifaceted 'all', of all other creatures, already-beloved and yet-to-be-loved – finally not she, it or they, but Rosenzweig's redemptive 'we'.

Back to Rosenzweig: Wolfson

At the conclusion of *Alef, Mem, Tau: Kabbalistic Musings on Time, Truth, and Death*, Elliot Wolfson cites a passage from the end of *The Star of Redemption* in which Rosenzweig attempts to describe what it means to live 'an eternal life, and not the temporal in time', to live 'outside time', refusing to be emplotted 'between beginning and end'. It is by inverting all beginnings and ends that Judaism, unlike Christianity, according to Rosenzweig, 'denies the omnipotence of the between and disavows time' (see *SR*, 443). Wolfson glosses the passage as follows:

> The disavowal of time does not imply an abrogation or even a dialectical surpassing of temporality, but rather its radical deepening, an eradication of time by rooting oneself more deeply in the ground of time. Eternity, accordingly, is not the metaphysical overcoming of or existential escape

from time but rather the merging of the three-dimensional structure of lived temporality through eternalization of the present in the continuous becoming of the being that has always been what is yet to come.[20]

Here and elsewhere in his work, Wolfson makes a new beginning out of Rosenzweig's ending, largely by reading his work *auf der Spur der Kabale*, seeking the trace of a medieval mysticism in the opus magnum of an early twentieth-century philosopher, so as to give voice to a postmodern 'grammar of becoming', as Wolfson dubs his own path of thought.[21] To read Rosenzweig postmodernly is to read directly into some of the greatest tensions in his text, which means reading him to the end and revisiting his beginning so as to rediscover a middle that is indeed *not* the static *between* of the conventional narrative eschatology that he ascribes to Christianity.[22] If the kingdom is always coming, then it must never simply arrive: eternity cannot be freed from its entanglement with time, nor time with eternity.[23] Yet the originary 'facticity' (*Tatsächlichkeit*) that Rosenzweig attributes to God, human and world, respectively, in order to safeguard the irreducible multiplicity and relationality of the 'all', may be undone by the very theory of 'the eternality of temporal becoming'[24] from which it arises, argues Wolfson.[25] Acknowledging that Rosenzweig attempts to preserve the viability of theological language as a signifier of an experienced human encounter with a 'real God' (*wirklichen Gottes*), Wolfson suggests that Rosenzweig nonetheless ultimately deconstructs his own theism. To follow Rosenzweig back to his ambivalently apophatic beginnings in nothing is also to lead him along paths not yet taken: 'To think in his footsteps – the thinking that is the highest mode of thanking – imposes on us the demand to inquire if it is feasible to speak of such a meeting when our ability to assert anything positive about the "reality" of God is compromised'.[26]

As Wolfson shows, the tension between theism and its negation becomes particularly acute at the very end of the *Star* – at the gateway of eternal life, as Rosenzweig names it. Here the articulated temporality of speech gives way to the timelessness of visual communion occurring at 'that border of life' where eternity impinges on time – where God can be glimpsed. And what does God look like? Rosenzweig tells us, or so it seems. Like light, like a face: a shining face peering out from an overwrought astral symbol, at once mirror and metaphor for the human – blatantly and almost parodically so, as Rosenzweig composes the scene, naming forehead and cheeks, ears, nose, eyes and a mouth sealed with a kiss. 'We are speaking in images', he notes. To meet God face to face, then, is to encounter the naked truth that God can only be revealed in and as the masking of becoming, through the poetics of figuration, argues Wolfson: 'The metaphysical concept of actual presence is transposed into a semiotic trope of mythopoetic metaphoricization'.[27] Indeed, although Rosenzweig insists that we 'not only may but must call it God's countenance' (*SR*, 445), the star is not a symbol of God any more than of humanity or world, but rather presents the 'all' of existence in its mobile and enmeshed relatedness – 'countenance that looks upon me and from out of which I look' (*SR*, 446). At the end of time we are also still in its middle, then. Rosenzweig continues: 'But what he gave me to see in this beyond of life is – nothing different than what I was permitted to perceive already in the center of life; the difference is only that I see it, no longer merely hear' (*SR*, 446). We are also back at the silent beginning, as Rosenzweig reminds us as well: 'And this last is not the last, but that which is always near, the nearest; not the last then, but the first. How difficult is such a first! How difficult is every beginning!' (*SR*, 446–7).[28]

If the end is the beginning, whence plenitudinous particularity emerges from nothing, then the beginning, once reversed, is also the dissolution of difference – something hinted at, to varying degrees, by Augustine's *nihil aliquid*, Rosenzweig's *Nichtnichts* or the Kabbalists' *Ein Sof*, 'inessential essence . . . origin that has no limit'.[29] For Wolfson, the interpretation of creation *ex nihilo* through the lens of temporal reversibility particularly characteristic of Kabbalistic mysticism and also resonant with Rosenzweig's thought is 'not simply a cognitive insight but a way of seeing that alters reality'.[30] Borrowing the words of Catherine Keller, he describes the resulting nexus of negative theology and negative cosmology as an 'apophatic panentheism' that affirms both the identity and the reciprocal transcendence of 'God' and 'world', each configured as the something of the other's nothing and the nothing of the other's something.[31] Such is 'the unfathomable ground where mysticism and atheism insidiously shake hands' that Rosenzweig tries, but fails, to avoid.[32] It is ground that Wolfson seems to tread with ease.

On the Rebound: Augustine

We entered Rosenzweig's *The Star of Redemption* through the opening of a discussion of miracles that invokes Augustine's *The City of God*. There miracles are signs of things to come – specifically of eternal life, which is where Augustine ends. We've just been there with Rosenzweig: on the rebound with Augustine, eternity looks both the same and different. *Looking* is still the relevant term, though here again Augustine proves the less abstract thinker. Whereas Rosenzweig offers a meticulously drawn

Gestalt of the abundance of life lived outside time, Augustine (perhaps foolishly) attempts a more literal rendering – depicted in the realest of real times, as it were – in which horror and wonder, beauty and the grotesque become very nearly indistinguishable. The prematurely born, the cannibally ingested, the gapingly wounded, the fat and the thin, the short and the tall – he considers all of these challenges and more, together with the fundamental problem of the apparent too-muchness resulting from eternity's all-at-onceness: just imagine the pile-up of hair and fingernails! (He actually tries to do so.) Yet Augustine is convinced that the resurrected saints will rejoice in gazing upon one another and that they will see not excess flesh but exceeding beauty – divine beauty. Indeed, the saints will see God '*in* the body itself (*in ipso corpore*)'. He wonders if they also see God '*by means of* the body (*per corpus*)'. If so, will their eternal eyelids never close? Alternately, if they look with spiritual sight, what *is* this, and how does it relate to bodily seeing? Is it a kind of X-ray vision, working even when the physical eyes are closed, capable of perceiving directly what is immaterial and thus invisible? Or is it more like the ability to sense the life force (*vita*) invisibly animating visible bodies? He inclines towards the latter option:

> Perhaps God will be known and visible to us in such a way as to be spiritually seen by each one of us in each one of us, seen by the one in the other, seen in him or herself, seen in the new heaven and the new earth, seen in the whole creation as it will be, seen also through bodies in every body, wherever the eyes of the spiritual body are directed with their penetrating gaze. (*City of God*, 22.29)[33]

Especially as illumined by the rays of Rosenzweig's *Star*, this is a striking, even a startling, assertion in its thoroughgoing theological incarnationalism – an apophatic panentheism that approaches a mystical atheism, as Wolfson suggests with regard to Rosenzweig. To meet the divine 'face to face', to see through the eyes of love, is to perceive God *fully embodied in creation*. To perceive bodies in their plenitudinous excess and poignant finitude – to live fully in the eternity of *this* day – is already to see God. There is no other path, and the path *(die Bahn)* – as Rosenzweig names the center of life to which we rebound in the end – is all there is.

Forward and Back: Jewish-Christian In/difference

What are the implications of temporal reversibility for Christian supersessionism? Has this back-and-forth reading escaped its dangers? Paula

Fredriksen argues for the relatively benign character of Augustine's historiciz-
ing view of Judaism: "By . . . embedding Jewish legal observance in history,
Augustine in effect demythologized, and so secularized, its implications:
carnal praxis was not a huge and enduringly indictable moral failing, but
divinely mandated action appropriate to those earlier times. Further, by
understanding this practice as incarnate prophetic enactment, Augustine
domesticated it for Catholic doctrine, relating ancient Jewish observances
to current Christian beliefs by way of conformation rather than contrast'.[34]
Famously, Rosenzweig very nearly embodied such a supersessionism,
determining to become a (practicing) Jew so as subsequently to become a
proper Christian, as he recounted to his cousin Rudolph Ehrenberg in
a letter of 31 October 1913: 'I declared I could turn Christian only *qua*
Jew'. Equally famously, he shifted his decision, so that the path towards
Christianity ultimately led him back to Judaism: 'It no longer seems
necessary to me, and therefore, being what I am, no longer possible.
I will remain a Jew'.[35] In a letter to his mother written soon after his
'conversion', Rosenzweig mentions both Tertullian and Augustine in the
context of a scathing (and very witty) denunciation of Christian supersessionism.[36] The *Star* implicitly turns the tables on Augustine, appropriating
the 'city of God' for Judaism while ceding historical-political agency to
Christianity: 'Our life is no longer interwoven with anything external, we
have taken root in ourselves, without roots in the earth, eternal wanderers
therefore, yet deeply rooted in ourselves, in our own body and blood. And
this rooting in ourselves and only in ourselves guarantees our eternity
for us' (*SR*, 324). Laying claim to an Augustinian *contemptus mundi*,
Rosenzweig thus also appropriates and transvalues the 'carnality' of 'body
and blood' that Augustine assigns to the Jews.[37]

Reading backwards from the vantage point of Wolfson's gaze forward,
one might suggest that neither Rosenzweig nor Augustine has pushed
the theory of time and eternity to its logical conclusion, in so far as each
retains a doctrine of election, whether privileging Jews or Christians. If, as
Wolfson argues, time's eternalization entails the overcoming of binaries
and eternity's temporalization mandates that there is no time but the
present, then difference and sameness are opposites that always already
coincide in a messianic moment ever yet to arrive, in 'the advent of the
absolute (non)event'.[38] And if Judaism and Christianity, like all dyadic
pairs, are revealed to be 'differently identical in a manner that is identically
different', as Wolfson puts it, what might that sound or look like?[39] A dialogue in which all speak and hear at once? A many-eyed face that gazes
and is gazed upon indistinguishably? The radical multiplicity of all-that-is
may be closer to *one* than to *two*, or even *three* – because it is closest of all
to *nothing*.

Notes

1   Elliot R. Wolfson, *Language, Eros, Being: Kabbalistic Hermeneutics and Poetic Imagination* (New York: Fordham University Press, 2005), xvi.

2   Ibid., 372.

3   Francesco Paolo Ciglia, 'Auf der Spur Augustins: *Confessiones* und *De Civitate Dei* als Quellen des Stern der Erlösung', in *Rosenzweig als Leser: kontextuelle Kommentare zum 'Stern der Erlösung'* (Martin Brasser (ed.); Tübingen: Max Niemeyer Verlag, 2004), 223–44. Ciglia suggests, on the evidence of Rosenzweig's journals (later published as the Paralipomena), that Rosenzweig was immersed in Augustine's texts starting circa 1916.

4   This is Rosenzweig's own description, from a letter of 2 September 1928 to Richard Koch, cited in Ciglia, 'Auf der Spur Augustins', 224. The fuller text reads: 'Nachdem ich 1913 plötzlich zum Philosophen geworden war . . . fiel mir Ende 1916 der Plan meines "Lebenswerks" ein . . . Der Plan ging auf ein Buch de omnibus rebus et quibusdam aliis, wie der Stern nachher geworden ist, aber in Form eines Bibelkommentars. . . . Vor nun zehn Jahren schrieb ich dann plötzlich überstürzter – aber, wie sich erst später herausgestellt hat, glücklicherweise den Kommentar unter Weglassung des Textes', Letter 526, *Franz Rosenzweig, Briefe* (Edith Rosenzweig (trans. and ed.); Berlin: Schocken Verlag, 1935), 618–20.

5   Ciglia comments: 'Man kann mit einigem Recht sage, dass Rosenzweig in Augustin nie nur eine Gestalt aus längst vergangenen Tagen, sondern immer auch einen lebendigen Gesprächspartner gesehen hat, von dem man Anregungen und Denkanstösse erhalten kann' ('Auf der Spur Augustins', 225).

6   Franz Rosenzweig, *The Star of Redemption* (Barbara Galli (trans.); Madison: University of Wisconsin Press, 2005), 119 [hereafter, *SR*]. German edition: *Franz Rosenzweig, Der Stern der Erlösung* (3rd edn; Heidelberg: Lambert Schneider, 1954). In his introduction to Galli's translation, Wolfson makes the link between speech-thinking and interpretation: 'The interpretative act – which bespeaks the essential nature of speech-thinking, the dialogical comportment unique to the human being, in its inscripted and oral forms – affords one an opportunity to experience time, and, more specifically, the moment, which encapsulates time in its most elemental cadence, as novel repetition' (Elliot R. Wolfson, 'Introduction to Barbara Galli's Translation of Rosenzweig's Star', in Franz Rosenzweig, *SR*, xix).

7   Norbert Samuelson makes the case for Halevi as a source, simultaneously dismissing the possibility of any significant Augustinian influence: '. . . those of us who are familiar with the writings of the church fathers will recognize at best some slight similarities between Rosenzweig's account of miracles and the still crude conceptual appeals to miracles by the church fathers. There is no question that Rosenzweig in fact has the theology of the church fathers in mind as his model for appeal to miracles in theological debate. But at the state that Christian philosophy had reached at the time of these spiritual giants, the concept of miracle was not what Rosenzweig said it was.' 'Halevi and Rosenzweig on Miracles', in *Approaches to Judaism in Medieval Times* (David R. Blumenthal (ed.); Chico, California: Scholars Press, 1984), 161. Samuelson's appeal to 'progress' stands in odd contrast to Rosenzweig's presentation of himself as retrieving an ancient insight that is appealing

precisely because it evades modern historicism's commitment to a narrative of progress. More to the point, he does not succeed in demonstrating that Halevi's theory of miracles explains all that is in Rosenzweig's, or that Augustine's explains none of it. As Ciglia argues, the influence of *City of God* 10, 21, and 22 is easily identifiable, texts on which Rosenzweig commented in his journals: 'Auf der Spur Augustins', 233–44.

8   'Transition' is the title of the conclusion of part 1. Among the ways Rosenzweig understands the transition is as the conversion of paganism to revelation. The Christian is, by origin, a converted pagan (*SR*, 419), and the Christian of antiquity still manifests a convert's zeal: 'No scholastic of the Middle Ages dares to treat the wisdom of the Greeks with such triumphant audacity as does Augustine' (*SR*, 298).

9   See Ciglia's description of the discussion of miracle: 'eine erstaunliche, offensichtlich herausfordernde und sozusagen "postmoderne" Rehabilitierung des altern und scheinbar überholten theologischen Themas des Wunders vorangetrieben wird', 'Auf der Spur Augustins', 233. The question of how 'postmodern' Rosenzweig's broader thought is, is fraught. I am going to suggest that Wolfson gives a postmodern revoicing of Rosenzweig's thought, yet, as we shall see, he does so by resisting what he himself acknowledges to be crucial to the very dialogism that others have hailed as postmodern, namely, Rosenzweig's positing of 'the "essential separateness" (wesenhafte Getrenntheit) or "transcendence" (Transcendent) of each of the elements vis-à-vis each other', Elliot R. Wolfson, 'Light Does not Talk but Shines: Apophasis and Vision in Rosenzweig's Theopoetic Temporality' in *New Directions in Jewish Philosophy* (Aaron W. Hughes and Elliot R. Wolfson (eds); Bloomington: Indiana University Press, 2010), 88.

10   The abyss is a recurring figure. In 1.1, Rosenzweig prevaricates: the originary 'nothing' is 'meant only as a nothing of knowledge, not as a positively placed nothing, not as a "dark ground", not as an "abyss of the godhead", but as a starting point for thinking about God, as a place of the setting of the problem' (*SR*, 36). In 3.3, as 'the last silence grows silent in us', he discovers 'the true abyss of the godhead' (*SR*, 407).

11   The discussion of love is only hinted at in the introduction to part 2, due to its structural positioning; it seems significant, however, that it cannot quite be left out. See *SR*, 105, 120–21. As Eric Santner puts it, with regard to Rosenzweig's theory of miracle, 'We might say that all Rosenzweig wanted to show was that truly inhabiting the midst of life . . . was actually a remarkable, even a miraculous achievement that required some form of divine support – ultimately a form of love – kept alive, in time, by a certain form of life', Eric L. Santner, 'Miracles Happen: Benjamin, Rosenzweig, Freud, and the Matter of the Neighbor' in *The Neighbor: Three Inquiries in Political Theology* (Slavoj Zizek, Eric L. Santner and Kenneth Reinhard (eds); Chicago: University of Chicago Press, 2006), 133.

12   On this point, see Ciglia, 'Der gordische Knoten der Zeit: Aspekte des Dialogs zwischen Rosenzweig und Augustin', in *Franz Rosenzweigs "neues Denken" : internationaler Kongreß, Kassel 2004* (Wolfdietrich Schmied-Kowarzik (ed.); 1; Freiburg, Munich: Karl Alber Verlag, 2004), 323–45.

13 Among the many other resonances with the *Confessions* that remain to be explored in more depth, I would highlight the breathtaking discussion of love, command, shame, confession and prayer in II.2 (*SR*, 290–302) as well as the discussions of music and poetry in 2.2 and 2.3. Elsewhere I have discussed at more length the resonances between Augustine's and Rosenzweig's theories of miracle ('Augustine and Rosenzweig on the Possibility of Experiencing Miracle', in *Material Spirit* (Carl Good, Manuel Asensi and Gregory Stallings (eds.); forthcoming).

14 Strictly speaking, the account is tripled, as humanity too has its nothing, according to Rosenzweig; yet creation is a process in which God and world are most directly implicated.

15 The figure of brooding, he notes, is garbed grammatically as 'Spirit' in 'the trailing attire of femininity' while also being attributed with 'an activity of the feminine tribe' (*SR*, 165). He adds subsequently, 'The maternal is always that which is there already, the paternal is only an addition' (*SR*, 172). The paternal seems to be associated here with act and event and the negation of the maternal – a scarcely unfamiliar gendered troping.

16 Albeit not the blandly universalizing kind: 'Revelation does not know of any father who is universal love; God's love is always wholly in the moment and at the point where it loves; and it is only in the infinity of time, step by step, that it reaches one point after the next and permeates the totality with soul' (*SR*, 177).

17 See Wolfson, 'Apophasis and Vision', 107.

18 Translations of Augustine are my own. Latin text: James J. O'Donnell, *Augustine: Confessions, Text and Commentary* (Oxford: Clarendon Press, 1992), also available online.

19 Regarding Augustine's nihil aliquid, see my 'Carnal excess: flesh at the limits of imagination', *Journal of Early Christian Studies*, 17/2 (2009), 247–65, as well as Virginia Burrus, Mark Jordan and Karmen MacKendrick, *Seducing Augustine: Bodies, Desires, Confessions* (New York: Fordham University Press, 2010), ch. 4, for a fuller discussion of time and desire in Augustine's *Confessions*.

20 Elliot R. Wolfson, *Alef, Mem, Tau: Kabbalistic Musings on Time, Truth, and Death* (Berkeley: University of California Press, 2006), 176–7.

21 Ibid., 175.

22 'It is Christianity that thus made the present into the epoch. Past is still only the time before the birth of Christ. All subsequent time from Christ's life on earth until his return is now that one great present, that epoch, that standstill, that extension of times, that between over which time has lost its power. Time is now pure temporality [bloße Zeitlichkeit]. . . . [T]ime has become a single way, but a way whose beginning and end lie beyond time, and hence an eternal way' (*SR*, 359). In the passage cited by Wolfson, he asserts that 'God's time' 'denies time . . . the same time that is experienced on the eternal way' (*SR*, 443).

23 See, most recently, Elliot R. Wolfson, *Open Secret: Postmessianic Messianism and the Mystical Revision of Menahem Mendel Schneerson* (New York: Columbia University Press, 2009), 267–8, attributing to Rosenzweig the

'paradoxical discernment that the goal can only be obtained by never being obtained. . . . On the one hand, redemption is predicated on a diremptive temporality that assures the possibility of the future being realized in the present, but, on the other hand, the future that is realized is precisely what remains constantly to come'.

24 Wolfson, *Alef, Mem, Tau*, 50.
25 Wolfson, 'Apophasis and Vision'. See also his earlier 'Facing the effaced: mystical eschatology and the idealistic orientation in the thought of Franz Rosenzweig', *Zeitschrift für neuere Theologiegeschichte*, 4/1 (1997), 39–81.
26 Wolfson, 'Apophasis and Vision', 123.
27 Ibid., 120.
28 See also Rosenzweig's 'New Thinking', reflecting on the *Star's* ending: 'Here the book ends. For what is still coming is already beyond the book . . . [T]he enraptured-terrified recognition that in this beholding of the "world-image in God's countenance", in this apprehension of all being in the immediacy of a moment [Augenblick] and blink of the eye [Augen-blick] the limit of humanity is entered. . . . An ending that is at the same time a beginning and a middle: to enter into the middle of everyday life', Franz Rosenzweig, *The New Thinking* (Alan Udoff and Barbara E. Galli (trans); Syracuse: Syracuse University Press, 1999), 100.
29 Wolfson, 'Apophasis and Vision', 114.
30 Wolfson, *Open Secret*, 55.
31 Wolfson, *Open Secret*, 66–129, citation at 82.
32 Wolfson, 'Apophasis and Vision', 123.
33 Translations my own. Latin text: Augustine, *Sancti Aurelii Augustini De civitate Dei* libri I-X (Corpus Christianorum, Series Latina, 47, 48; Turnhout: Brepols, 1955).
34 Paula Fredriksen, 'Secundum Carnem: History and Israel in the Theology of St. Augustine', in *The Limits of Ancient Christianity: Essays on Late Antique Thought and Culture in Honor of R. A. Markus* (William E. Klingshirn and Mark Vessey (eds); Ann Arbor: University of Michigan Press, 1999), 26–41.
35 Letter 59 in Rosenzweig, *Briefe*, 71–72, *Franz Rosenzweig: His Life and Thought* (Nahum Glatzer (trans); Indianapolis: Hackett Publishing Company, 1998), 25, 28.
36 Letter 57 in Rosenzweig, *Briefe*, 66.
37 Rosenzweig can also be explicit in his alignment of Augustine with the (in his view, distinctly Christian) conflation of worldly politics and divine providence: 'Augustine . . . now explains: for the Church . . . discord between one's own welfare and the faith that is loyal to one that is higher could not arise; for it "salus" and "fides" are united' (*SR*, 349). Despite Rosenzweig's strong and precise distancing of his own Jewish perspective from Augustine's Christian one with regard to eternal versus historical life, the very distinction owes much to Augustine, as Amos Funkenstein, *Perceptions of Jewish History* (Berkeley: University of California Press, 1993), 298–301, has shown: like Augustine, Rosenzweig posits a 'parallel but disjoint[ed]' history of divine and earthly peoples, in which the citizens of 'the city of God' are dispersed as

wanderers and aliens among the citizens of the world, having no real stake in the fortunes of political states but rather being rooted in a heavenly or eternal society.

38 Wolfson, *Open Secret*, 300.
39 Ibid., 290. See also his *Venturing Beyond: Law and Morality in Kabbalistic Mysticism* (Oxford: Oxford University Press, 2006), 129–85, on the complex and ambivalent relation of Jew to non-Jew in Kabbalistic tradition.

Part II

Reading Postmodern Thinkers in Parallel with Reading the Fathers

CHAPTER 4

EMMANUEL LEVINAS AND GREGORY OF NYSSA ON READING, DESIRE AND SUBJECTIVITY

Tamsin Jones

In this paper I explore some of the similarities between Emmanuel Levinas and Gregory of Nyssa, specifically in the rich nexus of interplaying themes of reading, desire and the formation of a particular subjectivity. Levinas and Gregory both articulate a theory of revelation and its interpretation that involves understandings of human desire and of self-formation, which overlap in significant ways. For both, selfhood emerges out of an infinitely structured desire for the other (or for God[1]) and is cultivated through a particular act of reading, of interpretation, most especially of reading Scripture (the primary site of revelation for both Levinas and Gregory).

I will argue that Levinas and Gregory start from the same basic assumption concerning the status of revelation: revelation, while taken as the holy word of God, nonetheless – or even, for that very reason – requires infinite translation in order to be completed. From this shared starting point, Levinas and Gregory can be compared on three consequent and interrelated loci regarding revelation and its reading: (1) the fact that revelation performs a transgressive rupturing of the finite world assumes an ontological gap between the 'infinite word' and the finite interpreter – revelation is thus inherently excessive and cannot be contained and an 'unrevealed' remainder perdures; (2) this understanding of revelation as transgressive summons a desirous response – the reader reacts to revelation by wanting more; and (3) this destabilizing response of infinitely expanding desire actually performs a kind of non-substantial subjectivity, one whose constitution comes from without and is not inherent to the person.

Methodological Preliminaries

Prior to beginning, let me identify one problematic methodological point. I am not only drawing connections between ideas situated at a vast historical distance from one another, but also connections between two different religious traditions and two different theoretical discourses. Gregory of Nyssa is a fourth-century Christian bishop, theologian and sometime mystic. Levinas is a twentieth-century Jewish philosopher informed by the dual traditions of Husserlian phenomenology and Heideggerean fundamental ontology, as well as the long tradition of Talmudic interpretation. Moreover, I am arguing that one can find points of commonality on the very contested site of Biblical interpretation – that is, the locus where Christians commenced a history of violence (rhetorical and actual) against Jews.[2] This is an audacious, and perhaps foolhardy, comparison, and the motivations behind such a decision ought to be interrogated. What am I doing, or attempting to do, when I read Levinas and Gregory together?

It is perhaps easiest to begin by clarifying what I am not doing. This is not a genealogical comparison. No doubt one could find some connection in the 'reception history' of Gregory of Nyssa that would link him to Levinas. This would be a fascinating and undoubtedly illuminating – if circuitous and indirect – study, but it is not the project of this essay. Nor am I reading Gregory through a Levinasian lens, applying the twentieth-century thinker's concepts and categories to the fourth-century writings. Nor am I using Gregory as a foil to expand upon or complicate Levinas's thought.[3] Rather, I am reading the two systematically, comparing in a synchronic fashion their understandings of revelation, its ontological assumptions, and consequences for their various understandings of reading, the human desire for God and the formation of a particular subjectivity. The question remains: why?

When one sets out to compare two texts or two thinkers, the comparison is usually employed as a means to identify either differences or similarities. In either case, there is often an implicit goal behind the comparison. If one is highlighting differences, it may be an attempt to show the innate superiority of one over the other; that is, the differentiation may serve as a basis for the exclusion of one. Or, one may demonstrate the similarities (as I am doing) with the goal of assimilating one text or thinker to the other – in other words, that Jewish thinker is 'right' because he agrees with this Christian thinker or vice versa. In this way, the comparison may serve as a basis for inclusion, or more violently, absorption of one thought world into another (a concern that critically motivates most of Levinas's thought). There is a third possibility: the comparison may be employed to make a claim about the 'truth' or 'error' found in both.

In this case, when I read these particular authors together, I am positing a normative claim: both Gregory of Nyssa and Levinas have something to teach me about reading. Specifically, both thinkers teach me that the creative paradox in which the polysemic and necessarily interpretative aspect of reading texts, *especially* normative texts, lies in the very excessiveness of the divine imprint found therein. More than this normative claim, however, my argument goes further to make an apologetic claim. The apologetics implicit in my argument become explicit through a brief excursus into a related theoretical discussion: the relationship between literary theory and the Jewish hermeneutical tradition of *Midrash*.

Levinas can be located within the tradition of Midrashic reading which will emphasize the polysemic quality of revelation found in both the Scripture and the Talmud. There has been some debate[4] in recent years as to the exact relationship between literary theory and Midrash, but there is no question that there is a legitimate comparison to be made. Moreover, in this immensely creative discussion, the Greco-Christian tradition (treated in the singular for the most part) is often unequivocally cast in the role of the nemesis to be overcome: Christianity means 'logocentrism'. Christian practices of allegorical readings – in which every text contains a single meaning, and behind one signifier there is always one single intended 'true' signified – instantiate the worst examples of this logocentrism. The apologetics implicit in my argument aim to complicate this dichotomy.

To be clear, I am not saying that there is no truth or usefulness to the basic contrast between a 'Jewish' polysemic hermeneutic and a 'Christian' logocentric one. This contrast expresses a necessary corrective – most obviously in beginning to challenge the violence of silencing that occurs with any hermeneutic that aligns and elides the 'Judeo-Christian' tradition.[5] Nonetheless, as with David Stern and Daniel Boyarin, who complicate this dichotomy from the perspective of nuancing the rich and diverse history of Jewish hermeneutics,[6] there are likewise many cases in which Christian exegetes do not read logocentrically (if we are to take 'logocentric' as shorthand for a one-to-one relationship between signifier and signified – a relationship of perfect presence, full disclosure and complete comprehension). There is, in other words, an implicit motivation in my choice to read Levinas and Gregory together, a desire to 'rescue' Gregory as at least one example from within the Christian tradition that ought not to be included within this overly broad critique.

Let me restate unequivocally what I am up to here. In a rather unsophisticated way, I do think both Gregory and Levinas are 'right': they both remind us forcibly of the limits and possibilities of reading excessive texts. They both share an insight across the centuries, and in widely different contexts, about – very broadly – what it would mean to call Scriptures Revelation (with a capital 'R') or 'word of God', the kind of reading such a text demands, how inherently destabilizing an event such a reading is and, thus, the kind of *reader* such a reading produces. There are undoubtedly many significant departures between the two – the most obvious of which is the fact that the Scriptures or revelation to which each refers are different. Nonetheless, I will argue that the structural overlaps between the two point to a shared insight that is helpful to think through the activity of reading and interpreting texts that are somewhat removed from us. I will begin with a discussion of Levinas's hermeneutics.

Levinas's Theory of Scriptural Interpretation

Levinas's essay, 'Revelation in the Jewish Tradition',[7] is framed around the question of the *possibility* of revelation. How can one explain the presence of revelation as that which comes from 'outside' this world – from outside all that we experience and know – and fissures or interrupts it, without taming the revelation of God, making it an object like other objects to be used, enjoyed, manipulated or ignored? How can revelation be given over to the world, how can it *appear*, without immediately being divested of its absolute alterity? In order to understand Levinas's concern and what is at stake in this question, one must first recognize his critique of philosophy as a 'totality'.

Western philosophy, according to Levinas, conceives of the world as a totality.[8] It is a transparent and contained whole, available to be grasped and possessed by the rational seeker. According to this view, 'our world lies before us, enabling us, in its coherence and constancy, to perceive it, enjoy it (*jouissance*), and think about it'.[9] Given such a totalizing view of the world, in *Totality and Infinity* Levinas articulates only two possibilities of relation between the self and the 'Other' – destruction or assimilation – both of which involve the objectification of the Other. The 'I' or self can either perceive the other as a threat and seek to destroy it, or it can assimilate the other to itself, regarding the Other as an object to be *enjoyed*.[10] In both, the 'I' experiences the world as a totality centred around the ego. And thus, continuous with this totalizing mode of Western philosophy is an understanding of human nature as most fundamentally acquisitional, constantly consuming – ironically, both to flex an innate power ('the world is mine to be possessed in thought') and in a futile attempt to satisfy a lack.

Levinas suggests that this way of being in the world is founded on a particular protological ontology. The world, and humans in it, originated from some whole, simple and one. The falling away from this whole ushered in a period of *sojourn* in which we are searching and seeking to return to that original wholeness. Here, desire is understood primarily as a *need* which 'characterizes a being indigent and incomplete or fallen from its past grandeur', and hence the fundamental motivation in life becomes one of 'nostalgia, a longing for return'.[11] Levinas traces this understanding back to its Greek philosophical roots. Because of its central emphasis on unity, Greek philosophical thought seeks to reduce the other to the same: 'The ideal of Socratic truth thus rests on the essential self-sufficiency of the same, its identification in ipseity, its egoism',[12] and philosophy becomes essentially 'egology'.[13] Thus, briefly, stands Levinas's (very) broad charge against most of Western thought. In *Totality and Infinity* he seeks to give an alternative way of doing philosophy by thinking of 'infinity' as that which ushers in the possibility of a relation which remains irreducible to comprehension and cannot be assimilated into a 'totality'.

By posing the question of the *possibility* of revelation, Levinas is getting at the same problem of totality and infinity from another angle. He wants to explore whether it is possible for something transcendent, exterior or 'other' to this totality to break into it without losing its alterity. His solution focuses on an analysis of 'the reader as the scribe', in which he argues that the need for intensive interpretative engagement with revelation means that the one who receives revelation, in some sense, also writes it.[14] In the Bible, Levinas argues that one finds a text whose structure both allows for and demands active interpretation. This interpretation, however, begins with close textual attention. Levinas insists that one must return from the translations of the Bible to the original Hebraic text in order to 'reveal the strange and mysterious ambiguity or polysemy which the Hebrew syntax permits'.[15] Such a return makes it clear that it is impossible to decide conclusively on the ultimate intention of a verse or text. The revelation contained within the book can thus be called a 'mystery', but one which, rather than resulting in a loss of clarity, demands a greater intensity in reading and interpretation.

Like Gregory of Nyssa, for Levinas the possibility of revelation requires a notion of divine accommodation. The 'marvelous contraction of the Infinite into the Finite' in revelation means that 'the Word of God can be held in language which created beings use among themselves'.[16] As a result, revelation is the site of a mutual self-exposure: both the content of the revelation itself, which is given over to be interpreted, and the reader, who in receiving the revelation is exposed to the demands of the text, find themselves in a vulnerable position.[17]

Levinas's understanding of 'reader-as-scribe' does not indicate a return to an elevation of will or subjective power in reading and interpretation. Indeed, as Susan Handleman points out, the opposite is the case: '. . . the reader is also no longer the willful, isolated, heroic pagan self but in turn hollowed out, opened, called by, and obligated to the text and author in responsibility and command'.[18] The fact that it is the reader who, in part, writes revelation presupposes that what I as the reader write is only partial; there are other I's, other readers, who are in turn scribes or interpreters of that which they encounter in the revelation of Scripture. And the fullness of revelation is generated only from a multiplicity of interpretations.[19] According to Levinas, revelation has been given – the Torah has been handed over and is somehow within Jewish consciousness[20] – and yet it must be infinitely interpreted.

The revelation of God can break into, interrupt and be given over to this world, without threatening its final absolute alterity because of this paradox: revelation is fully given over and yet incomplete without an infinite multiplicity of interpretations. The Talmud is written as a discussion of revelation, but that very discussion forms part of the structure of revelation. It records all the differences of opinion between various rabbis and repeats the rabbinical formula, 'These words and others are all words of the living God'.[21] The truth of revelation is polysemic.

Given the polysemic structure of revelation, in what can its unity be found? It is found, first, in the metaphysical claim that behind all the interpretations lies one ultimate voice: 'God spoke all these words' (Exod. 20.1). Further than this, however, there is a unity in the *content* of the infinitely open interpretations, in other words, in the Law (*Halakhah*).[22] Levinas's particular understanding of the Law is clarified through a consideration of the ethical implications of the reader-as-scribe.

Responsible Subjectivity: The Self as 'For-the-Other' and Metaphysical Desire

The significance of Levinas's notion of the reader-as-scribe runs deeper than the consequence of the necessity of an infinite multiplicity of interpretations; it also entails an understanding of that reader-as-scribe as one capable of response, and the *singularity* or *irreplaceability* of that reader-as-scribe. This response, regardless of the particularities of different interpreters, can be reduced to the following command: 'But to follow the Most High is to know, also, that nothing is of greater importance than the approach made toward one's neighbor, the concern with the fate of the "widow and the orphan, the stranger and the poor man"'.[23] The reader-as-scribe, precisely as the 'person to whom the word is said', is the summoned one, the one commanded to obedience. This summons consists solely in being *assigned* toward the Other. This assignment is unavoidable; one cannot refuse it.

The constitution of the self lies in this infinite responsibility, for it is only here that one is irreplaceable and utterly unique. What then is the response of the human person to this assignment? It is the 'here I am' (*hineni, me voici*). The response of 'here I am' issues forth a presenting of oneself without interest; it is an attitude of obedience due not to a categorical imperative, nor any universal law located within the confines of reason, but from an obligation towards one's neighbour.[24] The communication of response to the Other is not derived from affection for the Other or for the self. Rather, it is drawn out from the self by the revelation of the Other.

On this point, Levinas indicates the significant difference between 'need' and what he calls 'metaphysical desire'. The latter is 'an aspiration that the Desirable animates; it originates from its "object"; it is a *revelation* – whereas need is a void of the Soul; it proceeds from the subject'.[25] Need results from a lack, ontological in nature (i.e. in mythic terms, resulting from a fall away from original union and wholeness). *Eros,* in this understanding, is characterized as a hunger: it is based on a model of consuming or 'enjoying' which requires satisfaction and gratification.[26] It is inherently self-directed – a matter of drawing objects towards and into the self, a process of assimilation that originates from and is directed back towards the self.

Levinas opposes such needy desire with what he calls 'metaphysical desire'. Rather than trying to fill a lack or need, metaphysical desire goes out from itself 'toward a yonder',[27] and yet is not directed at any particular object because it is not satisfied by the consumption of any object; it is, in that sense, insatiable. Metaphysical desire tends towards the 'absolutely Other'[28] that cannot be assimilated or absorbed, that resists the self. There is no satisfaction to this desire, nor does it entail an approach of or lessening of the distance to the Other. Instead our desire is increased by the relation to the Other: 'It is a generosity nourished by the Desired, and thus a relationship that is not the disappearance of distance . . . for it nourishes itself, one might say, with its hunger'.[29]

It is a relation that feeds on its own desire. There is, in other words, no end, no terminus to this desire. It does not culminate in a final moment of satiated union, and there is no acquisition of the 'that' which is sought; it is 'not a Desire that the possession of the Desirable slakes, but the Desire for the Infinite which the Desirable arouses rather than satisfies'.[30]

Moreover, in the possibility of listening to, or rather of obeying, the call to responsibility, one can recognize 'that subjectivity is the very fracturing of immanence'.[31] This is what Levinas means by the awakening of the self by the Infinite by facing the Other. 'The face-to-face relation between the same and the Other, the I and the Other, does no violence to the I; rather through the response to the Other the self is constituted'.[32] The response of the I constitutes its singularity or uniqueness – the I becomes a definable personal self, and yet, a self that is a singular self only as a result of its relationality. The I remains under the sway of the Other, but the call of the Other to respond places the I in a position that no other I can fill, and thus calls this particular I into being:

> To utter 'I', to affirm the irreducible singularity in which the apology is pursued, means to possess a privileged place with regard to responsibility, for which no one can replace me and from which no one can release me. *To be unable to shirk: this is the I.*[33]

This is the command that comes in revelation from 'beyond' to respond to the Other: Levinas writes that revelation 'steals into me like a thief, despite the outstretched nets of consciousness, a trauma which surprises me absolutely, always already passed in a past which was never present and remains unrepresentable'.[34] This 'Glory of the Infinite' cannot be represented in any way; it can only be witnessed to precisely by saying 'here I am'. In this way, the polysemic revelation of God finds its unity in the content of the command (the Law). Levinas makes this explicit when he writes, 'To know God is to do justice to the neighbor'.[35] In many respects, this pithy statement encompasses the entirety of his religious thought. With this overview of Levinas's understanding of revelation sketched out, I turn now to Gregory to see how his thought on some of the same questions compares.

Gregory of Nyssa's Theory of Interpretation

Gregory of Nyssa's understanding of the dynamics of scriptural interpretation is interspersed throughout his writings, yet two texts are particularly instructive in this regard. Gregory's riposte to Eunomius in the second book of the *Contra Eunomium* (*CE* II)[36] establishes the philosophical, theological and linguistic assumptions behind Gregory's theory of Biblical interpretation. Secondly, in Gregory's more mature work, *The Commentary on the Song of Songs*, we find a complex interplay between divine incomprehensibility, allegorical scriptural interpretation and his understanding of the self formed in response to revelation. As divine incomprehensibility remains even with divine revelation, one's response is always both interpretative and inherently destabilizing. In other words, Gregory develops a notion of selfhood which, like Levinas's *summoned* and *subjected* self, is constituted in response to a prior call and which, as a result, lacks static or substantive identity apart from this summoning.

The most fundamental thesis of *CE* II is the claim that one can neither know nor name God's essence as a result of the basic 'gap' (διάστημα, *diastema*) between an infinite God and a temporally and spatially constituted creation.[37] This question about the origin and capacity of language is no abstract or insignificant matter; rather, it gets to the heart of Gregory's understanding of the relation between God and humanity.[38] The impossibility of naming God is not the result of human weakness or sin as much as a neutral statement of the 'irreducible opposition between God and creature'.[39] The limitation is primarily positive: it heralds the glory befitting God.[40] Hence Gregory also insists that the naming of God is not merely *impossible*, it is *impious*.

Significantly, the debate between Gregory and Eunomius about the origin and status of language is framed within a debate of how to properly interpret Scripture, specifically how to interpret the account of creation in Genesis. Gregory's position that language is derived from human concepts (ἐπίνοια, *epinoia*) is 'blasphemous' according to Eunomius, not only because it denies divine providence, but also because it contradicts the literal words of the Genesis narrative. Gregory must counter this critique with his own account of how Scripture is to be understood and interpreted.

To begin with, Gregory thinks that one must understand Scripture as revelatory only because in Scripture God graciously descends to the created order of language.[41] To properly understand what Gregory means here, one must first understand Gregory's depiction of the divine accommodation to the needs of creation in the *kenosis*, the divine self-emptying, of the Incarnation. As Sarah Coakley has demonstrated in an article tracking different Patristic models of kenosis, Gregory has a somewhat unique understanding of this doctrine. Gregory interprets Phil. 2.5–11 (in which the Incarnation is described as the kenosis of God) not as a divine self-limiting or constriction into human form, but as a filling, indeed overflowing, of divinity into the finite vessel of humanity.[42] Here the human is not taken over, but taken up and transformed in its ever-increasing capacity to receive the overflow of the divine being.[43] Gregory extends this understanding of kenosis to the divine accommodation in Scripture: revelation in Scripture expands to fill and saturate our capacity to receive it in an infinitely extensive way.

A second significant element of Gregory's understanding of divine accommodation in Scripture is that revelation does not take the form of dictation. The writers of Scripture act not as transcribers, but as translators – trustworthy co-workers through whom God entrusts his word.[44] In this way scriptural language also reflects a multitude of particular perspectives and contexts, while still laying claim to the inflection of God's truth. For instance, Gregory accepts that Moses writes in a particular way, using specific terms and concepts considered, in his human wisdom, sufficient for the uplifting of his readers:

> Thus Moses' speech *accorded with his upbringing and education*, but he attributes these words to God, as has often been said, because of the infancy of those recently brought to the knowledge of God, to present the divine will clearly, and in order to make the hearers readier to believe, once persuaded of the reliability of the account.[45]

In other words, embedded within Gregory's understanding of Scripture as the sacred and uniquely authoritative word of God is, nevertheless, a historicist, hermeneutical assumption that language arises out of particular contexts to which one must attend in order to better understand the meaning of the text. Thus, Gregory assumes that *scriptural texts are inherently interpretative* – both in their origin and in our reading of them.

It is significant that Gregory's explicit argument about the impossibility and impiety of singly naming God correlates with an implicit argument about the impossibility and impiety of singly interpreting Scripture. One must not expect attainment of a single truth in either case. Both phenomena (both God and God's revelation in Scripture) far exceed that which can be signified by one word or by one interpretation.

Against Eunomius's accusation that by limiting language of God to derivations of human concepts the Cappadocians are being disrespectful and impious, Gregory argues that true reverence is demonstrated through a willing acceptance of the limits of knowledge:

> As far above the touch of the fingers as the stars may be, so far, or rather much further, the nature which transcends mind rises above terrestrial reason. Having learnt, therefore, how great the difference of nature is, we should quietly stay within our proper limits. It is *safer* and at the same time *more reverent* to believe that the divine majesty is more than can be thought of, than to restrict his glory by certain ideas and think there is nothing beyond that.[46]

The claim to reach anything more is not only wrong-headed but also arrogant and idolatrous. One must take one's cue from Scripture, which teaches many things about God and 'clarif[ies] the way we apprehend God', but says nothing of God's essence.[47]

We may draw certain practical consequences from Gregory's Biblical hermeneutic: First, Scripture is to be interpreted diversely, and any interpretation involves a translation. Secondly, scriptural interpretation ultimately serves an apophatic function. There is no common language between

God and humanity; one can never hope to comprehend God's essence. Nevertheless, there is no sense that Gregory is at all in doubt about the ability to know that God exists, and moreover, that God shows God's self in and to creation. God's revelation is a paradoxical gift: a vision of the invisible. 'With this paradox, Gregory is operating at the boundaries of his language and conceptual framework, and yet at the same time he remains faithful to his core belief in the infinite transcendence of God and the infinite possibilities inherent in the never-ending human journey towards God'.[48]

Where Levinas struck the balance between unity and diversity in Biblical interpretation through reference to the Law, Gregory does it with reference to the inherent aim or intention (σκοπός, *skopos*) of a text. One's interpretation must be guided by this internal intention of the text; it is the circumscribing horizon of all possible meanings. This might seem to limit interpretations to a finite number except for the fact that, in the case of the Bible, its overarching *skopos* follows Gregory's understanding of the life of faith in a particular way: it is a journey into the unknown and requires a willingness to leave behind the safety of possessed knowledge into the darkness of ignorance in response to a summons. Thus, the Law of revelation and the skopos of revelation for Levinas and Gregory both relate to an individual's response to the Other/God, a response which is initiated through a response to the text. From this notion of Scripture as a limiting *horos* (ὅρος) or horizon, out of which arises an unlimited possibility of interpretations,[49] specific practices of reading follow which entail and produce Gregory's specific notion of what it is to be a self.

The Allegorical Constitution of Selfhood in In Canticum Canticorum

In one of his final works, *The Commentary on the Song of Songs*, Gregory deepens his understanding of the relation between scriptural interpretation and a subjectivity formed out of its desire for the ultimately desirable, yet finally unattainable, God. Reading through the series of homilies, the connection between Gregory's allegorical interpretation of the *Song of Songs* and his apophaticism is immediately clear. I argue that Gregory's insistence upon divine incomprehensibility, the cornerstone of Gregory's apophaticism, arises out of, justifies and is performed in, allegorical interpretation. Further, I argue that the intrinsic relation between the pluriformity of interpretation (especially allegorical interpretation) and apophasis, in Gregory's hands at least, yields a disruption of identity as much as a formation of it. Within Gregory's theological vision, the idea and experience of identity is transformed from a static reality to a dynamic and deeply destabilizing 'way' of approach which never arrives at a fixed point; further, this way of approach is not only announced in, but also actually formed through, allegorical interpretation.

For Gregory, like most other Christian interpreters of the *Song* before him, the bride in the *Song of Songs* is the soul yearning after the bridegroom, or Christ. The time in which the bride waits for her beloved is 'night', understood as the 'time of darkness . . . the contemplation of what is unseen . . . the darkness of God's presence'.[50] Unable to wait, the bride goes out into the city and asks the watchmen if they have seen 'the one whom my soul loves'. Yet the watchmen are silent. As the bride passes on through the city 'and did not perceive her love among *immaterial and spiritual beings* . . . she realizes that her sought-after love is known only in the *impossibility to comprehend his essence, and that every sign becomes a hindrance to those who seek him*' (italics added).[51] Here, language itself is the stumbling block. In other words, the bride, the soul, learns that her beloved, God, is known only in the recognition of the impossibility of knowing and the concurrent necessity of passing over every sign (whether literal or spiritual). It is clear, then, that an insistence upon divine incomprehensibility arises out of Gregory's allegorical interpretation of the *Song*. It is helpful to notice a curious methodological point about Gregory's understanding of allegory: allegorical interpretations always justify and strengthen the need for allegorical interpretation; it always shores up its own methodological foundation by pointing to limits of our understanding and the impropriety of claiming more than we should about our knowledge of God. Allegory does not, in Gregory's hands, correspond to a logocentric view that seeks out the one true meaning hidden behind the material text. Allegory is the furthest thing from being a method intent on delivering one single truth. Rather, allegorical reading evades any attempt to circumscribe knowledge, opens up onto diverse horizons and, in this way, underwrites its own necessity and usefulness. The argument is even more circular than this, however, for we shall also see that divine incomprehensibility is also the presupposition underlying the allegorical interpretation of scriptural texts.

As we have seen in Gregory's debate with Eunomius, the foundation of Gregory's apophaticism is his insistence upon the *diastema* between the infinity of God and the finitude of creation. The infinity of God necessarily thwarts all finite attempts at comprehensive knowledge and thus sends the creature spiralling infinitely towards God, in an endless and increasing desire for God. In the Fifth Homily of the *Song of Songs*, Gregory writes:

> So then, when God draws a human soul to participate in himself, he always remains in equal measure superior to the participating soul because of his superabundant goodness. For on the one hand, the soul continually grows through participating in what is beyond it and never stops growing. On the other hand, the good in which the soul shares remains the same [i.e. unlimited] so that the more the soul participates in it, the more she recognises that it transcends her as much as before.[52]

As many have observed, Gregory is one of the first Christian theologians to positively discuss God's infinity, to insist that God is limited by nothing.[53] Consequently, one never ceases moving towards God; one can never reach God because reaching would indicate a divine boundary or limitation. The 'perfection of knowledge attainable by human nature' only sparks the 'beginning of a desire for more lofty things'.[54] In other words, the culmination of the perfection of our *knowledge* is really only the beginning of our *desire* for God. Gregory thus speaks of an infinite deferral as well as an infinite attainment: 'They never cease to desire, but every enjoyment of God they turn into kindling of a still more intense desire'.[55]

Elsewhere Gregory distinguishes between desire based on lack and desire drawn out of one expansively, a desire grounded in excess rather than lack.[56] Similar to Levinas, the former kind of desire is to be expurgated, cleansed from the self, in order that one might be open to the experience of a desire which has no end and no satisfaction. The latter desire is propelled not by need, but by the excess of the desirable. The beloved, or desirable, is so infinitely; it thus attracts the self outwards towards the Other and this becomes the source of unceasing movement. The eternality or perpetuity of the progress of the soul towards God supplies the justification for allegorical interpretation of Scripture: one must continuously look behind the obvious in the search for the hidden. Furthermore, the eternality of the soul's progress also bridges over to the third characteristic of allegory: its constitutive capacity to transform the individual soul in the face of divine mystery.

As I have already alluded to, Gregory interprets the *Song of Songs* to celebrate the 'union of the human soul with God'.[57] However, this is more than an allegorical interpretation of the *Song of Songs*; Gregory takes it one step further by stating that the act of interpreting the Song is itself an act of unifying oneself with God. It is important to note that what Gregory is here describing is not abstract and speculative, but real and experiential. He is describing the act of interpreting a text together as a community – an activity in which he is presumably engaged simultaneously to writing and delivering these homilies. He writes that 'the interpretation of the Song's prologue according to the two preceding days had the benefit of washing and purifying from the flesh's mire our understanding of its words'.[58] Notice, it is not the prologue itself, but the (allegorical) interpretation of it which is purifying. In what way is allegorical interpretation formative? In what way does it affect the 'union' of the human soul with the divine? If such interpretation always leads to a profound acknowledgement of divine incomprehensibility, then it is by drawing the self out of any stable, conscribable definition – only by tearing it out of a defined communal identity into the ecstasy and vertigo which, Gregory insists, attends the mystical ascent to God.

Having detailed the outlines of Gregory's theory of interpretation, let me now try to highlight some specific points of similarity between him and Levinas. First, there is an immeasurable disjunction between an infinite revelation and its finite reception or landing place. Gregory addresses this disjunction through his notion of the divine accommodation, in which the divine Word comes according to one's capacity to receive it. This can be seen in Gregory's allegorical reading of the passage in the *Song* in which the bridegroom knocks at the door and, when it is opened, places his hand through the small opening available to him. Alluding to the Incarnation, Gregory writes that 'God's creative hand contracted itself to reside in our small, worthless human existence'.[59] The bride 'opens the door' signifying the 'veil of flesh' in order to bid the Word enter her chamber (heart). But the aperture is too small to contain the infinite Word, thus only the hand appears. More than this, however, the 'hand' draws the bride out, into the street, to seek her beloved further. It entails a response, in other words. One follows the summons: 'I opened to my beloved; my beloved was gone; my soul went forth at his speech, I sought him, but found him not; I called him, but he did not answer me' (Song 5.6). In this way, the hermeneutical key to the entire journey of the soul remains the kenotic movement of the Incarnation, the overflowing of divinity into the limited capacity of human receptivity. This overflowing, in itself, cracks open that limited capacity and enlarges it. Receiving revelation necessitates a response that is both transformative and destabilizing. Thus, for Gregory, Christ holds the same *functional* place – serving to unify structurally infinite interpretations of Scripture – as the Law does for Levinas.

Secondly, Gregory's strong emphasis on the inherent relation between allegorical interpretation and apophaticism means that for him as for Levinas there are an infinite number of possible interpretations of Scripture.

As interpretation is always performed by a finite and limited interpreter, he or she cannot rest with one particular interpretation.

Both Gregory of Nyssa's and Levinas's strong emphasis on the inherent relation between scriptural interpretation and divine incomprehensibility results in the necessity of an interpretative pluralism. Scripture is revelatory. But Scripture reveals only by filling and then overflowing our finite capacity to understand and interpret it. Through such interpretative practices, one engages the whole being, body, mind and soul without finding a solid place upon which to stand and rest. This very act also transforms and enlarges one's capacity to receive more. Scriptural interpretation thus displaces the self in a confrontation with divine incomprehensibility. It reveals a subjectivity which is called into this particular existence only through a displacement and rupturing of self as much as a formation of it. This, according to both Levinas and Gregory, is an endless movement: revelation, by filling and overflowing our finite capacity, summons a response which calls us into a new being, again and again.

Conclusion

This paper has explored the ways in which the respective theories of Biblical interpretation of Levinas and Gregory share certain structural similarities. Both insist on the active engagement with the text that obliges a re-translation; in some sense interpretation is necessary to the arrival of revelation. It comes from without and yet must be responded to by something within. This logically leads to both thinkers considering the possibility of a radical open-endedness to revelation. Both Levinas and Gregory battle against a similar foil or enemy: the over-reaching epistemological claims based on a lack of attention to the metaphysical chasm that separates the infinite from the finite. Thus both also underline the metaphysical reality of a disjunction between revelation (or its first source as coming from 'elsewhere' and revealing a God that remains hidden in the revelation) and its interpreters. The finitude of the interpreter requires an infinite amount of interpreters to complete revelation. Likewise, the act of interpreting revelation, of reading Scripture, is constitutive of a particular subjectivity and, at the same time, destabilizing. One's subjectivity does not come from within; one is drawn out of the self in a desirous movement that is directed from without. This movement defines us.

Revelation, in the hands of both Levinas and Gregory, accomplishes a 'breach of the totality',[60] an interruption of the infinite into the finite.

The truth of revelation (if we can for a moment speak inaccurately in the singular of such an event) is encountered only in the eternal dynamic of looking towards that which breaks in but which will never become visible: 'since the true sight of God consists in this, that the one who looks up to God never ceases in that desire'.[61] In the end, both Levinas and Gregory of Nyssa speak to the same concern – avoiding a singular reading of revelation which implies a view of the human person as necessarily acquisitive and selfish and for whom satiation is a possibility – and the same answer – stretching out the movement toward the Other infinitely, of making the end no end at all.

Notes

1 Herein lies one important difference between Levinas and Gregory: for the former, God can only ever be encountered in and through one's response to another (human) person. Hence, 'ethics' is the primary starting place always for Levinas.
2 For a nuanced indictment of the history of Christian hermeneutical violence to Jewish texts, see Daniel Boyarin, *A Radical Jew: Paul and the Politics of Identity* (Berkeley: University of California Press, 1994).
3 Elsewhere I have employed a reading of Gregory of Nyssa for this purpose vis-a-vis a comparison of John Milbank and Jean-Luc Marion on the subject of the 'gift'. See 'Revealing the invisible: Gregory of Nyssa on the gift of revelation', *Modern Theology,* 21/1 (2005), 67–85.
4 See for instance, Daniel Boyarin, *Intertextuality and the Reading of Midrash* (Bloomington: Indiana University Press, 1990); Susan A. Handelman, *The Slayers of Moses: The Emergence of Rabbinic Interpretation in Modern Literary Theory* (Albany: SUNY Press, 1982); Sanford Budick and Geoffrey Hartman (eds), *Midrash and Literature* (New Haven: Yale University Press, 1986); David Stern, *Midrash and Theory: Ancient Jewish Exegesis and Contemporary Literary Studies* (Evanston: Northwestern University Press, 1996).
5 On the forced suppression of Jewish voices that goes unacknowledged in the term 'Judeo-Christian', see D. Boyarin: 'The valorization of midrash as interpretation and indeed as a model of interpretation means as well revoicing of a Jewish discourse in the discourse of the West. The liberal term "Judeo-Christian" masks a suppression of that which is distinctly Jewish. It means "Christian", and by not acknowledging that much, renders the suppression of Jewish discourse even more complete' (*Intertextuality*, xi).
6 For instance, both Stern and Boyarin are critical of Susan Handleman et al. who claim that *Midrash* is the definitive Jewish hermeneutic. They point out that *Midrash* itself was often silenced within Rabbinical Judaism.
7 Emmanuel Levinas, 'Revelation in the Jewish Tradition' in *The Levinas Reader* (Sean Hand (trans.); Oxford: Blackwell, 1989), original publication in *Révélation* (Bruxelles: Editions des Facultés Universitaires Saint-Louis, 1977), 55–77.

8 Much of the following summary of Levinas's critique of western philosophy as a 'totality' is drawn from Emmanuel Levinas, *Totality and Infinity: An Essay on Exteriority* (Alphonso Lingis (trans.); Pittsburgh: Duquesne University Press, 1969).

9 Levinas, 'Revelation', 191.

10 Levinas, *Totality and Infinity*, 38.

11 Ibid., 33.

12 Ibid.

13 Ibid., 44.

14 On this central point Levinas locates himself broadly within the Midrashic tradition of reading Scripture. Daniel Boyarin encapsulates Midrash in the following way: 'Midrash most frequently (not always) does not proceed by paraphrase, by giving the "meaning" of a passage, but rather by expanding the text via the production of more narrative on the same "ontological" level as the text itself' (167). See Boyarin, 'Midrash' in *The Handbook for Postmodern Biblical Interpretation* (A. K. M. Adam (ed.); St Louis, Mo.: Chalice Press, 2000).

15 Levinas, 'Revelation', 193.

16 Levinas, *L'au delà du verset: Lectures et discours talmudiques* (Paris: Éditions de Minuit, 1982), 7.

17 In *Fragments of Redemption: Jewish Thought and Literary Theory in Benjamin, Scholem, and Levinas* (Bloomington: Indiana University Press, 1991), Susan Handleman observes the way in which this understanding of revelation as held captive to the power of another force parallels Levinas's understanding of the self in relation to the Other: 'Exegesis opens the text to the other voice; in Levinasian terms it is also the "ethical" *self-exposure* of the text, analogous to the way subjectivity is defined in the philosophical works as traumatized, broken up, vulnerable, exposed, and opened to the other' (*Fragments*, 285).

18 Ibid., 288.

19 Levinas writes: 'It is as if a multiplicity of persons . . . were the condition for the plenitude of "absolute truth", as if each person, by virtue of his own uniqueness, were able to guarantee the revelation of one unique aspect of the truth, so that some of its facets would never have been revealed if certain people had been absent from mankind . . . I am suggesting that the totality of truth is made out of the contributions of a multiplicity of people' ('Revelation', 195).

20 This givenness of revelation, the fact that it has been handed over, makes sense of the famous Talmudic story found in B. Baba Mezi'a 59 a-b (paraphrased by Stern in *Midrash and Theory*) in which the direct divine intervention into a dispute between rabbis goes unheeded. Correct interpretation of revelation is not decided finally by its source, but by those to whom it has been given. 'Since the Torah has already been given from Mount Sinai, we do not pay attention to heavenly voices, for You have already written at Mount Sinai, "after the majority incline" (Exod. 23.2)' (*Midrash*, 30). As Stern astutely expresses, 'Rabbi Yermiyah effectively invokes Scripture against God' (*Midrash*, 30).

21 Levinas, 'Revelation', 198.

22 As we shall see, this is one site of differentiation from Gregory of Nyssa who locates the hermeneutical unity of a necessarily infinite diversity of interpretation of Revelation in Christ, not the Law.

23 Ibid., 202.

24 Ibid., 206.

25 Levinas, *Totality and Infinity*, 62.

26 Ibid., 58.

27 Ibid., 33.

28 Ibid. Levinas refers sometimes to the Other and sometimes to Infinity; both express the same reality.

29 Ibid.

30 Ibid., 50.

31 Levinas, 'Revelation', 204.

32 Levinas, *Totality and Infinity*, 197.

33 Ibid., 245.

34 Levinas, 'God and Philosophy' in *The Levinas Reader*, 184.

35 Levinas, *God, Death and Time* (Bettina Bergo (trans.); Stanford: Stanford University Press, 2000), 199.

36 I will follow the translation by Stuart George Hall in *Gregory of Nyssa: Contra Eunomium II: An English version with Commentary and Supporting Studies, Proceedings of the Tenth International Colloquium on Gregory of Nyssa (Olomouc, 15–18 September, 2004)*, (Lenka Karfíková, Scot Douglass and Johannes Zachhuber (eds); Leiden: Brill 2006). Hall separates the text into paragraphs. I will cite the paragraph followed by the page number.

37 Gregory of Nyssa, *CE* II 67, 74 (*GNO* 1, 245).

38 *CE* II 290–1, 124 (*GNO* 1, 312).

39 Hans Urs von Balthasar, *Presence and Thought: An Essay on the Religious Philosophy of Gregory of Nyssa* (Mark Sebanc (trans.); San Francisco: Ignatius Press, 1995), 27.

40 'That he transcends every effort of thought, and is found to be beyond the reach of naming, stands as a testimony to mankind of his ineffable majesty', *CE* II 587, 192 (*GNO* 1, 397).

41 See *CE* II 418, 153 (*GNO* 1, 347).

42 On this point, Gregory is actually closer to Jean-Luc Marion, with his notion of saturated phenomenality, than Levinas who uses the language of rupture and/or transgression more than saturation to talk of revelation. Yet, both Gregory and Levinas share the attempt to think through the surprising and unpredictable advent of this excessive revelation into the finite. And for both, it speaks to us as a summons to respond, and a summons which comes from without and yet calls us particularly or uniquely, in such a way that no one else can respond in our place.

43 See Sarah Coakley, 'Does Kenosis Rest on a Mistake? Three Kenotic Models in Patristic Exegesis' in *Exploring Kenotic Christology* (C. Stephen Evans (ed.); Oxford: Oxford University Press, 2006), 246–64.

44 See Ari Ojell, 'Service or Master? "Theology" in Gregory of Nyssa's *Contra Eunomium II*' in *Gregory of Nyssa: Contra Eunomium II: An English Version with Supporting Studies, Proceedings of the 10th International Colloquium on*

Gregory of Nyssa (Olomouc, September 15–18, 2004) (Leiden; Boston: Brill, 2007), 473–84.

45 CE II 261, 117 (my emphasis) (*GNO* 1, 302).

46 CE II 95-96, 80–1 (my emphasis) (*GNO* 1, 254).

47 CE II 105, 83 (*GNO* 1, 257).

48 Ivana Noble, 'The Apophatic Way in Gregory of Nyssa' in Petr Pokorny (ed.), *Philosophical Hermeneutics and Biblical Exegesis* (Tübingen: Mohr Siebeck, 2002).

49 For a far more detailed discussion of the paradoxical relationship between unity and diversity of scriptural interpretation in Gregory of Nyssa, see Morwenna Ludlow, 'Theology and allegory: Origen and Gregory of Nyssa on the unity and diversity of Scripture', *International Journal of Systematic Theology*, 4/1 (2002), 45–66: '. . . there is in [Gregory's] theology both a sense of control and openness: particularly with regard to human reason he stresses both its limits *and* its endless dynamic in its path towards understanding God', 65.

50 Gregory of Nyssa, *In Canticum Canticorum* 6, 130 (*GNO* 6, 181). I am following, with some caution, Casimir McCambley's translation, *Commentary on the Song of Songs* (Brookline: Holy Cross Press, 1987).

51 Gregory, *In Cant.* 6, 131 (my emphasis) (*GNO* 6, 183).

52 Gregory, *In Cant.* 5, 119 (*GNO* 6, 158).

53 Ibid., 5, 118 (*GNO* 6, 157). For the definitive work on Gregory as a thinker of infinity see, Ekkehard Mühlenberg, *Die Unendlichkeit Gottes bei Gregor von Nysse: Gregors Kritik am Gottesbegriff der Klassischen Metaphysik* (Gottingen: Vanderhoek & Ruprecht, 1966), especially p. 103. More recently, see David Bentley Hart, *The Beauty of the Infinite: The Aesthetics of Christian Truth* (Grand Rapids: Eerdmans, 2003).

54 Ibid., 6, 130 (*GNO* 6, 180).

55 Ibid., 1, 51 (*GNO* 6, 32).

56 See Gregory of Nyssa, *On the Soul and the Resurrection* (Catherine P. Roth (trans.); Crestwood, N.Y.: St Vladimir's Seminary Press, 1993).

57 Ibid., 1, 47 (*GNO* 6, 22).

58 Gregory, *In Cant.*, 3, 75 (*GNO* 6, 71).

59 Ibid., 11, 208 (*GNO* 6, 338).

60 Ibid., 23.

61 Gregory of Nyssa, *The Life of Moses* (Abraham Malherbe and Everett Ferguson (trans); The Classics of Western Spirituality; New York: Paulist Press, 1978), 116.

CHAPTER 5

THE COMBINATORY DETOUR: THE PREFIX Συν- IN GREGORY OF NYSSA'S PRODUCTION OF THEOLOGICAL KNOWLEDGE

Scot Douglass

A Theoretical Framing of Theology as συνθεωρία.[1]

Martin Heidegger began his analysis in *Kant und das Problem der Metaphysik* on a cautionary note: '. . . all attempts to extend the pure knowledge of reason must first be held back until the question of the inner possibility of this science is clarified'.[2] This typical Heideggerian question, part of his larger interrogation of the laying of a foundation for metaphysics (*die Grundlegung der Metaphysik*), provides a relevant frame in at least two ways for reading Gregory of Nyssa. First of all and in a very straightforward manner, Gregory repeatedly sounded the same cautionary note against the over-extended rational ambitions of Eunomius. Explicitly throughout the *Contra Eunomium*, but pervading his entire output, Gregory constantly 'clarified' how severely limited is the 'inner possibility' of pure reason in knowing the essence of God.[3]

At the same time, Heidegger's project proves relevant to reading Gregory in a second, much more fundamental manner: the methodological demand to interrogate the inner possibility of Gregory's own approach to knowing. In particular, what inner possibilities for speaking about God did Gregory discover, develop and employ in the wake of his radical critique of the 'inner possibilities' of Eunomian reasoning. That is, what productive possibilities emerged for Gregory in his denial of language's mastery over essence. This more fundamental framing would need to investigate, therefore, not only what theological conclusions Gregory presented as an alternative to Eunomius, but all of the following as well:

- Given that Gregory's critique of Eunomius's conclusions, the critique of his Neo-Arian *what,* was rooted in challenging the inner possibility of Eunomius's rational *how,* how did Gregory undertake his own *how* of arriving at his alternative Nicene *what* so as to avoid the same critique?
- How did Gregory's methodological *how* emerge from his own examinations into the inner possibility of theological thinking? (That is, what

theoretical connections can one find between his interrogation of theological language and how he employed theological language?)
- What, as a result, was the status of Gregory's theological *what?*
- How was Gregory's theological *what* dependent upon *how* he presented it? And, of course (closely related), how did Gregory want his readers, both contemporary and future, to read/engage his theological *what?*[4] Or, perhaps more precisely (and overlapping with Tamsin Jones's essay in this volume),[5] what did Gregory want to happen to those who read him properly?
- In short: *how* did Gregory arrive at his theological *what?* What is the status of this *what* in light of *how* it was produced? How, therefore, should someone read this *what?*

None of these questions, of course, needed Heidegger to have first asked them of Kant for my making such an inquiry into Gregory.[6] If the connection being drawn between Gregory and Heidegger, separated as they are by one and a half millennia, were to be left at simply borrowing a question, then it would be quite arbitrary to assume any comparative/dialogical value. Putting them in conversation, though, proves extremely productive for a number of reasons that further advance a 'responsible reading' of Gregory, even if (perhaps especially if) one's scholarly ambition is to understand him better within his own historical context (the goal, for example, of Matthieu Cassin's contribution to this volume and his much larger project on the third book of Gregory's *Contra Eunomium*[7]). What justifies such a dialogical method in this case is a certain resonance between Heidegger's and Gregory's assumptions, assertions and critiques of language's relationship to truth. Both thinkers are wrestling with variations of the same problem: in light of the complex relationships among language, concrete existence and time, what type of access (noetic, experiential, types of fidelity) can someone have to truth in the ongoing project of becoming? That is, they both reject what Heidegger would call the ontotheological in the name of wrestling with a phenomenology of truth: the outworking and manifestation of truth within the context of creation/existence in the world. Both are concerned, therefore, with the inseparable connection between origins and the project (the projection out of this origin) of becoming. Because this common ground is cultivated in different contexts with divergent goals, each develops certain aspects of the problem more than the other – aspects that are frequently latent in the other. One of my methodological wagers (justified by exemplum, I think, in Virginia Burris's essay[8]) involves the following chain of thinking: (1) certain ideas/questions/themes always exceed any single investigation;[9] (2) these single investigations belong to a reception history of past investigations; (3) any single investigation is steered in certain directions by historical contingencies; and (4) the insights of different thinkers wrestling with overlapping problems can open up latent potentialities in a text that are implicitly true to the text, even though the author did not develop these potentialities. This methodological process can be seen in the Trinitarian controversy itself. With the development, for example, of Nicene Christology and Trinitarian theology, church fathers find Nicene orthodox meaning in scriptural passages whose original articulations were not framed around the questions and problems of the fourth century. Paul and John are understood to be Trinitarian even though this is, strictly speaking, anachronistic.[10] On a more pedestrian level, this is no different than the following common exchange: 'Well, based on what you are saying about x, I think you would be interested in what so and so says about x', followed by, 'I never thought about it in that way or in that context, but yes . . . now that I do, that's exactly what I was saying, or at least an extension of what I was saying, even though I wouldn't have said it that way'.[11] In the case of reading ancient texts, given Plato's observation in the *Phaedrus* that written texts are like abandoned orphans, the work of opening up these latent potentialities must be done by the reader and not the author.[12] Johannes Zachhuber's essay on reception history in this volume indicates to me that there are key interpretative forks in the road of reception that simultaneously magnify and suppress different aspects of a thinker.[13] This implies, among other things, that possibilities of a text are lost almost immediately – possibilities that can be re-opened by later thinkers wrestling with similar questions and problems. I would argue that this can be legitimately ('responsibly') understood as 're-openings' and not merely as eisegetical constructions.

The resonance, therefore, in this case is both methodological and thematic, despite a difference between Heidegger and Gregory regarding the possibility of a revelation of the type claimed within Christianity.[14] This distinction, though, is not quite as distinctive as it might first appear. The emergence of the so-called post-secular and the (re)turn to religion in continental philosophy as seen, for example, in the renewed interrogation of the Messianic and the 'absolute other', demonstrates a persistence of the deep structures of the problem of revelation. That is to say, Heidegger's contribution to reading Gregory better is not dependent upon being able to make some sort of plastic substitution of 'God' for 'being'. The question is whether or not there is something usefully in common: the (sub)structure of truth becoming knowable. When explicit belief in the possibility of divine revelation is in play, as is clearly the case with Gregory, such questions must formally negotiate the bidirectional components of any knowledge of God. That is, one must examine the relationship between revelation as the movement from God to human beings – from the invisible to the visible, from the transcendent to the phenomenological – and theology as the responsive movement from the believer towards God in the service of others – from the visible to the invisible, from the phenomenological to the transcendent. This back and forth movement became particularly problematic and uniquely productive in Gregory's thinking because of the radical ontological division he drew between uncreated and created being in his polemic against Eunomius.[15] Gregory's belief in divine revelation, though, functions merely as a variable within the common ground one can find between him and Heidegger – a variable that examines a particular application of the question of truth. Revelation for Gregory, despite its problematic relationship to the transcendent and its disruptive character, always and completely obeys the rules of creation in its manifestation, including language's form, origin and limitations.

In his *Homilies on Ecclesiastes*, Gregory identified the impenetrable barrier between Creator and creation and its phenomenological impact on a created being's ambition to ever know its Creator:

οὕτω καὶ πᾶσα ἡ κτίσις ἔξω ἑαυτῆς γενέσθαι διὰ τῆς καταληπτικῆς θεωρίας οὐ δύναται, ἀλλ' ἐν ἑαυτῇ μένει ἀεὶ καὶ ὅπερ ἂν ἴδῃ, ἑαυτὴν βλέπει· κἂν οἰηθῇ τι ὑπὲρ ἑαυτὴν βλέπειν, τὸ ἐκτὸς ἑαυτῆς ἰδεῖν φύσιν οὐκ ἔχει. οἷον τὴν διαστηματικὴν ἔννοιαν ἐν τῇ τῶν ὄντων θεωρίᾳ παρελθεῖν βιάζεται, ἀλλ' οὐ παρέρχεται. παντὶ γὰρ τῷ εὑρισκομένῳ νοήματι συνθεωρεῖ πάντως τὸ συγκαταλαμβανόμενον τῇ ὑποστάσει τοῦ νοουμένου διάστημα· τὸ δὲ διάστημα οὐδὲν ἄλλο ἢ κτίσις ἐστίν.

Thus the whole created order is unable to get out of itself through a comprehensive vision, but remains continually enclosed within itself, and whatever it beholds, it is looking at itself. And even if it somehow thinks it is looking at something beyond itself, that which it sees outside itself has no being. One may struggle to surpass or transcend diastemic conception by the understanding of the created universe, but one does not transcend. For in every object one conceptually discovers, it always comprehends the diastema inherent in the being of the apprehended object, for diastema is nothing other than creation itself.[16]

In this much-examined passage, Gregory identified two separate noetic strategies, both rooted in the word θεωρία (to ascend from creation to God). Both attempts decisively failed, bouncing back at the diastemic border, because of the impossibility of creation ever transcending its own constitution. The first θεωρία-based noetic[17] strategy was the straight-forward ambition of creation to 'get outside of itself' (ἔξω ἑαυτῆς) through a 'comprehensive vision', through a θεωρία that was καταληπτική (a word related, of course, to καταλαμβάνω).[18] Far from 'getting outside of itself', created being never got beyond the futility of only seeing itself (ἑαυτὴν βλέπει).[19] Conceding the impossibility of a direct, transcending vision, created being attempted a second strategy: a θεωρία able to perform a self-transcending analytic of creation from within creation.[20] This second θεωρία also failed for the same reason (γάρ) as did the first, with the unequivocal result that the practitioner 'does not transcend' (ἀλλ' οὐ παρέρχεται[21]). Neither strategy succeeded because every attempt to have a θεωρία necessarily resulted in a συνθεωρία. This 'seeing with' is underlined in the double usage of the prefix συν- attached by Gregory to the desired but futile θεωρία–καταλαμβάνω combination: the verb συνθεωρεῖ and its direct object τὸ συγκαταλαμβανόμενον διάστημα. And just to make sure the reader understood the self-reflexive limitation inherent in διάστημα, Gregory immediately added: τὸ δὲ διάστημα οὐδὲν ἄλλο ἢ κτίσις ἐστίν. Every θεωρία, therefore, is always a συνθεωρία, a συνθεωρία σὺν διαστή-ματι. The desire, therefore, for a θεωρία καταληπτική results, necessarily, in a συνθεωρία συγκαταλαμβανομένη. This doubling of the prefix συν-, the impossibility of seeing anything in an isolated purity (the impossibility of thinking anything fully abstracted from its manifold manifestation in creation), not only provided a radical critique of Eunomian reason (Eunomius's attempt, for example, to isolate ἀγέννητος as a pure theologeme), but implicated Nyssen's own production of theology in a number of important noetic economies whose extension of knowledge of God (to borrow the language of Heidegger's question) simultaneously held itself back by embracing the limitations of its own inner possibilities while forging new ways of producing knowledge of God that exploited the source of these limitations. Gregory's employment of these new ways in a section from the *Contra Eunomium II*, ways that are rooted in the significance of the prefix συν-, will be the site later in this essay for exploring all of the questions posed above.

The world of mathematics (differential equations, in particular) provides an interesting picture of Gregory's theological construction in respect to the fate of both revelation and theology: the circular asymptote. In a circular asymptote, there is a function (e.g. $r = a\theta^2/[\theta^2 - 1]$) such that any value within the circle belongs to an outward spiral that gets infinitely closer to the circle without ever touching it, let alone crossing it. This is the nature of theology for Gregory. Within the circle of creation, the theologian συνθεωρεῖ συγκαταλαμβανόμενον διάστημα—(in which) τὸ δὲ διάστημα οὐδὲν ἄλλο ἢ κτίσις ἐστίν, never transcending the diastemic limit. The following graph plots the attempt and failure of creation to transcend the circle of creation.

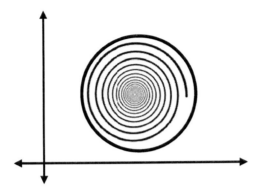

At the same time, any value outside the circle belongs to a spiral that infinitely moves away from and converges upon the circle without, again, ever touching it. This is the unknowable realm of the 'οὐσία' of God, that which is ineffably adiastemic and akinetic.

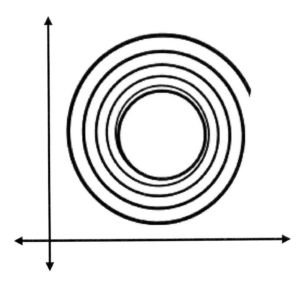

When we extend this into three dimensions, we get a spherical asymptotic boundary in which the sphere functions as the untouchable boundary separating inside from outside and outside from inside. For Gregory, of course, the inside of the sphere is entirely diastemic and kinetic, the realm of creation and συνθεωρία; that which is 'outside' the sphere is, for all of creation constitutionally bound within it, unspeakably adiastemic and akinetic. This outside realm in which God is 'otherwise than being'[22] is a 'realm' in itself for Gregory, without language. The second graph, the spherical asymptote that approaches the boundary from the outside, traces the constitutional limitation upon the Creator to make an adiastemic revelation inside the circle of creation. The question, therefore – especially given that nothing within the circle can get out – is what happens when God's revelation crosses the boundary and moves into the diastemic realm.[23] What transformation/deformation necessarily occurs in this moment of ontological transgression? What type of theological knowledge is (im)possible? As Tamsin Jones lays out in her essay, the metrics of this question so concerned Levinas that he interrogated the very possibility of revelation.[24]

Jean-Luc Marion, arguably the best contemporary reader of the phenomenological tradition in terms of its applicability to the production of theology (and the subject of Johannes Zachhuber's essay), begins the preface to his study *La Croisée du Visible* with the following:

> La question de la peinture n'appartient ni d'abord, ni uniquement aux peintres, moins encore aux seuls esthéticiens. Elle appartient à la visibilité elle-même, donc à tous, à la sensation commune.[25]

This movement from the invisible to the visible – from outside the diastemic boundary to inside it, from the eternally unknowable to the temporally knowable – requires revelation to take on[26] διάστημα. In fact, it only becomes revelation as it crosses the diastemic border. In the language of Gregory's comments on Ecclesiastes, the desire to have a θεωρία καταληπτική of what is outside the diastemic boundary results in a συνθεωρεί συγκαταλαμβανόμενον διάστημα of that which God has revealed within the diasteme. As a result, the question of art in its widest sense – the visual arts, poetry, rhetoric, literature and music – is first and foremost a question for the Christian theologian, especially those, like Gregory of Nyssa, who affirm the Nicene divinity of Christ – affirm the coming together of that which was outside the circle of creation with that which was within, a coming together that the orthodox fathers called the οἰκονομία of Christ.[27] This aesthetic turn, the recourse to the epinoetic, was made necessary by the diastemic turn of revelation, by the necessary material culture of revelation. Always inside the diastemic boundary, revelation inspires a theological response that is equally dependent upon and contained within the material culture of διάστημα.

In 'Der Ursprung des Kunstwerkes', Heidegger began his analysis with an interrogation of the material aspect of all works of art:

> Alle Werke haben dieses Dinghafte . . . Aber auch das vielberufene äestheti-sche Erlebnis kommt am Dinghaften des Kunstwerkes nicht vorbei. Das Steinerne ist im Bauwerk. Das Hölzerne ist im Schnitzwerk. Das Farbige ist im Gemälde. Das Laudtende ist im Sprachwerk. Das Klingende ist im Tonwerk.[28]

For Heidegger, truth's dependence upon the thingly character of its manifestation not only impacts its general structure but also the fabric of its production and the horizon of its reception. Heidegger argues that the truth of art cannot be separated from its thingly manifestation, it cannot be abstracted into a portable and self-contained propositional truth. In the language of Gregory, the truth of theological art is intrinsically tied to its diastemic manifestation and cannot be abstracted into an adiastemic proposition (which would be an impossibility for Gregory, of course, because language, the very thing propositions are made from, belongs to the material culture of creation).[29] The significance of this for Gregory can hardly be overstated; revelation as revelation is constitutionally separated from God – its ultimate origin. The truth of art, therefore, is never directly and comprehensively representational (it is never a θεωρία καταληπτική) of the true essence of that being explored. As a result, the truth revealed in art is always and simultaneously both a truth and an untruth:

> Der Satz: Das Wesen der Wahrheit ist die Un-wahrheit, soll dagegen nicht sagen, die Wahrheit sei im Grunde Falschheit. . . . Die Wahrheit is Un-Wahrheit, insofern zu ihr der Herkunsftbereich des Noch-nicht (des Un-) Entborgenen (Derrida's Supplement) im Sinne der Verbergung gehört. In der Un-verborgenheit al Wahrheit west zugleich das andere 'Un-' eines zweifachen Verwehrens. Die Wahrheit west als solche im Gegeneinander von Lichtung und zweifacher Verbergung.[30]

As I have observed elsewhere,[31] this understanding of the status of truth within the diasteme has a clear resonance with Gregory as exemplified in his reading of David's comment in Psalm 115.2: πᾶς ἄνθρωπος ψεύστης ('All men are liars').[32] Gregory, in contrast to Paul in his letter to the Romans, does not see this as a text about depravity, but rather one about the constitutional limitations of diastemic/dimensional beings. 'All men lie' οὐχὶ τῷ μίσει τῆς ἀληθείας, ἀλλὰ τῇ ἀσθενείᾳ τῆς διηγήσεως ('not in any hatred of the truth, but in the feebleness of being able to set out a description').[33]

For Heidegger, there is a moment of partial unconcealing of truth within art in which 'Die Kunst ist das Sich-ins-Werk-Setzen der Wahrheit' ('Art is the setting-itself-to-work of truth').[34] In a similar fashion for Gregory, theology as poetic art is truth setting-itself-to-work. How this 'works' in Gregory will become more clear, I hope, via an extended case study that returns to the initial set of questions about the various but interrelated *whats* and *hows* of his production of theological meaning. That is, I would like to return to Heidegger's methodological interrogation of the inner possibility of the *how* of Gregory's theological production via a close reading of how Gregory structures that section of the *CE* II surrounding his use of the Abraham narrative (roughly paragraphs 67–170). By looking again at the same passage that Morwenna Ludlow so aptly addressed at the 2004 Gregory of Nyssa Congress held in Olomouc,[35] I hope to further examine the question of Gregory's method. Whereas Ludlow situated her reading of ascent within the whole corpus of Gregory's output, I will limit myself to just those passages from Gregory that appear within this section of the *CE* II, to just this one portion of his thingly theological art.[36] What follows, therefore, is really nothing more than a footnote, albeit a rather lengthy footnote, to her excellent analysis and the questions she posed.

The Extended Footnote

In the *CE* II, Gregory extended methodological caution beyond his critique of Eunomian reason to his own epinoetic approach, directly addressing the question of the inner possibility of any method, including his own, of forming knowledge about God:

> Καὶ ἄλλως δ' ἄν τις ἀσφαλὲς εἶναι φήσειεν ἀπολυπραγμόνητον ἐᾶν τὴν θεί αν οὐσίαν ὡς ἀπόρρητον καὶ ἀνέπαφον λογισμοῖς ἀνθρωπίνοις. τὸ μὲν γὰρ τῶν ἀδήλων καταστοχάζεσθαι καί τινα τῶν ἀποκρύφων γνῶσιν ἐξ ἐπινοίας ἀνθρωπίνων λογισμῶν ἐρευνᾶσθαι πάροδον καὶ ἀκολουθίαν καὶ ταῖς διεψευσμέναις τῶν ὑπολήψεων δίδωσιν, διότι τῶν ἀγνοουμένων ὁ στοχασμὸς οὐ μόνον τὸ ἀληθές, ἀλλὰ καὶ αὐτὸ πολλάκις τὸ ψεῦδος ὡς ἀληθὲς ὑπολήψεται.

> In another way, one might argue that safety lies in leaving the divine nature unexplored, as being inexpressible and beyond the reach of human reasoning. Speculating about the obscure and using the epinoia of human reason to search for some kind of knowledge of things hidden, allows admission and currency to false ideas, since speculation about the unknown understands not only what is true to be true, but often also what is false.[37]

Fully aware of this risk, Gregory's desire for God trumped his caution, but not without implications for how he went about this pursuit. As a result, he constantly qualified almost every assertion he made about God with phrases like αὐτὸ ὅπερ ἐστὶ ('whatever that is'[38]) or the employment of the indefinite τις, and he consistently chose vocabulary that downgraded the epistemological status of his own remarks. For example, Gregory states:

ἐκ τῆς πολυειδοῦς καὶ ποικίλης κατ' αὐτοῦ σημασίας ἐναύσματά τινα πρὸς τὴν κατανόησιν τοῦ ζητουμένου θηρεύοντες.

. . . as we hunt amid the pluriform variety of terms applying to him for sparks to light up our understanding of the object of our quest.[39]

Theological desire takes on the role of a hunter (θηρεύοντες) whose stalking of illumination in the midst of spiritual darkness, despite the multiplication of theological signs, is reduced to the gathering of some sparks (ἐναύσματά τινα).[40] In respect to methodology, there is a double downgrade in operation here: the believer hunts for sparks of truth from words already dedicated to speaking about God. Gregory described a bonfire of theological language in which words and phrases about God burn, giving off their own semantic light while simultaneously casting their own semantic shadows. In the language of Heidegger, language veils and unveils at the same time; it reveals a truth that is also an untruth whose untruth does not reduce its truth to falsehood. As a result, the reverent believer hunts through this pile, poking the burning logs, for the few sparks that contain some truth. Consistent with this image, the section of the CE II surrounding Gregory's reading of the Abraham narrative is best understood as the well-crafted productive conflict of not only images but also ideas and entire frameworks of meaning (his own collection τῆς πολυειδοῦς καὶ ποικίλης κατ' αὐτοῦ σημασίας) – all sources of light in themselves, whose incommensurable interaction produces some sparks of truth.[41] In the larger framing of this study, Gregory produces a text whose meaning requires συνθεωρεῖν. That is, he links together multiple modes of ascent (Biblical, Platonic, biographical, natural), various false modes of descent, numerous illustrative figures, competing conceptual images of containment, along with many Biblical and philosophical references into a complex layering and overlapping of allusions whose fundamental theological value is their generative interplay (not their particular meaning).[42]

Gregory describes this process with various verbs that focus on the idea of 'making use' of multiple sources, frequently within the compass of some combinatory impulse: συμφέρω, χράομαι + plural object, ἁρμόζω and ποιέω + plural object. In a key passage (which uses all four of these words

and happens to be the sentence that the above 'sparks' clause modifies),
Gregory described his epinoetic methodology, his epinoetic approach, to
using language in the service of knowing God:

> While avoiding every kind of concurrence (συνενεχθῆναι) with any wrong
> notion in our views about God, we make use (κεχρήμεθα) of a great variety
> of names for him, adapting (ἁρμόζοντες) our terminology to various concepts.
> Since no one title has been discovered to embrace the divine nature by
> applying directly to the subject, itself, we therefore use (ποιουμένου) many
> titles . . . as we hunt amid the pluriform variety of terms applying to him
> for sparks to light up our understanding of the object of our quest.[43]

Gregory 'makes use' of these various images and systems of thought; in the
language of Heidegger, he sets them to work. He first delimits their
meaning and then makes them mean something new by bringing them
together. In doing so, he cautiously engaged the main positive problem
raised by his critique of Eunomian reason: namely, having established
again and again that human beings are confronted with an unbridgeable
gap between Creator and creation that makes knowledge of essence impossible, how can human beings live out their God-given desire and hope to
know God? That he must do so cautiously is reflected in the juxtaposition of
συνενεχθῆναι with ἁρμόζοντες. Both words contain the notion of bringing
together, the latter combination being appropriate and fitting, harmonious, while the former combination does violence to God and must be fled
(συμφέρω was frequently but not exclusively rooted in martial linkage).
This clear epinoetic construct of employing a plurality of names, 'employing'
with the clear reference of giving them a particular job,[44] becomes something of a methodological cipher for reading Gregory's employment of
image and allusion. The multiform usage of concepts and names is matched
by the plural, multiform usage of images. As Morwenna Ludlow remarks,
Gregory's usage here of ἁρμόζοντες also fits well with the larger argument
of this paper in that 'its basic meaning – to fit one thing to another – always
seems to me to suggest a basic materiality and recalls the work of what we
might call an "artisan" rather than an "artiste" (a carpenter or "joiner"
making a cupboard – that kind of thing). The former term which should
not be used pejoratively, but which often is, is a useful corrective to the
notion that "art" is somehow divorced from materiality'.[45]

Central, therefore, to Gregory's method of producing theological meaning
is the concept of linkage. This is reflected in Gregory's own words (which, in
turn, conceptually reflect the συνθεωρία passage from his commentary on
Ecclesiastes) leading up to his employment of the Abraham narrative: 'What

is the link between things of contrary nature?' (τί τὸ μεσιτεῦον τοῖς παρηλλαγμένοις τῇ φύσει;).[46] The word translated 'link' (τὸ μεσιτεῦον), although not a common New Testament word, brings with it a disproportionately rich Biblical heritage, referring in five of its six New Testament usages to the mediating role of Christ.[47] One of these, 1 Timothy 2.5, εἷς γὰρ θεός, εἷς καὶ μεσίτης θεοῦ καὶ ἀνθρώπων, ἄνθρωπος Χριστὸς Ἰησοῦς, is particularly relevant to Gregory's project.[48] The mediation that must take place is clearly identified to be between God and man (θεοῦ καὶ ἀνθρώπων), and the mediating role of Christ is clearly a linkage–function of the divine Christ being ἄνθρωπος. In a similar manner, Gregory explicitly organized his many references to 'ascent' in this section of the *CE* II both around and in the biographical, in the ἄνθρωπος Abraham. This, of course, finds an analogue in the dramatic appearance of Alcibiades at the end of *The Symposium* and his encomium to Socrates as the concrete manifestation of enlightened ἔρως.[49] As he does here and throughout his works, Gregory consistently turns to the resources of the diastemic to overcome the problem of being diastemic. In the *CE* II, this takes the form of his exploiting the limitations of language to overcome the limits of language; using a 'lesser' type of thinking, ἐπίνοια, to overcome the limitations of thinking; using concrete images to imagine that which is beyond the concrete; and using a particular ἄνθρωπος, Abraham, to model the possibility of a type of transcendence that remains linked to the earth. In the larger language used in the early centuries of Christianity to speak about Christ and adopted by Gregory, the Incarnation is an οἰκονομία. As an 'economy' of linkage (divine and human), Christ becomes paradigmatic for all revelation belonging to a diastemic economy. That is, language belongs undeniably to the anthropological component of the economy of revelation.

Gregory negotiates this problem of finding a link between 'things of contrary nature', God and man, by forging multiple linkages that generate meaning through their being put together. He does this with words and he does this with images and concepts. This generation of meaning, therefore, is fundamentally literary in nature and irreducible to analytical re-articulation. As Ludlow develops in her Olomouc essay,[50] this entire section is a 'refraction' of received images woven together in a series of true and false ascents. It is a carefully constructed interplay of natural ascents, philosophical ascents and Biblical ascents presented as a recursive tapestry of images, allusions and arguments that both clarify and complicate their generative interaction. Gregory's ideal reader should allow these linkages to produce a new meaning whose impact requires a response more than seeking the discovery of clarified notions that require arbitration and critical judgement of their truth claim.[51] Gregory, therefore, has Abraham conclude:

τοῦτο σημεῖον ἐποιήσατο τῆς τοῦ θεοῦ ἐπιγνώσεως ἀπλανές τε καὶ ἔκδηλον, τὸ κρείττω καὶ ὑψηλότερον παντὸς γνωριστικοῦ σημείου τὸν θεὸν εἶναι πιστεῦσαι.

. . . and he (Abraham) took as his indicator, infallible and manifest, of the knowledge of God just this – that he believed God to be greater and higher than any epistemological indicator.[52]

Gregory turns Abraham's conclusion into a guideline for doing theology:

τὸ γὰρ σπουδαζόμενον ἐν τοῖς περὶ θεοῦ λόγοις ἐστὶν οὐχὶ ῥημάτων εὐφωνίαν εὔκροτόν τε καὶ ἐναρμόνιον ἐπινοῆσαι, ἀλλ' εὐσεβῆ διάνοιαν ἐξευρεῖν δι' ἧς τὸ πρέπον τῇ ὑπολήψει τῇ περὶ θεοῦ φυλαχθήσεται.

The purpose of theology is not to think up resounding and harmonious verbal beauty, but to identify a reverent notion by which what befits the thought of God may be kept intact.[53]

What is striking about this maxim emerges more clearly when it is linked with an earlier statement regarding the ultimate goal of Abraham's journey: τὸ πρωτότυπον κάλλος ἰδεῖν ἐπεθύμησεν ('he yearned to see the original model of beauty').[54] There is a distinct difference between the beautiful and the euphonic, between God and words about God – though both are linked by desire (σπουδαζόμενον and ἐπεθύμησεν). That which is negated as the goal of theology, οὐχὶ ῥημάτων εὐφωνίαν εὔκροτόν τε καὶ ἐναρμόνιον ἐπινοῆσαι, makes explicit a particular seductive risk of ἐπίνοια: the making of false linkages (ἐναρμόνιον) whose real goal is a θεωρία καταληπτική. That is, theology for Gregory must reject the hope that harmonious linkages could ever bring about noetic closure – that they would be fully harmonious. Quite to the contrary, his productive use of linkage (συνθεωρία) creates sparks of theological truth that resist closure and totality.

Gregory's first mention of ascent in this section of the *CE* II that centred on Abraham's journey turns to the natural world and involves setting up a hierarchy from the earth to the heavens, literally moving from the dirt to the winged exploration of the sky. This demonstrates on a very basic level Gregory's epinoetic strategy of beginning with that which is known and using it to move towards the divine. Ludlow lays out this pattern very clearly in her Olomouc article. After putting forth the general negative thesis: 'Human nature does not have the potential in it to understand precisely the being of God' (*CE* II:67), Gregory then states: 'One might understand this from examples near at hand'.

On a more sophisticated level, this natural illustration cuts allusively in at least two directions. The first direction connects this passage, both conceptually and through the word γῆ, with the central illustration of Abraham. Just as the birds rise significantly higher than the worms, they make negligible progress in terms of reaching the stars:

> εἰ δὲ πρὸς τὰ ἄστρα καὶ τὴν ἀπλανῆ σφαῖραν ἡ σύγκρισις εἴη, οὐδὲν ἔλαττον κεχωρίσθαι τοῦ οὐρανοῦ τὸ μετεωροποροῦν διὰ πτήσεως τῶν περὶ γῆν νομισθήσεται ζῴων.

> . . . if however the comparison were with the stars and the fixed sphere, the high-flyers with wings would be reckoned just as far from heaven as the animals on the ground.[55]

When later discussing Abraham's ascent, the patriarch's 'using (ποιέω again) all these as means and staircase for his upward journey' (πάντα ἐφόδια πρὸς τὴν ἄνω πορείαν καὶ ὑποβάθρας ποιούμενος, *CE* II:89), Gregory amplifies the context and scope of a remark made by Abraham in Genesis 18 by making it Abraham's conclusive remarks regarding his journey toward God: Ἐγὼ δέ εἰμι γῆ καὶ σποδός ('I am but earth and ashes').[56] In doing so, Gregory links Abraham firmly with the initial illustration, particularly with those within the natural ascent who 'dwell on the ground':

> ἡ γὰρ γῆ δοκεῖ μοι καὶ ἡ τέφρα τὸ ἄψυχον καὶ τὸ ἄγονον ἅμα διασημαίνειν, καὶ οὕτω νόμος πίστεως γίνεται τῷ μετὰ ταῦτα βίῳ, διδάσκων τῇ κατ'αὐ τὸν ἱστορίᾳ τοὺς τῷ θεῷ προσιόντας ὅτι οὐκ ἔστιν ἄλλως προσεγγίσαι θεῷ, μὴ πίστεως μεσιτευούσης καὶ συναπτούσης δι' ἑαυτῆς τὸν ἐπιζητοῦντα νοῦν πρὸς τὴν ἀκατάληπτον φύσιν.

> Earth and cinders seem to me together to signify what is at once lifeless and sterile, and thus a law of faith is generated for subsequent history, using Abraham's story to teach those who approach God that there is no way to come near to God, unless faith interposes and of itself joins the enquiring mind to the incomprehensible nature.[57]

Gregory's interpretation of Abraham's claim of being 'earth and ashes' directly addresses the larger question already cited: 'What is the link between things of contrary nature?' (τί τὸ μεσιτεῦον τοῖς παρηλλαγμένοις τῇ φύσει;). The contrary natures of 'earth' (γῆ) and the 'incomprehensible' (τὴν ἀκατάληπτον φύσιν) can be 'joined' (μεσιτευούσης) via the linking capacity of faith as exemplified by Abraham. The idea of mediation, of linking together, is again central to Gregory's project both in terms of *what* and *how*.

A second allusion in the illustration of natural ascent can be located in the multiple references to wings. This is an echo of the ascent of the soul in Plato's *Phaedrus* in which ascent is facilitated by the soul's growing of wings. This begins a comprehensive program of placing Platonic ideas of ascent next to Biblical ideas of ascent. Such a placement naturally invites an analysis of what fits and what does not fit. In this case, Gregory somewhat distances himself from Plato in the service of his epistemological critique of Eunomius. The ascent made possible by being 'winged' ultimately proves to be inadequate and ineffectual in terms of reaching the stars. Even the winged angels, in the next illustration, soar to heights regarded as being superior only when reckoned in comparison to the earthbound and lesser-winged beings. This method of reading Platonic allusions, sorting out what does and doesn't fit, has a very real but limited utility in getting at how Gregory employs these allusions. That is, Gregory is doing more (and less) with these Platonic allusions than simply standing on Plato's shoulders, building upon his insights and referencing him as an authority.

Deciding how to read these allusions proves increasingly critical because the number and complexity of linkages Gregory forges begin multiplying. He creates generative links not only between images within the text and ideas outside of the text, but also between multiple images entirely within the text. And, of course, what we're really talking about is much more complex than that. We have images linked to images that are linked to ideas, ideas linked to ideas that link back to images that are linked to more ideas, and so on. I would like to focus briefly on examples of generative linkages with the Platonic and then return in conclusion to the theoretical question of how to read them.

As with Diotima and Socrates, Abraham 'yearned to see the original model of beauty' (τὸ πρωτότυπον κάλλος ἰδεῖν ἐπεθύμησεν).[58] Gregory's usage of the metaphor of seeing, here and throughout this section, resonates with both the *Symposium* and 'The Allegory of the Cave'. Plato's ubiquitous cave also appears in the above-mentioned illuminative value of fire-generated 'sparks' (*CE* II.145), in the layered identification that 'words are a kind of shadows of reality, matching the movements of things which exist' (*CE* II.150) and in the constant employment of the sun – the heliotrope – throughout his illustrations. Gregory's illustration, for example, of children trying to catch the sunlight[59] functions on at least two very different levels. It is a critique of Eunomius's arrogant and childishly immature attempt to grasp and contain truth. It also presents a model of ascent that, like Abraham's, functions horizontally through time, maturing from childishness to adulthood. Like almost all images that Gregory links together, the image of the child reaching for the sun implicates itself in multiple directions throughout the surrounding passage.

Other allusions to Plato include references to the mixed nature of the birth of Ἔρως who is neither beautiful nor ugly, but something in-between. In Gregory, ἄνθρωπος is neither fully divine nor fully base. He marvels at how

> . . . the same being both reaches up above the heaven in enquiring into invisible things and also slides toward material passions, dragged down by the weight of the body, towards wrath and fear, pain and pleasure, pity and hardheartedness, expectation and memory, cowardice and daring, love and hatred, and all those things which produce contradiction in the soul's power. (*CE* II.107)

What functionally defines both personified Eros and humanity as experienced in this life is being located in an in-between state of need, consumed with desire to fill that need. Repeating the basic argument of Socrates to Agathon in the *Symposium*, Gregory remarks:

> ἡ δὲ τῶν Χριστιανῶν πίστις οὐχ οὕτως· οὐ γὰρ τῶν γινωσκομένων, ἀλλὰ τῶν ἐλπιζομένων ἐστὶν ὑπόστασις. τὸ δὲ διακρατούμενον οὐκ ἐλπίζεται· Ὃ γὰρ ἔχει τις, φησί, τί καὶ ἐλπίζει;

> Christian faith is different: its assurance is not of things learnt, but of things hoped for. What is possessed is not hoped for: 'Why should one hope', it says, 'for what he has?'[60]

What needs to be noted in this supplanting of desire with hope is that Gregory transformed his reading of Paul in a manner that nudged it towards Plato. That is, in this quotation of Paul by Gregory – Ὃ γὰρ ἔχει τις, φησί, τί καὶ ἐλπίζει; – he exchanged Paul's usage of βλέπω in Romans 8.24, ὃ γὰρ βλέπει τίς ἐλπίζει; for the Platonic ἔχω of the *Symposium* (εἴτε ἐπιθυμεῖ τε καὶ ἐρᾷ, ἢ οὐκ ἔχων;).[61] This also cuts two ways. The usage of διακρατέω and ἔχω at one level are directed against Eunomius's claim to have 'grasped and possessed' the truth, also linking itself back to the child/sunlight image. At the same time, Gregory alludes to the Apostle Paul in a moment that deeply affirms Abraham's ascent via faith and grounds it, as does Socrates, in the conscious and desperate acknowledgement of need.

As Socrates embodies philosophical ἔρως, so Abraham embodies Christian hope. And hope is intimately linked with faith, while remaining deeply rooted in desire. It is the investment of a soul in something that has been promised, something that is future and not presently possessed.

Conclusion

Gregory has structured this section of the *CE* II in such a manner that theological meaning is produced in the very messy process of images being linked together. As Morwenna Ludlow has argued (so I will not rehearse the details here), Gregory not only alludes to Platonic ascent throughout this section, he also alludes to the ascent of Jacob's staircase, possibly conflating the trajectories of Abraham, Isaac and Jacob, as well as to the Psalms and David. In doing so, Gregory forges a new fourth-century Christian ladder, but not in the sense of making a highly determined combination of specifically identified elements from multiple sources to forge a new clear and definite ladder of Christian ascent. That is, the conclusion of this section is not that Gregory's ladder is 15/32 Platonic, 3/8 Jacob's ladder, 1/16 natural arguments and 3/32 miscellaneous Biblical. Nor can it be analytically reduced to the following type of conclusion: it is largely Platonic with these three major qualifications, these two substitutions and this minor reframing. Gregory, of course, does make these qualifications and regards them as important. But he also has created something of an impossibly multidimensional ladder that can only exist in one's imagination but is nonetheless rooted in the experience of Abraham – the Abraham, it is important to note, who inhabits the text of Genesis. The various ladders that contribute to this multidimensional ladder themselves come from ladder factories that already complicate their own clarity. The 5-D ladder that Gregory creates cannot and should not be reduced into a single image. It can only be created by the linkage of multiple images and only exists, therefore, in the space that the combination of these images creates – a linkage that resists full synthesis, resists a Hegelian *Aufhebung*. The believer's proper response, therefore, to the 5-D ladder is not to reduce it to a manageable Christian 3-D, but rather to be so overwhelmed by the 'yearning to see the original model of beauty' as to be willing to enter this strange and impossible space, buttressed by the fact that the ἄνθρωπος Abraham has already done it, cautioned by the fact that Abraham didn't know where he was going either and was reduced to crying out: 'I am earth and ashes'. Like Kierkegaard's 'Knight of Infinite Resignation', Gregory resigns himself to the impossibility of having a pure θεωρία that is καταληπτική; that is, he resigns himself to the theoretical axis of incommensurability in which the gap between sign and referent precludes the naming of essence. And, then, like Kierkegaard's 'Knight of Faith',[62] Gregory somehow regains God via a narrative detour through the incommensurable axis of the productive – an axis intimately linked with the manoeuvre associated with the prefix συν-. That is, he exploits the incommensurable gap of bringing together multiple signs (images, allusions, philosophical systems, modes of being, etc.) – a bringing together that is productive of a certain type of meaning, a meaning generated by what Paul Ricœur called the semantic impertinence (*impertinence sémantique*) of living metaphors (*métaphore vive*). Resonant with Gregory's use of image, Ricœur concludes: 'Le symbole donne à penser'[63] – 'symbole' best understood in Heidegger's etymological reading of it as συν + βάλλω: 'to throw together'.[64]

The notion that 'the symbol gives rise to thought' (a notion rooted in the idea that living linkages within texts still give) returns us to the larger question of how to read an ancient text from the twenty-first century. At the outset of such a question, one must acknowledge that all methods have their particular historical context – whether it be the postmodern, the scholastic, the Enlightenment or the scientific-philological. Additionally, whatever the method, no one is making the claim that they are employing the same methods of reading as the ancient author did. Because that is not the goal – even for the scholar whose primary goal is to understand the method/meaning of the ancient author – the question of method can never be straightforward, simple or self-evident in respect to claims of being the 'right' method. In the case of Gregory of Nyssa (and Augustine, for that matter), the methodological question of using Heidegger to pursue a better reading of Gregory is not a question of Gregory anticipating or foreshadowing Heidegger. It is rather a question of Gregory's insights and impulses, which remained undeveloped in ways that were not useful to his context, being exposed and clarified by a thinker like Heidegger whose different context allowed a more sophisticated development.

Notes

1   This essay functions as something of a sister study to an article to be published by Brill in 2011: 'Heidegger and Gregory of Nyssa's *Ad Ablabium: quod non sint tres Dei*' in *Gregory of Nyssa's* Opera Minora. *Proceedings of the 11th International Colloquium on Gregory of Nyssa (Tübingen and Freiburg, September, 2008)* (Supplements to Vigiliae Christianae; Leiden; Boston: Brill, forthcoming). What that means in practical terms is that both articles use the same passage from Gregory's commentary on Ecclesiastes, in conjunction with Heidegger's 'Der Ursprung des Kunstwerkes' in *Holzwege* (Gesamtausgabe; Frankfurt am Main: Klostermann, 1994) as the starting point. This essay goes on to apply this framework to my reading of a passage from the *Contra Euno- mium* II, whereas the Tübingen article applies it to a passage from the *Ad Ablabium: Quod non sint Tres Dei*.

2 Martin Heidegger, *Kant and the Problem of Metaphysics* (5th edn; Richard Taft (trans.); Bloomington: Indiana University Press, 1997), 6. The full sentence from which this quotation is taken: 'Angesichts der ständigen "Verunglückung" aller Anschläge in dieser Wissenschaft, ihrer Unstimmigkeit und Wirkungslosigkeit müssen jedoch alle Versuche, die reine Vernunfterkenntnis zu erweitern, zunächst unterbunden werden, bis die Frage nach der inneren Möglichkeit dieser Wissenschaft geklärt ist'. Martin Heidegger, *Kant und das Problem der Metaphysik* (Gesamtausgabe 3, Klostermann, Frankfurt, 1991), 9.

3 One of the clearest statements of this limitation: Gregory of Nyssa, *Contra Eunomium* II:106 in *Gregory of Nyssa, Contra Eunomium I and II* (Werner Jaeger (ed); *Gregorii Nysseni Opera*, I; Leiden: Brill, 1960), 257.26–258.1: Διὰ τοῦτο πᾶσάν τις θεόπνευστον φωνὴν ἐρευνώμενος οὐκ ἂν εὕροι τῆς θείας φύσεως τὴν διδασκαλίαν οὐδὲ μὴν ἄλλου τινὸς τῶν κατ' οὐσίαν ὑφεστηκότων· ὅθεν ἐν ἀγνοίᾳ πάντων διάγομεν πρῶτον ἑαυτοὺς ἀγνοοῦντες οἱ ἄνθρωποι, ἔπειτα δὲ καὶ τὰ ἄλλα πάντα. References to *Contra Eunomium* [henceforth *CE*] in this chapter are by book and paragraph number, followed by volume, page and line numbers of the Jaeger edition of *Gregorii Nysseni Opera* [henceforth *GNO*], thus: *CE* II:106 (*GNO* I. 257.26–258.1).

4 Matthieu Cassin's essay in this volume (Chapter 6, 'Text and Context: The Importance of Scholarly Reading. Gregory of Nyssa, *Contra Eunomium*') approaches this question from Gregory's own comments in his *Letter 29* in which, among other things, he invites a teacher of rhetoric to read certain passages for the pleasure of their rhetorical allusions.

5 Tamsin Jones, 'Emmanuel Levinas and Gregory of Nyssa on Reading, Desire and Subjectivity' (this volume, Chapter 4).

6 Kant, for example, asks three excellent questions that it would be good for us to ask Gregory as well: 'What can we know? What ought we to do? What can we hope for?' But Kant and Gregory, except in respect to the epistemological role of imagination, do not share the type of productive resonance that exists between Gregory and Heidegger.

7 Matthieu Cassin, 'Text and Context' (this volume, Chapter 7). See also, Cassin, 'L'Écriture de la Polémique à la Fin du IVe Siècle: Grégoire de Nysse, Contre Eunome III' (Thèse de doctorat, Université Paris IV – Sorbonne, 2009).

8 Virginia Burris, 'Seeing God in Bodies: Wolfson, Rosenzweig, Augustine' (this volume, Chapter 3).

9 There are two elements to this observation: Derrida's idea of the supplement and the subsequent discursive impossibility to achieve containment/totality and Marion's idea of the super-saturated, of phenomenological excess.

10 This, of course, is very tricky on multiple levels given that Paul and John, in this case, are also understood to be a source of Trinitarian truth. What is ultimately being asserted by the Orthodox is that if Paul and John had been exposed to the questions and concerns of the fourth century, they would be able to explain how their own writings are consistent with Nicene orthodoxy, and possibly admit they might have avoided phrases like 'the first born of all of creation', 'the only-begotten', etc. – or at least qualified them more clearly – if they could see how subject to heretical misunderstanding they were. To the degree, I think, that one asserts that the Nicene fathers are correct in reading

Paul and John to be in support of Nicene orthodoxy, one has to acknowledge that the later refinement of theological assertions allows a reader to read backwards into a text on the basis that they are wrestling with the same problem/ truth from different historical moments and contingent concerns.

11   In this case, the chronological relationship between the two texts is irrelevant. The referenced author could be an ancient text or the two conversants could be revisiting a conversation and the author could have written subsequent to it.

12   Plato, *Phaedrus* 275e (Harold North Fowler (trans.); Loeb Classical Library, 36; Cambridge, Mass.: Harvard University Press, 1930–1935).

13   Johannes Zachhuber, 'Jean-Luc Marion's Reading of Dionysius the Areopagite. Hermeneutics and Reception History' (this volume, Chapter 1).

14   Dietrich Bonhoeffer *Act and Being: Transcendental Philosophy and Ontology in Systematic Theology* (Wayne Whitson Floyd Jr. and Hans-Richard Reuter (eds); Martin Lukens-Rumscheidt (trans.); Works, 2 (Minneapolis: Augsburg Fortress, 1996), therefore, was too hasty (in my opinion) in rejecting Heidegger as a source for his work on revelation because Heidegger's thought precluded divine revelation. I think this type of strict criteria of a thinker's relevance ignores the potential contribution of someone like Heidegger who is intensely interrogating questions of the disclosure of truth via an event of truth.

15   'The entire battle and doctrinal controversy, then, between the church and the *anomoeans* turns on this: Should we regard the Son and the Holy Spirit as belonging to created . . . or uncreated existence?' (δεῖν ἢ κτιστὸν νοεῖν τὸν υἱὸν καὶ τὸ πνεῦμα κατὰ τὸν λόγον τῶν ἐναντίων ἢ τῆς ἀκτίστου φύσεως). CE I:220, GNO I.90.20–24.

16   Gregory of Nyssa, *In Ecclesiasten Homiliae* in *In Inscriptiones Psalmorum; In Sextum Psalmum; In Ecclesiasten Homiliae* (J. McDonough and P. Alexander (eds); *Gregorii Nysseni Opera*, V; Leiden: Brill, 1962), 412.6–14.

17   I am not using 'noetic' here as the less-freighted substitute for 'allegory' (as is emerging in current Patristic scholarship), but rather in contrast to Gregory's *epinoetic* strategy and something of a gloss for the totalizing rationality he accuses Eunomius of advocating.

18   This is the same verb, as Gregory well knew, in the Johannine prologue: καὶ τὸ φῶς ἐν τῇ σκοτίᾳ φαίνει, καὶ ἡ σκοτία αὐτὸ οὐ κατέλαβεν (John 1.5). Gregory frequently accused Eunomius, in respect to his positivistic/optimistic view of knowing, of noetic violence (this theme is subtly repeated in the second strategy, revolving around the word βιάζεται).

19   Balthasar mapped this out in his groundbreaking 1946 work on Gregory of Nyssa: *Présence et pensée: Essai sur la philosophie religieuse de Grégoire de Nysse* (2nd edn; Paris: Beauchesne, 1988).

20   This second method is also rooted in a sense of notional violence (βιάζεται). βιάζω from Homer to Aeschylus to Sophocles, from Thucydides to Xenophon to Plato, denotes the use of violence to force a desired outcome.

21   The larger usage of παρέρχομαι is interesting in this context, especially the sense of 'overstepping' and 'transgressing' and 'passing over or beyond': see Liddell and Scott's *Greek English Lexicon*, 1337, column 2.

22   This phrase, of course, comes from the title of Levinas's book: *Autrement qu'être ou au-delà de l'Essence* (The Hague: Nijhoff, 1974).

23 See my *Theology of the Gap: Cappadocian Language Theory and the Trinitarian Controversy* (Theology and Religion; New York: Peter Lang AG, 2005) for a more thorough exploration of the implications of this limitation, especially in respect to the Nicene claim of the deity of the incarnated Christ.

24 Jones, 'Emmanuel Levinas and Gregory of Nyssa' (this volume, Chapter 5).

25 Jean-Luc Marion, *La Croisée du Visible* (Paris: La Différence, 1991), 1. Translation: 'The question of painting does not pertain first or only to painters, much less only to aestheticians. It concerns visibility itself, and thus pertains to everything – to sensation in general', *The Crossing of the Visible* [La Croisée du Visible] (James K. A. Smith (trans.); Stanford: Stanford University Press, 2004), ix.

26 'Take on' both in the sense of possess/incorporate/be dependent upon and as something that challenges the *diastemic* order.

27 Agamben's recent book, (*Il regno e la gloria. Per una genealogia teologica dell'economia e del governo. Homo sacer 2,2.* Neri Pozza. 2007), addresses, from the perspective of the formation of Western political institutions, the reversal of the terms μυστηρίον and οἰκονομία in the fathers (that begins as early as Irenaeus) from the Pauline ἡ οἰκονομία τοῦ μυστηρίου το τὸ μυστηρί ον τῆς οἰκονομίας. Gregory continues this usage in the *CE* III (e.g. *CE* III.1.46) in a manner that has significance to his understanding of theological language: language, itself, belongs to an economy that mirrors the divine economy of the person of Christ – the combination of the *adiastemic* with the *diastemic*.

28 Martin Heidegger, 'Der Ursprung des Kunstwerkes', 9. Translation: 'All works have this thingly character . . . even the much vaunted aesthetic experience cannot get around the thingly aspect of the art work. There is something stony in a work of architecture, wooden in a carving, colored in a painting, spoken in a linguistic work, sonorous in a musical composition', 'The Origin of the Work of Art' in *Poetry, Language, Thought* (Hofstadter, Albert (trans.); New York: Harper Row, 1994), 19.

29 There is a very real resonance here between Gregory's understanding of language within the theological task and two famous but frequently misunderstood statements, by Derrida – 'Il n'y a pas de hors-texte' – and Heidegger – 'Die Sprache is das Haus des Seins'. Neither Derrida nor Heidegger is saying that there is no reality outside of language, but that the intimate and inseparable connection between understanding and language requires that understanding can never transcend the inescapable mediating and constituting influence of language. In the case of Gregory, all theology is inextricably bound to the limitations of language; for Gregory, human thought as well belongs to the *diasteme* and contains διάστημα. Not only does this mean that the referent always transcends its reference, but the act of referring necessarily distorts the truth value of what can be known about the referent via the reference in a way much more complicated and invasive than Plato's concern for *mimetic* degradation.

30 Heidegger, 'Der Ursprung des Kunstwerkes', 43, 49. Translation: 'The proposition, "the nature of truth is untruth", is not, however, intended to state that truth is at bottom falsehood. . . . Truth is un-truth, insofar as there belongs to it the reservoir of the not-yet-uncovered, the un-uncovered, in the sense of concealment. In unconcealedness, as truth, there occurs also the other "un-" of

a double restraint or refusal. Truth occurs as such in the opposition of clearing and double concealing'.

31 Douglass, *Theology of the Gap*, 83.

32 Gregory of Nyssa, *De Virginitate* in *Opera Ascetica* (W. Jaeger, J. P. Cavarnos and V. W. Callahan (eds.); GNO VIII/1; Leiden: Brill, 1963), 290.13–14. Translation mine.

33 Gregory of Nyssa, *De Virginitate*, GNO VIII/1:290.13–14.

34 For example, Heidegger, 'Der Ursprung des Kunstwerkes', 25.

35 Subsequently published as Morwenna Ludlow, 'Divine Infinity and Eschatology: The Limits and Dynamics of Human Knowledge According to Gregory of Nyssa (CE II:67–170)' in *Gregory of Nyssa: Contra Eunomium II: An English Version with Supporting Studies, Proceedings of the 10th International Colloquium on Gregory of Nyssa, (Olomouc, September 15–18, 2004)* (Karfíková, et. al (eds); Supplements to Vigiliae Christianae; Leiden; Boston: Brill, 2007), 217–37.

36 Because of Gregory's understanding of language and his privileging of ἐπίνοια, I would argue that all theology for Gregory is 'theological art' – even those aspects of his theological rhetoric that are the construction of philosophical arguments.

37 CE II:97 (GNO I.255.1–8).

38 See CE II:70 (GNO I.246.29–30).

39 CE II:145 (GNO I. 267.26–28).

40 Even a cursory glance at the *Thesaurus Linguae Graecae* (TLG, www.tlg.uci.edu/) for various forms of θηρεύω demonstrates that Gregory is not at all alone among the church fathers in using the image of a hunter to describe the work of the theologian. The point here is the type of hunting that Gregory says is required – that one is hunting amidst language already dedicated to speaking about God.

41 Gregory takes the particular θεωρία with all its inherent limitations and forces a συνθεωρία that produces a new meaning irreducible to a new θεωρία. That is, the production of new meaning resists a Hegelian *Aufhebung*. It is only in the irresolvable tension of the συν that Gregory's combinatory method produces meaning as a truth/un-truth.

42 Matthieu Cassin's essay in this volume shows, via his analysis of Gregory's invitation in a letter for a trained rhetorician to pay particular attention to certain passages for their allusive cleverness alongside the referenced passages from the CE III, that Gregory was very conscious of how he constructed his texts and that he paid particular attention to the combination of subtle references.

43 CE II:144–145 (GNO I.267.18–28). συνενεχθῆναι (the aorist passive of συμφέρω) carries with it an ambiguous emphasis on both meeting in agreement and in conflict, to be of one mind or to meet in battle. As Gregory stated (see above), ἐπίνοια is always ambiguously unsafe. κεχρήμεθα is an interesting word because it not only refers to 'making use of something' but does so from the position/idea of need and out of a sense of yearning. It also is used frequently in the context of war.

44 I am using the idea of words 'working' in the aesthetic sense of Heidegger in 'Der Ursprung des Kunstwerkes' in which he defines art as that which 'puts the

truth to work': 'Die Kunst ist das Sich-ins-Werk-Setzen der Wahrheit' (e.g. 'Der Ursprung des Kunstwerkes', 25).

45   Email discussion with author.

46   *CE* II:76 (*GNO* I.249.11).

47   Gal. 3.20; Hebrews 8.6, 9.5, 12.24; 1 Tim 2.5. In Gal 3.19, μεσίτης refers to the mediating role of angels in delivering the Law. That half of these references are from the Letter to the Hebrews only reinforces Morwenna Ludlow's contention that Gregory's comments regarding Abraham's faith should be read in light of Hebrews 11 (Ludlow, 'Divine Infinity', 222).

48   Gregory directly quotes 1 Tim. 2.5 towards the beginning of the *CE* III (*CE* III.1.92) in his deconstructive argument against Eunomius's self-subverting claims about the title of 'Son of Man'. It is also central to the question being examined here from the *CE* II and the idea of the Incarnation as an 'economy', an οἰκονομία. The very idea of οἰκονομία embeds the discussion of Christ in terms of negotiating a combination.

49   Ludlow, 'Divine Infinity', 228, demonstrates how Gregory has framed his argument in this section of the *CE* II around the Platonic idea of ascent/ staircase as laid out in the *Symposium* and originally explained to Socrates by Diotima. When Alcibiades, in his drunken state, crashes the party, he agrees to make a speech as long as he can praise Socrates instead of 'Love'. As it turns out, his description of Socrates exactly mirrors the representation of 'Love' in Socrates' speech.

50   Ludlow, 'Divine Infinity', 225–232.

51   That is, the larger question of responsible reading gets turned on its head, as Tamsin Jones develops, into a Levinasian question of the reader's responsiveness (Jones, 'Emmanuel Levinas and Gregory of Nyssa', this volume, Chapter 4).

52   *CE* II:89 (*GNO* I.253.14–17).

53   *CE* II:136 (*GNO* I.265.7–10). Gregory is not drawing a distinction in this passage between the bad thingy-ness of articulated words (ῥημάτων εὐφωνίαν εὔκροτόν τε καὶ ἐναρμόνιον) and the good immateriality (non-thingy-ness) of διάνοια. Human thought, itself, has a diastemic nature to it, and even unarticulated human thought belongs to a linguistic economy.

54   *CE* II:89 (*GNO* I.252.29–253.1).

55   *CE* II:68 (*GNO* I.246.4–7).

56   *CE* II:90 (*GNO* I.253.20). Abraham says this in Gen. 18.27 following the conversations with the three visitors regarding the promise of Isaac and the destruction of Sodom and Gomorrah. Gregory's usage here follows something of a rabbinic hermeneutical technique (no direct dependency is being claimed).

57   *CE* II:91 (*GNO* I, 253.22–8).

58   *CE* II:89 (*GNO* I.252.29–253.1).

59   See *CE* II:80 (*GNO* I.250.10–6) for Gregory's use of this image, and *CE* II:81–3 (*GNO* I.250.16–251.14) for his negative application of it to Eunomius.

60   *CE* II:93 (*GNO* I.254.4–8).

61   Plato, *Symposium*, 200a (W. R. M. Lamb (trans.); Loeb Classical Library, 166; Cambridge, Mass.: Harvard University Press, 1925).

62 A motif which recurs in more than one of Kierkegaard's works, but especially in *Fear and Trembling* (C. Stephen Evans and Sylvia Walsh (eds); Sylvia Walsh (trans.); Cambridge: Cambridge University Press, 2006).

63 Ricœur returns again and again in his thinking to this felicitous and complex phrase. It is the title of an essay that appeared in *Esprit* 27/7–8 (1959) as well as the title of the concluding section of his *La symbolique du mal*, the second part of his *Finitude et culpabilité*: Ricœur, Paul, *Philosophie de la volonté*, Volume 2. *Finitude et culpabilité (1. L'homme faillible. 2. La symbolique du mal)* (Paris: Aubier, [1949]–1960).

64 Heidegger, 'Der Ursprung des Kunstwerkes', 43.

Part III

Reading the Fathers Reading Themselves

Chapter 6

Text and Context: The Importance
of Scholarly Reading.
Gregory of Nyssa, Contra Eunomium[1]

Matthieu Cassin

Between 379 and 383, Gregory, bishop of Nyssa in Cappadocia, wrote three books aimed at answering the successive parts of the *Apologia Apologiae* published by Eunomius of Cyzicus. The *Apologia Apologiae*, as its title indicates, was the defence of a previous apologetic work (the *Liber Apologeticus*) published by Eunomius in 360 or 361, in response to a critique of it written around 364 by Basil of Caesarea, the elder brother of Gregory of Nyssa. It is noteworthy that we have so many texts from this polemical series: *Liber Apologeticus* by Eunomius, the three books *Contra Eunomium* by Basil and three volumes of *Contra Eunomium* by Gregory of Nyssa.[2] Only the *Apologia Apologiae* of Eunomius is missing, surviving only in fragments recorded in Nyssen's *Contra Eunomium*. Two texts, written a little later and in a slightly different literary genre, completed this series: the *Expositio Fidei* (*Profession of Faith*) by Eunomius, proposed during the 'synod of heresies' summoned by the Emperor Theodosius in 383,[3] and Gregory's answer, the *Refutatio Confessionis Eunomii* (*Refutation of the Profession of Faith of Eunomius*).[4] We may add to this list a speech delivered by Gregory in Constantinople, *De deitate filii et spiritus sancti et in Abraham*, just before the opening of this 'synod of heresies'.[5]

Many other works were devoted to the refutation of Eunomius's theses which, for the most part, have not survived. In contrast, having all the Cappadocian texts just mentioned supplies us with a complete organic set from which to follow the various stages of the controversy, nearly step by step. Because this is so rare for this period, one might expect that access to such a complete grouping of texts would arouse readings that differ substantially from that of other Patristic texts equally concerned with controversies. In effect, the situation here is very similar to the study of modern religious controversies in which researchers are able to study the writing strategies, or even the publishing strategies, specific to each of the protagonists; the answers or voluntary omissions of one step or another of the controversy; and the relations, confessed or not, which go through the various steps and successive texts.[6] Until these elements are separated and clarified, it is impossible to explain and describe the theological and philosophical positions of the protagonists. Such a complete survey draws a map of religious history, literary history, history of the book, intellectual practices, social networks and so on.

However, Gregory of Nyssa's *Contra Eunomium* was most often read, at least until the modern era, through a single frame: research on the history of Christian doctrine – the history of dogma, according to an older name. Such a context implies a distinct orientation of reading and a clear limitation of its objectives: the work was studied in order to find elements of a coherent, even systematic, theology specific to Gregory of Nyssa[7] – which would also allow Gregory to be used as a source to reconstruct the doctrinal positions of his heretical opponent, Eunomius. The book, in such a reading, is no longer seen as an organic whole inserted in a larger series but only as a source from which to draw isolated elements, fragments, each to illustrate this or that point of the systematic scheme. One must note, in particular, that since the *Contra Eunomium* was generally categorized as a Trinitarian work, its Christological content was most often left aside; the book was isolated from its editorial context and its paratext, whether authorial or editorial;[8] and it was cut off from its belonging both to a tradition and to contemporaneous history, that is to say, to the ongoing dispute. Even when the history of the tradition was taken into account in the history of dogma, the immediate history of a controversy as dense as this one disappears almost entirely because the history of doctrine favours the characteristic features of the doctrinal position of an author or a work and leaves aside the fluctuations and adaptations of positions in a given controversy.

In order to be exempt from these important limitations and so as to unfold more possible readings of a text as rich as Gregory of Nyssa's *Contra Eunomium*, a method that would take into account the requirements of literary and Patristic history seems to be more appropriate and more promising. Without pretending to be exhaustive, I will proceed in three steps:

- Study the paratext of the work in order to distinguish the different stages and the different times of its composition and connect it to the paratext of other works in the same controversy in order to clarify the links that are no longer evident for a modern reader.[9]
- Set the book back in its own literary genre so as to underline the generic features and the author's adaptation of some traditional elements – such a perspective may indeed help to read the book not only as a technical, theological work, but also as literature.
- Explore the history of *Contra Eunomium*'s reception in order to show how some readings did gradually stand out and how others have been forgotten.

I do not claim I have reached a neutral and exhaustive reading of Nyssen's texts, nor a reading that would enable us to reach the original book, freed from the layers of successive interpretations. Such a hope would only lead to a new fabric as artificial as the former. I do not want to bleach the text of Gregory, as the German archaeology at the end of the nineteenth century did with Greek temples. But if hermeneutic work implies that the reader gets involved in his work and approaches it with his own prejudices, tools and the span of history that separates him from the text, it does not imply that we must merely record these facts and, thus, freely interpret ancient texts. The degree of elaboration found in the works of the Cappadocians, and in particular those by Gregory of Nyssa, forbids all straight reading as well as any attempt of reduction. If it is not impossible to apply tools borrowed from contemporary philosophy to these texts, for example, or to confront them with thinkers from different eras, it is first necessary, I think, to use the tools of a historical and literary reading in order to emphasize the elements hidden to our modern eyes, so as to display the complexity of the texts.

The Paratext of Gregory of Nyssa's Contra Eunomium: *Nyssen's Hints about How to Read His Text*

Author

The study of the *paratext* of a recent document is, in general, not too difficult if it is not extended to the concerns of a history of reception (*epitext*). It is different, however, for an ancient text because of its long transmission and the devices characteristic of an ancient edition. Although the question of the name of the author of *Contra Eunomium* is not a problem – 'Gregory, bishop of Nyssa' – the elements added later ('our father among the saints', etc.), which are not without interest, must be considered using a separate approach.[10]

Title

The title of the work (or rather the titles of the three works) is not as simple to define because the variations in the manuscripts are greater than the various indications of the author. It is particularly difficult to determine how far the formulation can be attributed to the actual author. One can establish that the text is characterized as a λόγος ἀντιρρητικός,[11] not only through manuscripts but also by Gregory himself in his *Letter* 29: the text is a refutation, an element of a controversy.[12] The work, therefore, was presented as an answer to the λόγοι of Eunomius and, more precisely, to those he had published. This means Gregory's text was not an answer to doctrinal positions held by Eunomius, but to a well-defined written piece, the *Apologia Apologiae*. Finally, the succession of Gregory's books and titles suggest that the refutation of Eunomius's work follows each part, book by book; the *Apologia Apologiae* is not taken by Gregory as a whole.

Internal divisions of the Contra Eunomium *(Books, Parts, Chapters)*

Each of the three books is granted a proper title, which is not constituted by a simple numerical variation within a fixed model, unlike modern designations (*Contra Eunomium* I, II and III). They were three distinct entities, tied together but circulating separately for at least some time.

Book III is the only one that also has main internal divisions, called τόμοι (parts). The whole manuscript tradition has seen them as if they were on the same level as the division between Book I, II and the *Refutatio*. But the indirect tradition and some elements of internal commentary have allowed F. Diekamp[13] and then W. Jaeger to restore the original structure of the work. One text, extant only in Syriac, which had not yet been edited when W. Jaeger was working, allows us to trace back to the first half of the sixth century the difficulties and confusions we find in the manuscripts.[14] The incoherencies that this division introduces suggest that the organization of Book III into ten parts was not due to Gregory himself.[15]

Besides the division of Book III, the different manuscripts present a list of titles for the different chapters (κεφάλαια). A large number of manuscripts indicate the chapters of Book I in the margins, proposing converging positions for them.[16] Furthermore, it is acknowledged that the chapters of Book I are by Gregory himself,[17] and I have shown that their position goes back at least to the sixth century. If this is accurate, it would be a very valuable testimony to the way Gregory understood his own text. However, the chapters of the other books are obviously not by the same hand.

These elements of paratext confirm, therefore, the division of the work into three books, each of them belonging to a much larger but relatively autonomous group. They also provide us, at least for Book I, with a reading aid by or proximate to the author himself, thanks to the titles of the chapters and their positions in the text. This first series of elements provides readers with hints of the literary genre and reminds them of the genealogy of the work, written over almost five years, in three (or four if we take the *Refutatio* into account) distinct steps.

Preface(s)

If the first elements listed above give only clues about the possible readings of Nyssen's tract, some associated texts provide more significant tools. An actual preface or a dedication for any of the three books of the *Contra Eunomium* did not exist. If each book starts with an exordium, it does not seem that there is any proper introductive paratext inside the books. On the other hand, the manuscripts, in most cases, interpreted a letter from Gregory and the answer from his brother Peter as a kind of preface to the three books. Almost all the manuscripts put the two letters just before the table of contents or before the first book *Contra Eunomium*.[18] However, this fact remained largely unnoticed, since W. Jaeger had preferred not to edit the letters with *Contra Eunomium*. As a result, they only appear in the editions of the letters of Gregory.

Letter 29 is a cover letter for the first book *Contra Eunomium* and was sent to Gregory's brother Peter.[19] It was on his advice that Gregory had undertaken the refutation of Eunomius's books. In the second part of the letter, Gregory expressed some doubts about how appropriate it was to publish his work because he had answered Eunomius's attacks against Basil so violently. In the third part, the bishop of Nyssa presented the structure of his first book: a first section that dealt with the accusations against Basil – it is what the modern critics have called the 'historical section' – and a second that dealt with doctrine.

Peter's answer[20] did not bring any new elements, but it confirmed the relevance of Gregory's text and the legitimacy of his anger, justified by Biblical patterns. The two letters have been, therefore, since late antiquity, a kind of preface, whether or not this was Gregory's intention. They confirmed the nature of the text – it is a refutation of a given book by Eunomius – and underlined the long history of the controversy and the place held by the paternal figure of Basil. Above all, though, a large part of *Letter* 29 is dedicated to the justification of polemic (μάχη).[21] Gregory said that he had tried to confine polemic within a delimited place, the first part of Book I, in which he refuted the slanders against Basil. Even if the first part of Book I shows more polemical content than the rest of the book, the oratorical violence is not completely absent from the second part of Book I, and is widely present in Books II and III. One can notice, however, that

Gregory tried to separate the debate about doctrine from the possibly violent answers to Eunomius's personal attacks.

There is another letter by Gregory, however, concerning the *Contra Eunomium*, even though it has never been used to throw light on the nature of the books or their possible readings. It is *Letter* 15,[22] addressed to two unknown young people, John and Maximianos, students of an unknown sophist.[23] In this letter, Gregory clearly distinguished two purposes of the book. For John and Maximianos, who were Christians, the book was an 'invitation meant to hearten those who are in the full vigour of youth to do battle with our adversaries';[24] for the sophist, certain passages will be read with pleasure. The first reading was plain and Gregory did not add any more details: it was the obvious reading of the book in its original context, a refutation of a heretical text to be read by Christians. The second reading, on the other hand, demanded more explanations from the letter's author. Gregory specified, in fact, which parts of the book may especially interest the master of the young men. He first mentioned τὰ πρὸ τῶν ἀγώνων, specifying the chosen style. He then suggested reading some passages taken from doctrinal parts which were elegantly explained. With these indications, even if the sophist – who was the master of the two young men – was not a Christian, the reading proposed by Gregory involves a literary and rhetorical approach, without taking too much into account the doctrinal or properly Christian content.

If the doctrinal reading of the *Contra Eunomium* was for Gregory himself the most evident one, which asks neither for explanation nor justification, it was also possible to read the books in another way which belonged more properly to the literary sphere and overtakes the confessional frontiers. The second reading required putting forth specific passages because the whole work cannot be read in such a way. The book is at once composed of elements dealing with Christian doctrine and, more precisely, refutation of the heresy of Eunomius, as well as passages where anger and ill humour are prominent. In the first book, Gregory wanted a strict distinction between the two elements: refutation of Eunomius's accusations first, then a response to his theology. The text of Book I, however, shows that the two threads were woven together and alternated in the framework of the three books.

Considering this double bipartition, it is tempting to think these elements correspond to each other, at least in part. We would thus have some polemical parts, which require literary skill on the part of the reader, and some doctrinal parts, needing above all a Christian interpretation. However, as we have discussed, we also find literary elements in the doctrinal parts and Christian references being utilized in the polemical sections. These three letters, however, open new perspectives for reading the *Contra Eunomium* that scholarly studies have, up until now, barely mentioned.

Cover letter of Basil's Contra Eunomium

These letters are of even greater interest in light of a correspondence by Basil, a letter that directly concerns the *Contra Eunomium* and was addressed to a sophist, Leontios (*Ep. 20*).[25] The letter is quite different from the one Gregory sent several years later to John and Maximianos. In particular, Basil clearly emphasized the doctrinal content, and the sophist addressed was obviously Christian. We find here, however, some points which make one wonder if Basil sent his work to this man not only because he was a Christian but also because he was a teacher of rhetoric. The recipient is named at the beginning of the letter by his profession, a sophist. This title suggests that the work was not written exclusively for a Christian reader or, at the very least, that it can be evaluated by a specialist of literature and rhetoric.

If the Basilian paratext does not permit a separation of the two spheres of reading as clearly as Gregory's letters, it should not greatly surprise us. In fact, the pure literary elements, mainly the polemical elements, are much more discreet in Basil's *Contra Eunomium*; they do not form polemical clusters as in Gregory's work.

Conclusion

This study of paratext confirms the nature of Nyssen's books: a refutation that follows Eunomius's text through several books written by both adversaries. It also provides us with indications as how to read the first book which may go back to Gregory himself. At last, and above all, the cover letters emphasize the multiplicity of readings: one that is more doctrinal, and another one, more literary; each fit in some passages of the books. However, both interpretations are interwoven through the main part of *Contra Eunomium*.

What new light do these elements shed on the text? First of all, it is essential not to neglect the literary components in the interpretation of the *Contra Eunomium*. Gregory himself emphasized this point. In the second place, we should not neglect the indications given by the different manuscripts, above all when the relative unanimity of the accounts confirms that these elements are ancient enough. If they do not bring us to

Nyssen's understanding of the text, they at least support a historical interpretation of the book, which is of some significance to a true hermeneutical
approach.

Doctrinal Controversy, Secular References and Elaboration of a Christian Satire

We must therefore pay attention not only to the theological content but
also to the process of refutation, its tools and the actual polemic. A close
reading of the three books *Contra Eunomium* allows us to make the
following point: if Gregory did not hesitate to sprinkle his text with more
or less insulting terms to his opponent, gathering his main polemical attack
in some specific passages, these *loci* are the most elaborate, on a literary
level, of the whole book. Here we find the richest vocabulary, the most
elaborated images, the most numerous secular references. If indeed the two
threads, theological and polemical, are closely woven together throughout
the three books, they nonetheless alternate in the framework of the *Contra
Eunomium*. The theology is clearly influenced by the polemic that
surrounded it, and this last point plays an important role in the actual
refutation of Eunomius's positions. However, their relative separation
points to an interpretation that differentiates one from the other and
aims to bring to light the proper functions of the two levels of writing
and their reciprocated ties.

The Elaboration of a Christian Polemic

Long before Gregory, other Christian authors had already developed
literary tools designed for fighting adversaries within the church itself.
These tools and their historical and doctrinal conceptions during the first
three centuries of our era have been masterfully studied by A. Le Boulluec.[26]
Such a study has not been undertaken about authors of subsequent centuries, though the material is at least as rich as any in the first three centuries.
I will study here several examples – mainly, three passages from the third
book of *Contra Eunomium* – paying particular attention to the literary
tools and to the literary references that support Gregory's text.

Eunomius, New Circe

The first text, which takes place in the second part of the third book
(*CE* III.2.75–81), is built upon a series of images whose thematic unity is

supported by what immediately precedes it:[27] Gregory had just compared two fragments from Eunomius to show that his opponent contradicted himself. The bishop of Nyssa said he was surprised that men could follow Eunomius's doctrine when he so obviously contradicted himself. Here is the sequence: quotation of Eunomius's fragment; emphasis on the contradiction; colourful attack against the misleading master, Eunomius; theological refutation of the quoted fragment. The polemical segment of this sequence occurs therefore as a preparation of the actual refutation; it is meant to be a tool capable of discrediting the opponent before entering into the actual discussion of ideas. The reader, thus warned against Eunomius, will be more easily convinced that Gregory's refutation is sound.

The clearly polemical passage is built on a rational chain of images, most of which rely on secular references rather than Biblical quotations or allusions. The attack is opened with a quotation from Psalms 34.15: 'They were divided but they had no compunction'. It is the only Biblical reference in the whole section. Here is a short list of arguments used in the passage, combined in such a way as to emphasize the weakness of those who follow Eunomius, while also asserting their relative innocence:

- First, 'being pulled by ear, like amphorae' is a proverbial formula that goes back to Bion of Borysthenes[28] and is used several times by Plutarch.[29]
- 'Drowsy people who agree with contradictory proposals' is a theme common since the Classical era. One can find a close parallel in Lucian's *Necyomancia siue Menippus*,[30] in which the main character is confronted with contradictory philosophical proposals.
- Eunomius's followers are compared with shadows that automatically follow the movements of bodies. The origin of this image is more difficult to establish.[31]
- The heart of the passage is a rather long comparison between Eunomius's disciples and Odysseus's companions turned into beasts by Circe's spells.[32] Leaning on previous interpretations of the Homeric episode, Gregory represents Eunomius as a sorcerer who belittles men to the bestial level of passions. The development of this connection finishes with a new formulation of the famous theme of the relationship between the respective positions of human and animal, and their relation to the divine: one is the face turned up to the sky, and the other is the snout lowered to its food.[33]
- Eunomius's companions are then likened to those put to sleep by a mandrake; here again, the image has clear Platonic sources (*Republic*, VI, 488c), but is also present in Demosthenes.[34]

- Finally, they are compared to fish that, fooled by bait, also swallow the hooks because of their gluttony. This is one of Gregory's favourite images;[35] it allows variations in the way the dangerous element is concealed (bread and poison, honey and poison[36]).

One can observe several common elements in this list. First of all, most of the colourful attacks are supported by secular sources whose images had already been used in a satirical or polemical context before their Christian usage. In order to fight Eunomius, Gregory reused literary tools developed by secular authors and he adapted them without apparent difficulty to a controversy internal to Christianity. Secondly, such a text shows great skill in composition and writing, able to hold the attention of a literate reader, whether pagan or Christian. Finally, such a series seems to have a clear goal in the controversy with Eunomius: it belittles and depreciates the opponent, but presents those who follow him as unwilling victims to deception who have at least partially escaped. Therefore, it would be enough for Gregory to open their eyes so that they can get back to the church's bosom and abandon the opposing party. The intended audience of Gregory's book included, therefore, Eunomius's followers, not only Eunomius himself. The literary means used here cleared them of responsibility for their adherence to doctrinal error and prompted them to recover their full use of reason, their rational abilities, which are a distinctive characteristic of men, in order to escape the one who had deceived them.

The various functions, therefore, of such a passage are as follows: discrediting the main opponent, who does not seem to be the essential addressee of this section; winning back his followers, who are the supposed readers of such a text; and gaining the reader's respect with the literary and rhetorical skill displayed here by Gregory. As a result, there is evidence in the text of social and cultural concerns, while the text is at the same time a polemical weapon.

Critique of Eunomius's Style: Heresiological and Comic Background

The structural situation is almost identical in the text to which I shall now turn. In the fifth part of the third book (*CE* III.5.18–26),[37] Gregory first quoted a passage from Eunomius. He then introduced an initial series of attacks against him, focused on one of Basil's passages which he had slandered. After quoting Basil's entire text, Gregory presented a second series of attacks. After these consecutive polemical passages, a new passage from Eunomius is quoted, which is then refuted on both theological and philosophical grounds. Gregory's virulence is undoubtedly excited here by the attack Eunomius had directly made against Basil – true to his habits, the bishop of Nyssa did not explicitly quote Eunomius's passage that contained the insults and slanders, but only mentioned its existence.

The two polemical passages differ a bit in their construction. In the first one, Gregory, addressing Eunomius for attacking Basil, used a technique close to the one previously analysed from the second part of Book III. The series opened with a Biblical reference: 1 Cor. 3.19, citing Job 5.13, 'he who seizes the wise men in their cleverness'. This sequence of attacks followed:

- Eunomius's attacks are compared to someone who fights his own shadow; the image, which is well known in secular literature,[38] was already used by Basil in his *Contra Eunomium*[39] to describe the fictional situation of Eunomius's *Apologia*.
- Gregory then compares the struggle with trampling an opponent already on the ground; the image is already a proverb in that time and well documented in secular literature.[40]
- The next image is developed at length: Gregory compares Eunomius's attacks against Basil with children who throw clods of earth towards the stars and, when the dirt falls back down, think they have hit the stars. Here again, the classical literary source is clear: a passage from Herodotus[41] which, along with some other texts, had given birth to a proverb, εἰς οὐρανὸν τοξεύεις, pointing out the vacuity and the vanity of an action.[42]
- This image is reinforced by the common representation of a child as a being whose reason is unachieved and imperfect. One finds several parallels, including similar images, in Plutarch.[43]

Several of these images were reused with variations in other parts of the *Contra Eunomium*, whether in combination with others or alone. Whereas the images of fighting shadows or trampling those who are already on the ground reappeared without great change, interesting variations appeared in the case of the children and the sky. In *Contra Eunomium* I.74–5, children throw stones towards the sun or reproach him for shining – again, it is Basil who is the sun, as he was the stars in *Contra Eunomium* III.5. In a context that no longer concerned Basil, Gregory likened Eunomius's action to children who try to trap a ray of sun in their hands and are disappointed when nothing remains (*CE* II.79–81). Because of such echoes, it is very important to read these three books as a whole and pay attention to theological parallels as well as to literary parallels in order to understand precisely their construction and meaning.

I have already studied the main part of this section elsewhere and I shall not repeat my demonstration here.[44] It may be enough to say that Gregory picked up some features of ancient literary criticism, particularly as far as corrupted and artificial styles were concerned, and propped them up with heresiological Christian features – in particular, the accusation of composing a cento. He gave fresh new colours to these Christian abuses with the help of references borrowed from comic or satiric secular literature. This section ends on a very beautiful image, dear to Gregory: drops of air in the water that pop up as soon as they arrive at the surface;[45] this image figured the vacuity of Eunomius's reasoning.

Even though Gregory's text did not immediately lose its polemic tone, the paragraphs which came after the violent attack dealt again with the debate of ideas. Gregory put forward a distinction between God and creation, studying the names that correspond to the two realities. The refutation went on but left aside for a time the almost complete focus on the polemic, itself.

The two main functions considered above remain: discrediting the opponent prior to the examination of a doctrinal point, and asking for literary recognition for those who could identify Gregory's sources and recognize his skill. The fact is clearer here, because Gregory precisely accuses Eunomius of not knowing how to write properly.

Demosthenes: Parodic Eulogy and Cappadocian Reference

Gregory's critique of Eunomian style naturally leads to my last example. Nyssen concluded his third book with a new but short attack. Eunomius was depicted as another Demosthenes, with all the features that such a literary critique attributed to the orator. Gregory, by contrast, showed himself as a poor provincial man – not very clever – speaking in a local dialect. The charge is violent, but this is a short ending for the immense corpus of the three books against Eunomius. As is usual in the works of the bishop of Nyssa, there is no actual conclusion, at least no conclusion proportionate to the size of the book, especially if we compare it to the size of the exordium that opens it.[46]

Gregory played again with literary practices, excessive eulogies that named any orator 'a new Demosthenes', and every poet 'a new Homer'. Long before the fourth century, such eulogies were already parodied and used in a satirical mode.[47] Gregory was also playing with the origin of his opponent. In fact, Basil had called Eunomius a 'Galatian' in his refutation;[48] Eunomius rebuked this accusation of quasi-barbarianism and specified the place of his birth. Gregory, who had already answered him in *Contra Eunomium* I.105, mentioned again his origin to contrast it with Demosthenes' birthplace: Eunomius is the new prince of orators, born not in Attica but in the fringes of Cappadocia. By contrast, Gregory used old prejudices against the Cappadocians and their language to better show his competence as a writer and a speaker. So, a theological book ends with a literary game.

This section on Demosthenes is split into two passages, which surrounded the last doctrinal point, and the last quotation from Eunomius. But this last quotation is no more refuted than those that precede it. There is no doctrinal conclusion to the debate, no recapitulation of the main subjects, no reminder of a Credo. We cannot know whether Gregory had refuted the whole third book of Eunomius or if he had stopped long before the end.[49]

Literary Polemic and Doctrinal Refutation

The points I have just elaborated may be clearer if we compare them with the elements of the letters that stand out as an informal preface to the *Contra Eunomium*. To begin with, I noted the relative isolation of the polemical passages, their relative autonomy considering the theological sections that surround them. Secondly, most of the secular literary references and most of the rare and unusual words are found in these polemical passages. Lastly, they are mainly located at the beginning of the argument, before the theological discussion. This position fits, therefore, exactly what is indicated in *Letter* 15 to John and Maximianos: the passages that may interest a sophist, that is to say, the passages with some literary work, are isolated, placed before the debates (πρὸ τῶν ἀγώνων) and show the main elaboration.[50]

The composition of the book fits well with the program outlined in the letter to Peter of Sebasteia (*Letter* 29). Sometimes, Gregory's anger was brought to the foreground, especially when Basil was directly attacked by Eunomius. These passages, however, are quite clearly separated from the main theological stream of the book. The polemic, of course, is not missing in these other pages and is an integral part of some of the methods used to refute Eunomius. Gregory, nonetheless, tried to persuade his reader that his book, except the openly polemical sections, was free from any bias against Eunomius, that the refutation ran only at a theological or philosophical level.

Furthermore, these sections of literary elaboration, rare but well chosen vocabulary and, sometimes, beautiful images – in particular the children and the stars, or the children and the light – created some pauses and occasions for rest in a long and arduous book. Besides, the frequent references to secular literature supported Gregory's self-representation as a cultivated bishop, belonging to the same cultural elite as the pagans. Eunomius, by contrast, was set apart, among men of drudgery and little learning. A little later, Simplicius disparaged John Philophonus with the same insults.[51]

Such a reading cannot be neglected: the theological and philosophical problems of this controversy must be seen in the context of the literary polemic. The literary weapons are all as essential as the theological discussions. The cultural and social setting is important in order to convince the addressees of the book. Even though Eunomius was not the fugitive slave that Gregory pictured, in order to understand properly Gregory's undertaking, we should take into account his being so keen on showing the inanity of Eunomius's pretentions to learning and speech.

It must also be noted that Basil's *Contra Eunomium* shows very few marks of literary elaboration, in particular, very few references to secular literature. There is no large polemical section such as the one in Gregory's book. Of course, there are several attacks against Eunomius, but they are scattered throughout the book and always very brief and sketchy. So, Gregory's writing seems specific, distinct from his brother's way; this comparison reinforces the potential importance of my conclusions.

The literary genre of the book is not enough to define all its potentialities, even to provide a secure guide to exploit the content of *Contra Eunomium*. It is a literary work – thus a complex work – which implies a multiplicity of interpretations, projects and envisioned perspectives. A limited reading of the book, as that of the history of dogma, if it is partially valid, would not be enough to offer a complete or satisfactory approach to Gregory's work. Furthermore, some important elements of Nyssen's theology and exegesis would pass unnoticed. The importance given to the literary elements, the playing with literate secular culture, the elaboration of images and entire passages devoted to an extremely worked polemic show that the *Contra Eunomium* is not a purely doctrinal text, fully absorbed in a church controversy without any opening to literature or the secular world.

Such remarks must prompt us to be very cautious when using isolated passages of *Contra Eunomium* in order to illustrate one aspect or another of the thought of Gregory, or of the Cappadocians. It is difficult to think of an interpretation for the whole book, or for Gregory's thoughts, without doing first the slow work of identification of the sources, references and links to the various theological, philosophical and literary traditions. To put it differently, a work of global interpretation cannot be completed before a critical approach to the Greek text is complete. Furthermore, this patient work of elucidating what is not clear to our eyes more than sixteen centuries after the original writing is already a fruitful part of interpretation: it should open forgotten perspectives.

The Byzantine Reception of Gregory of Nyssa's Contra Eunomium

The last part of my paper shall deal with the Byzantine reception of Gregory's book. The most fruitful approach is also the most difficult, namely studying the reception of the thought and theology of Gregory in later literature. But an initial and easier survey should be done first: which passages of Nyssen's *Contra Eunomium* did the Byzantines quote? Is there some direct reading of the book or a tradition of anthologies, second-hand quotations? I offer here the results of a first investigation, which is far from complete.[52]

Unsurprisingly, the passages that subsequent authors quoted were selected according to the theological interests of their readers. During the Christological debates of the sixth century, texts dealing with union and distinction of natures – human and divine – were used; the texts from the palamite dispute quoted passages about divine substance, human knowledge of God and manifestation of divinity in a created world; in the fifteenth century, and in the context of the Union of Churches, we find quotations dealing with the relation of the Holy Ghost to Father and Son. Furthermore, the exegetical *catenae* used important parts of *Contra Eunomium* III, even if these texts did not deal directly with the relevant part of Biblical text the *catena* commented upon.[53] So, we have both a use of Gregory's text in direct relation to the theological concerns of the time and an extended usage that suggests a deep knowledge of Nyssen's works. We must also mention a very important testimony on the *Contra Eunomium*:[54] Peter of Callinicus, at the end of the sixth century, used Gregory's books throughout his debate with Damian of Alexandria. In the context of the tritheist controversy, the Trinitarian debates from the end of the fourth century were of direct interest.[55]

Beside theological uses of Nyssen's books against Eunomius, we should also speak of some literary links between the Cappadocian and some authors of the palamite controversy. They not only quoted theological passages from *Contra Eunomium*, but they also reused some polemical elements of the books. We are sure then that they had read Gregory's work thoroughly and had not just used some older anthologies. Theodore Dexios reused in his *Appellatio* Gregory's mention of Circe's potion in order to describe the effect of the book of his adversary.[56] Nicephorus Gregoras rewrote in the first books of his *Antirrhetics* a passage of Nyssen's *Contra Eunomium* III in order to add allusions to contemporary theological debate (ἐνέργειαι) and to Palamas himself, whose name was added to Eunomius's name (τοιοῦτος ὁ Εὐνομίου καὶ Παλαμᾶ θεός).[57] This precise text was used because Gregory had established a link between Eunomius's doctrine and the Judaic doctrine of Philo of Alexandria; Gregoras reused it in order to link Palamas and the Jews. So the text of Gregory was not only used as a theological source, but also as a literary – and polemical – model that could be adapted to new patterns.

Contrary to this pattern, Nyssen's *Contra Eunomium* does not seem to have been used in Byzantine theological compendia such as Euthymios Zygabenos's *Panoplia Dogmatica*. This author prolifically quoted Nyssen's *On the Divinity of the Son and of the Holy Spirit* for his section on Trinitarian doctrine, and he used Basil's *Contra Eunomium*, but he nowhere mentioned Gregory's *Contra Eunomium*.[58] We find a somewhat similar situation in the manuscripts: there are few annotations in the margins of Nyssen's books against Eunomius. For example, a codex (*Vaticanus gr.* 424) that was used by Isidore of Kiev bears notes by him in the margins of Basil's book, but there are none in the margins of Gregory's.

A larger survey will, of course, bring more elements and correct some of these conclusions, but we have already here a first idea of the way Nyssen's *Contra Eunomium* was read in a Byzantine context. The further reception of this text will require a proper investigation: the *Contra Eunomium* was not translated in Latin before the first edition of the Greek text, together with a Latin translation, in 1615 and 1618. How was Gregory's book used in the modern era? We should find some partial answers in the book of M. Ludlow,[59] but a comprehensive study is still needed.

These preliminary results, however, bring two points to the front: first, the perspective of the history of dogma, which picks up some separate elements form the continuous text, is not new; it was already the way that some of the Byzantine readers read the text by Gregory, collecting the passages that could be seen as evidence for their own theological positions. Yet these readers were not interested solely by the Trinitarian content; they found material about Christology, the Holy Spirit and so on. In addition to this, we get a testimony to another way of reading which takes into consideration both the theological core of Nyssen's book *and* the literary and polemical way of writing it.

Conclusion

My conclusion is to be placed on two different grounds: first, my investigations around Gregory's *Contra Eunomium* have shown that this book should not be read as a solely technical, theological tract. The author himself suggested that other readings were not only possible but also necessary. Literature had its place in the writing of such a book and shapes the theological content: it is prominent in polemical sections and present throughout the book. If Gregory of Nyssa pretended to a strict separation between theology and polemic, a closer reading shows that they are actually thoroughly intertwined. It is almost impossible to pull apart a theological aspect of the books without first investigating the way this theological reflection is colored by polemic. On the other hand, a reading that only takes into account the properly theological section, leaving aside the polemical ones, will remain unaware of a major part of Gregory's work: this tract, polemical and theological as it is, should also be read as part of the creation of a Christian literature.

Secondly, with a more panoramic view, I hope I showed that philological, historical and literary methods – what I have called a 'scholarly reading' – do not lead to sterility of interpretation, but open up new vistas. Or, rather, open up new vistas *again*: the quick survey of the history of the reception of Gregory's *Contra Eunomium* has shown that Byzantine readers already used this tract as a theological *and* literary model for their own work, for example. These methods also point out to modern readers who would be glad to have direct access to texts from late antiquity that, without the tools and methods proper to philological and historical reading, they risk being blind to decisive aspects of the works they comment upon. We may also remember that, before putting a work in the drawer of a given literary genre and historical setting, we must investigate with fresh eyes the eventually divergent directions the author put into this particular tract. Of course, Gregory of Nyssa's *Contra Eunomium* deals with the Trinitarian theology of his opponent, Eunomius, but this is not the only relevant aspect of the books. A first step may be to read it as an organic whole, looking for hints inside rather than in our own literary or theological concerns, not in order to recover the original Gregory, but only to have the chance to hear what has not been heard for many years or even centuries.

Notes

1 The initial translation of this text from the French was done by Takako Hirokawa, junior studying engineering physics, and Erik Bergal, sophomore studying civil engineering, both at the University of Colorado at Boulder; subsequent revisions were made by the editors in consultation with the author.

2 Editions of Greek texts: Eunomius, *The Extant Works* (R. Vaggione (ed. & trans.); Oxford Early Christian Texts; Oxford: Clarendon Press, 1987); Basil of Caesarea, *Contra Eunomium: Contre Eunome:Basile de Césarée* (Bernard Sesboüé, Georges-Matthieu de Durand and Louis Doutreleau (eds); Bernard Sesboüé (trans.); Sources Chrétiennes, 299, 305; Paris: Les Éditions du Cerf, 1982–1983); Gregory of Nyssa, *Contra Eunomium* (Werner Jaeger (ed.); Gregorii Nysseni Opera [henceforth *GNO*], I–II; Leiden: Brill, 1960). For translations of works by Gregory of Nyssa, see the General Bibliography.

3 See M. Wallraff, 'Il "Sinodo de tutte le eresie" a Costantinopoli (383)' in *Vescovi e Pastori in Epoca Teodosiana: In Occasione del 16 Centenario de la Consecrazione Episcopale di S Agostino, 396–1996: 25 Incontro di Studiosi dell 'Antichità Cristiana, Roma, 8–11 maggio 1996, vol.2* (Studia Ephemeridis Augustinianum, 58; Roma, 1998), 271–9.

4 Eunomius, *Profession of Faith* in *The Extant Works* (Vaggione (ed.); Gregory of Nyssa, *Refutation* (W. Jaeger (ed.); *GNO* II; Leiden: Brill, 1960).

5 *On the Divinity of the Son and the Holy Spirit and on Abraham* (Ernestus Rhein and Friedhelm Mann (eds.); *GNO*, X/2; Leiden: Brill, 1996).

6 For a modern example, see Mathilde Bombart, *Guez de Balzac et la querelle des "Lettres", écriture, polémique et critique dans la France du premier XVIIe siècle* (Lumière Classique, 76 ; Paris: Honoré Champion, 2007).

7 See Bernard Pottier, *Dieu et le Christ selon Grégoire de Nysse. Étude systématique du* Contre Eunome *avec traduction inédite des extraits d'Eunome* (Ouvertures; Namur, Belgium: Culture et Vérité, 1994).

8 Cf. Gérard Genette, *Palimpsestes: la littérature au second degré* (Paris: Seuil, 1982) and *Seuils* (Paris: Seuil, 1987).

9 Some modern editorial choices may explain that the links between paratext and main text have been missed: Gregory's *Letter* 29 and his brother's answer, *Letter* 30, had been cut off from *Contra Eunomium* until W. Jaeger's publication. But *Letter* 15 seems to have never been linked to *Contra Eunomium* until it was written.

10 In particular, the titles in the manuscripts clearly pit the saintliness of Gregory against the heretical status of his opponent (κατὰ τοῦ δυσεβοῦς Εὐνομίου [*Eun.* I, mss. BT] / πρὸς τὸν Εὐνομίου τοῦ δυσσεβοῦς . . . [*Eun.* II, ms. M], πρὸς τὸν Εὐνομίου τοῦ ἀσεβοῦς... [*Eun.* II, mss. CTS]).

11 Unanimously for *Eun.* I, by ms. M for *Eun.* II, and apparently not for *Eun.* III.

12 Gregory of Nyssa, *Letter* 29.3, *Lettres. Grégoire de Nysse* (Pierre Maraval (ed. & trans.); Sources Chrétiennes, 363; Paris: Les Éditions du Cerf, 1990), 310–11. Gregory designates his book in the same way in *Letter* 15.2: τῆς πρὸς τὴν αἵρεσιν ἀντιρρήσεως (ibid., 208–9).

13 F. Diekamp, 'Literargeschichtliches zu der Eunomianischen Kontroverse', *Byzantinische Zeitschrift* 18 (1909), 1–13.

14 Peter of Callinicus, *Petri Callinicensis Patriarchae Antiocheni Tractatus contra Damianum II–III* (Rifaat Y. Ebied, Lionel R. Wickham and Albert van Roey (eds); Corpus Christianorum Series Graeca, 29, 32, 35, 54; Turnhout; Leuven: Brepols; Leuven University Press, 1994–2003).

15 Pottier, *Dieu et le Christ selon Grégoire de Nysse*, 40. On internal divisions in Byzantine writings, see the stimulating perspectives of A. Failler, 'Origine et authenticité des titres dans l'*Histoire* de Georges Pachymérès', *Revue des études byzantines* 66 (2008), 95–123.

16 Matthieu Cassin, *L'écriture de la polémique à la fin du IVᵉ siècle: Grégoire de Nysse*, Contre Eunome *III* (Thèse de doctorat, Université Paris IV – Sorbonne, 2009), vol. I, 135–7.

17 See J. A. Röder, *Gregor von Nyssa, Contra Eunomium I, 1–146, eingeleitet, übersetzt und kommentiert* (Patrologia 2; Frankfurt am Main: Peter Lang, 1993), 73–4.

18 Cassin, *L'écriture de la polémique*, vol. I, 130–1.

19 Gregory of Nyssa, *Lettres. Grégoire de Nysse* (Pierre Maraval (ed. & trans); Greek text with French translation), 308–15; English translation in *Gregory of Nyssa: The letters: Introduction, Translation, and Commentary* (Anna Silvas (trans.); Supplements to Vigiliae Christianae 83; Boston: Brill, 2007), 206–8.

20 Gregory, *Lettres*, 314–19; *Gregory of Nyssa: The Letters*, 208–10.

21 Gregory, *Letter 29*, 7.

22 Gregory, *Lettres*, 208–11; *Gregory of Nyssa: The Letters*, 158–9.

23 I will not deal here with the discussion about the identity of the sophist. Giorgio Pasquali, 'Le Lettere di Gregorio di Nissa' in *Studi Italiani di Filologia Classica* n.s. 3 (1923), 111–12, thinks it was Libanios, but there is no definitive evidence.

24 Gregory of Nyssa, *Letter 15.3*: προτροπή, ὥστε σφριγῶντας τῇ ἀκμῇ τῆς νεότητος καταθαρσῆσαι τῆς πρὸς τοὺς ἐναντίους μάχης (*Lettres*, 208–11; *Gregory of Nyssa: The Letters*, 159).

25 Basil of Caesarea, *Saint Basile, Lettres* (Yves Courtonne (ed. & trans.); Paris: Les Belles Lettres, 1957), Vol. I, 50–1.

26 Alain Le Boulluec, *La notion d'hérésie dans la littérature grecque, IIᵉ-IIIᵉ siècles* (Études Augustiniennes, Série Antiquité 110–111; Paris: Institut d'études Augustiniennes, 1985).

27 For a fuller analysis, see Cassin *L'écriture de la polémique*, vol. I, 260–8.

28 Bion of Borysthenes, *Bion of Borysthenes: A Collection of the Fragments with Introduction and Commentary* (Jan Fredrik Kindstrand (ed.); Acta Universitatis Upsaliensis; Studia Graeca Upsaliensia, 11; Stockholm: Almqvist and Wiksell International, 1976), frag. 51, with commentary, 259–60.

29 Plutarch, *De Vitioso Pudore* [On Compliancy] 536A in *Plutarch Moralia, Volume VII* (Phillip H. de Lacy and Benedict Einarson (trans); Loeb Classical Library; Cambridge, Mass.: Harvard University Press, 1959); *Quaestiones Conviviales VII.5* (705D-E) in *Plutarch Moralia, Volume IX: Table-Talk, Books 7–9, Dialogue on Love* (Edwin L. Minar Jr., F. H. Sandbach and W. C. Helmbold (trans); Loeb Classical Library, 425; Cambridge, Mass.: Harvard University Press, 1959); cf. also *Vita Aesopi Westermanniana* 98:11–13 in *Aesopica. A Series of Texts Relating to Aesop or Ascribed to Him or Closely Connected with the Literary Tradition that Bears his Name. Collected and Critically Edited, in Part Translated from Oriental Languages, with*

a *Commentary and Historical Essay* (B. E. Perry (ed.), Urbana: University of Illinois Press, 1952).

30 Lucian, *Necyomancia sive Menippus,* 4 in *Luciani Opera* II (M. D. MacLeod (ed.); Oxford: Clarendon Press, 1972).

31 See, for example, Clement of Alexandria, *Stromates,* VII.13.82.7 (A. Le Boulluec (ed. and trans.); Sources Chrétiennes, 428; Paris: Les Éditions du Cerf, 1997), 254–5.

32 Homer, *Odyssey* (A. T. Murray and George Dimock (trans); Loeb Classical Library, 104–5; Cambridge, Mass.: Harvard University Press, 1919), X:208–319.

33 Cf., for example, Plato, *Republic,* IX, 586a–b (Paul Shorey (trans.); Loeb Classical Library, 237, 276; Cambridge, Mass.: Harvard University Press, 1930–5); *Timaeus,* 91e-92a (R. G. Bury (trans.); Loeb Classical Library, 234; Cambridge, Mass.: Harvard University Press, 1929); Xenophon, *Memorabilia,* I.4.11–12 in *Xenophon Volume IV: Memorabilia. Oeconomicus. Symposium. Apology.* (E. C. Marchant and O. J. Todd (trans); Loeb Classical Library, 168; Cambridge, Mass.: Harvard University Press, 1923); Cicero, *De legibus,* I. 27 in *Cicero Volume XVI: On the Republic. On the Laws.* (Clinton W. Keyes (trans.); Loeb Classical Library, 213; Cambridge. Mass.: Harvard University Press, 1928); *De Natura Deorum,* II. 140 in *Cicero Volume XIX: On the Nature of the Gods. Academics* (H. Rackham (trans.); Loeb Classical Library, 268; Cambridge. Mass.: Harvard University Press, 1933); Ovid, *Metamorphoses,* I. 76–88 (Frank Justus Miller and G. P. Goold (trans); Loeb Classical Library, 42–3; Cambridge, Mass.: Harvard University Press, 1916). See also, Gregory of Nyssa, *De Hominis Opificio,* VIII, Patrologia Graeca [henceforth *PG*], 44:144B.

34 Demosthenes, *Philippics,* IV.6 in *Demosthenes Orations, Volume I* (J. H. Vince (trans.); Loeb Classical Library, 238; Cambridge, Mass.: Harvard University Press, 1930). See also, Clement of Alexandria, *Protrepticus,* X.103.1–2 in *The Exhortation to the Greeks. The Rich Man's Salvation. To the Newly Baptized* (G. W. Butterworth (trans.); Loeb Classical Library, 92; Cambridge, Mass.: Harvard University Press, 1919).

35 For its Christological usage, cf. Gregory of Nyssa, *Oratio Catechetica* (Ekkehard Mühlenberg (ed.); *GNO* III/4; Leiden: Brill, 1996), 62.8–10; *De Tridui Spatio* in *Sermones Pars I* (Gunther Heil et al. (eds); *GNO* IX; Leiden: Brill, 1992), 281.12–16; and the indications of R. Goulet in *Macarios de Magnésie. Le Monogénès. Édition et Traduction* (Richard Goulet (ed. & trans.); Textes et Traditions, 7; Paris: J. Vrin, 2003), 208–209 and n. 3. Cf. also some other uses in Gregory of Nyssa, *Contra Usurarios* in *Sermones Pars I* (E. Gebhardt (ed.); *GNO* IX; Leiden: Brill, 1967), 197.27–198.1; 207.1–7; *In Ecclesiasten Homiliae* in *In Inscriptiones Psalmorum; In Sextum Psalmum; In Ecclesiasten Homiliae* (J. McDonough and P. Alexander (eds); *GNO* V; Leiden: Brill, 1962), 345.12–16; *De vita Moysis,* II. 297, *The Life of Moses* (Abraham Malherbe and Everett Ferguson (trans); The Classics of Western Spirituality; New York: Paulist Press, 1978); *Oratio Catechetica, GNO* III.4 56.22–57.1; *De Instituto Christiano* in *Opera Ascetica* (W. Jaeger, J. P. Cavarnos

and V. W. Callahan (eds); *GNO* VIII/1; Leiden: Brill, 1952), 75.22–76.2; *De Oratione Dominica* V (Johannes F. Callahan (ed.); *GNO* VII/2; Leiden: Brill, 1992), 73.9–12, 26–8; *Contra Eunomium*, I.53.

36 See Gregory, *Contra Eunomium*, II.57; III.2.132; *Refutatio Confessionis Eunomii* 75, *GNO* II.116; and *De Hominis Opificio* XX PG 44.200A–201A.

37 See the full analysis in Cassin, *L'écriture de la polémique*, 268–87.

38 Cf. Plato, *Apologia Socratis* 18d (Harold North Fowler (trans.); Loeb Classical Library, 36; Cambridge, Mass.: Harvard University Press, 1914); *Republic* VII, 520c–d; *Laws* VIII, 830c (R. G. Bury (trans.); Loeb Classical Library, 187, 192; Cambridge, Mass.: Harvard University Press, 1926); Plutarch, *Quaestiones Conviviales*, 735C; *De Tuenda Sanitate Praecepta* in *Plutarch Moralia, Volume II* (F. C. Babbitt (trans.); Loeb Classical Library, 222; Cambridge, Mass.: Harvard University Press, 1928), 130F; *De Garrulitate*, 514D in *Plutarch Moralia, Volume VI* (W. C. Helmbold (trans.); Loeb Classical Library, 337; Cambridge, Mass.: Harvard University Press, 1939); *Adversus Colotem*, 1114A (*Reply to Colotes in Defence of the Other Philosophers*) in *Plutarch Moralia, Volume XIV* (Benedict Einarson and Phillip H. De Lacy (trans); Loeb Classical Library, 428; Cambridge, Mass.: Harvard University Press, 1967), etc.

39 Basil of Caesarea, *Contra Eunomium*, II.1.12–24.

40 Cf. Aristophanes, *Nubes* (*Clouds*) 549–50 in *Aristophanes Volume II* (Jeffrey Henderson (trans.); Loeb Classical Library, 488; Cambridge, Mass: Harvard University Press, 1998); Aelius Aristides, *Or.* 3 (46), 498 in *Works* (C. A. Behr (trans.); Loeb classical library, 458–61; Cambridge, Mass.: Harvard University Press, 1973); Philostratus, *Vitae Sophistarum* II, 31, 2 (C. L. Kayser (ed.); Hildesheim, N.Y.: G. Olms, 1971), 116.24 [English translation: *Lives of the Sophists* in *Philostratus Volume IV* (Wilmer C. Wright (trans.); Loeb Classical Library, 134; Cambridge, Mass.: Harvard University Press, 1921)]; Libanius, *Orationes* I.91 in *Orations* (Jean Martin (ed.) and Paul Petit (trans.); Paris: Les Belles Lettres, 1979); *Progymnasmata* IX.2.16; XI.5.6 (Richard Foerster (ed.); Libanii Opera 8; Bibliotheca Scriptorum Graecorum et Romanorum Teubneriana; Leipzig: Teubner, 1903–27); Choricius of Gaza, *Orationes* 35, 61 in *Choricii Gazaei Opera* (Richard Foerster and Eberhard Richtsteig (eds); Biblioteca Scriptorum Graecorum et Romanorum Teubneriana; Stuttgart: Teubner, 1972). See also, Basil of Caesarea, *Homilia in Martyrem Julittam*, PG, 31.257.23.

41 Herodotus, *Historiae*, IV.94 (Haiim B. Rosén (ed.); Bibliotheca Scriptorum Graecorum et Romanorum Teubneriana; Leipzig: Teubner, 1987–1997). English translation: *The Histories* (Carolyn Dewald (ed.); Robin Waterfield (trans.); Oxford World's Classics; Oxford: Oxford University Press, 2008).

42 Cf. Zenobius in Paroemiographi Graeci III.46 (E. L. Leutsch and F. G. Schneidewin (eds); Göttingen: Vandenhoeck et Ruprecht, 1839–51), vol. I, 68–9.

43 Cf. Plutarch, *Amatorius*, 766A (*Dialogue on Love*) in *Plutarch Moralia, Volume IX* (Edwin L. Minar Jr., F. H. Sandbach and W. C. Helmbold (trans); Loeb Classical Library, 425; Cambridge, Mass.: Harvard University Press,

1965); *De Pythiae Oraculis*, 409C–D (*The Oracles at Delphi No Longer Given in Verse*) in *Plutarch Moralia, Volume V* (Frank Cole Babbitt (trans.); Loeb Classical Library, 306; Cambridge, Mass.: Harvard University Press, 1936).

44 Matthieu Cassin, '"Plumer Isocrate": usage polémique du vocabulaire comique chez Grégoire de Nysse', *Revue des études grecques*, 121 (2008), 783–96.

45 See Henri-Dominique Saffrey, '*Homo bulla*, une image épicurienne chez Grégoire de Nysse' in *Epektasis, mélanges patristiques offerts au cardinal Jean Daniélou* (Jacques Fontaine and Charles Kannengiesser (eds); Paris: Beauchesne, 1972), 533–44.

46 See a fuller analysis in Cassin, *L'Écriture de la Polémique*, vol. I, 288–97.

47 See Louis Robert, 'Une épigramme satirique d'Automédon et Athènes au début de l'empire', *Revue des études grecques* 94 (1981), 338–61; R. Merkelbach, 'Der neue Euphranor in Bargylia und Euphranor, der Admiral von Caesars rhodischem Geschwader', *Epigraphica Anatolica* 1 (1981), 29–32.

48 Basil of Caesarea, *Contra Eunomium*, I.1.32–3.

49 It is to be noted, however, that Basil ended his *Contra Eunomium* in a similar manner: there is no proper conclusion and it ends with the refutation of the last quotation, which is not the end of Eunomius's *Apologia*. But Basil had not used here a particularly elaborate image nor a reference to the secular culture; his development ends with the evocation of the eschatological knowledge of God, which seems a more proper ending for a theological tract than a reference to Demosthenes and comedy.

50 It is true that other passages, among doctrinal developments, use a rare vocabulary and develop particularly elaborate images, like the comparison with the feathers and tail of a peacock (Gregory of Nyssa, *Contra Eunomium* III.1.25–7). They are not, however, as common as in the polemical sections.

51 See Phillipe Hoffmann, 'Sur quelques aspects de la polémique de Simplicius contre Jean Philopon: de l'invective à la réaffirmation de la transcendance du ciel', in *Simplicius, sa vie, son œuvre, sa survie : actes du colloque international de Paris (28 sept.–1ᵉʳ oct. 1985)* (Ilsetraut Hadot (ed.); Berlin; New York: de Gruyter, 1987), 183–221.

52 See the survey in Cassin, *L'écriture de la polémique* vol. I, 169–214.

53 Cf., for example, Nicetas of Heraclea, *Catena Nicetae in Lucam*, extract 371, in *Synagôgê Paterôn eis to kata Loukan Euangelion* (Christou Th. Krikônê (ed.); Vyzantina keimena kai meletai, 9; Thessalonike: Kentron Vyzantinou Ereunôn, 1973), citing Gregory of Nyssa, *Contra Eunomium* III.2.45–57 on the Christological title of 'First-Born'.

54 This text, Peter of Callinicus, *Tractatus contra Damianum II–III* (see n. 14), brings us back before the archetype of the Greek manuscript tradition and supplies some sections now lost in Greek.

55 For the context of this debate, see the introduction of the first volume: Peter of Callinicus, *Tractatus contra Damianum II–III* (R. Y. Ebied, Lionel R. Wickham and Albert van Roey (eds); Corpus Christianorum Series Graeca, 29; Turnhout; Leuven: Brepols; Leuven University Press, 1994).

56 Theodore Dexios, *Appellatio aduersus Iohannem Cantacuzenum* 37.23–25, in *Theodori Dexii Opera Omnia* (Ioannis D. Polemis (ed.); Corpus Christianorum Series Graeca, 55; Turnhout; Leuven: Brepols; Leuven University Press, 2003).

57 Nicephor Gregoras, *Antirrhetica I*.II.1.13 (Hans V. Beyer (ed. & trans.);
    Wiener Byzantinische Studien, 12; Vienna: Österreichischen Akademie der
    Wissenschaften, 1976).
58 See Jacob Wickert, 'Die *Panoplia dogmatica* des Euthymios Zygabenos.
    Untersuchung ihrer Anlage und ihrer Quellen, ihres Inhaltes und ihrer
    Bedeutung', *Oriens Christianus* 8 (1908), 278–388, here 303–4 and
    A. N. Papabasileiou (Papavasileiou), *Euthymios-Iōannēs Zygadenōs: Vios,
    Syngraphai* (Leukōsia: Papavasileiou, 1979), 108–9.
59 M. Ludlow, *Gregory of Nyssa, Ancient and (Post)Modern* (Oxford: Oxford
    University Press, 2007).

CHAPTER 7

ANATOMY: INVESTIGATING THE BODY OF TEXTS IN ORIGEN AND GREGORY OF NYSSA

Morwenna Ludlow

Origen declares in the fourth book of *On First Principles* that 'just as a person consists of body, soul and spirit, so in the same way does the Scripture'.[1] In the same book he appears to suggest that Scripture's 'body', 'soul' and 'spirit' are three kinds, or levels, of meaning, which were implanted in the text by the Spirit. He also suggests that the different meanings are for different kinds of readers and are accessible by different kinds of reading strategies.

So runs Origen's own summary of his hermeneutics in *On First Principles* IV. However, there is much about this summary which is problematic. First, there has been much debate as to how the three levels of meaning relate to Origen's exegesis in practice, since he frequently only delineates two levels. Secondly, Origen is not quite clear as to how these three levels of meaning relate to different ways of reading the text and, in particular, how they relate to the apparent contrast that he makes between 'literal' and 'spiritual' exegesis. That the latter is connected with allegorical reading seems clear from the general tenor of *On First Principles* IV, but the exact nature of that relationship is clouded both in Origen's own writing and by its later reception. For example, the Cappadocian fathers showed an awareness that the allegorical method was controversial in the fourth century ; the Protestant Reformers showed outright hostility to Origen's use of allegory; and even Origen's *ressourcement* defenders in the past century show caution, some arguing that more weight should be placed on his use of typology as distinct from allegory.[2] Thirdly, even the nature of the body of the text is unclear: sometimes 'body' seems to refer to the literal meaning of the text (although exactly what 'literal' means is debatable). At other times, 'body' language seems to represent Origen's concern for the body of the text in another sense, that is, its literary qualities, such as its use of metaphor, number, unusual words and strange punctuation. In this latter sense, the 'body' of the text seems to refer to what modern critics would refer to as form, as opposed to content.

In this chapter I will use Gregory of Nyssa as a dialogue partner with Origen on the subject of hermeneutics, since it is in Gregory's theology in particular that one finds several sustained reflections on the nature of

Biblical interpretation in which he is clearly reckoning with and adapting Origen's hermeneutical ideas. One consequence of this process of critical reception seems to be Gregory's reluctance to use the body–soul–spirit trichotomy in as bold a way as Origen did – even though the idea of the 'bodily' aspect of the Biblical text is evident in some of Gregory's analogies, as we shall see.

In this chapter I will first suggest that Origen's and Gregory's conceptualization of Scripture can helpfully be set in the context of a classical and late antique debate about the status of texts – a debate which gave rise to the analogy of texts with humans' own compound nature (Part I). I argue in Part II that attention to the different ways in which Origen and Gregory use, or fail to use, language about body, soul and spirit usefully highlights important aspects of their hermeneutics. Furthermore, I claim that one can draw from Origen a hermeneutical model which not only illuminates how Origen reads Scripture but might become a useful method for reading Origen himself (and other early Christian writers). One can find a slightly different model in Gregory, which again could have interesting applications to modern readings of the fathers. Finally, in Part III, I conclude that these two models can be effectively used to critique each other in order to highlight the possibilities and pitfalls of reading ancient Christian texts.

I. Philosophy, Rhetoric and the Body of a Text

As is well known, Plato raised the issue of the problematic nature of texts in, for example, the dialogues *Ion*, *Republic* and *Gorgias* in which he portrays Socrates as hostile to poetry and rhetoric.[3] But the matter is notoriously complex: in the *Republic*, Socrates acknowledges the skill and influence (if not the truthfulness) of Homer (*Republic*, 606e); in the *Phaedrus*, Socrates admits the usefulness of rhetoric on certain conditions (*Phaedrus*, 277b–278c). And of course Plato himself committed his philosophy – including these very debates about texts – to a textual form. Indeed, there are many passages in Plato that could easily be described as rhetorical or even poetic (e.g. his use of myth in Book X of the *Republic*).[4] In the dialogues there is also a strong ethical current to the debate: Do the poets promote immorality? Are sophists ethically disengaged? Can you be a good rhetorician without knowing about the soul and about truth? Underlying these practical ethical queries are more fundamental questions about the relation of beauty and truth: can a 'good' poem or speech be beautiful, witty or entertaining without being truthful? Thus the Platonic corpus created space for a discussion about good texts and bad texts, while still holding out the possibility that no text is as good as dialectic (at least for the purposes of philosophy – the study of the truth).[5]

One particular aspect of Plato's writings about texts is the way in which he connected them with bodiliness. Socrates' literary critique associated texts as such with the body (in particular with the senses) and associated the truth they should try to express with the soul. The idea that writing is the image of living and breathing discourse (*Phaedrus*, 275) suggests the notion that texts are like a vehicle or body for an inner life-giving principle – the soul. The connection of both poetry and rhetoric with pleasure, and the subsequent argument that the pleasurable form of a text can hinder the perception of the truth, closely parallels Socratic scepticism about the use-fulness of the senses in epistemology and his warnings about the way in which the body can hinder ethical progress.[6] However, just as the human body could also be viewed rather more positively by Plato, so could the 'textual body'. In the *Phaedrus*, Socrates praises Pericles for having grasped the 'soul' of rhetoric (270b). His further comment (270e), that rhetoric targets the souls of its hearers and that rhetoricians must understand the soul, suggests the idea that the composition of a speech is akin to a body which serves the soul, the soul being what the speech is really 'about'. Here the body is more an instrument of, rather than a hindrance to or a veil of, the soul.

Later writers also used body and/or soul analogies in connection with the discussion of texts – usually in connection with the latter 'instrumental' view of the text having a 'body' serving the more important 'soul'. Thus, Aristotle uses 'body' language for the construction of a speech: for example, the *prooimion* 'articulates the subject in summary form, so that it [the prooimion] is like the head of a body'.[7] In the *Poetics*, the plot (*muthos*) of a drama is described as a 'kind of soul'.[8] The author of the *Rhetorica ad Herennium*, while distinguishing the *verba* and the *res* of a speech, stresses that the two should be held firmly together; it is the vulgar and half-educated who 'separate words from thoughts as one might sever body from mind'.[9] Quintilian describes the preparatory exercises in rhetoric, which took the form of preparing bits of speeches before attempting a whole speech, as, 'so to speak, limbs, or parts of larger wholes'.[10] Finally, several sources cite Porphyry as having declared that 'since speech is thought to have a soul and a body, one could justly regard the invention of thoughts as the soul of speech and expression as its body'.[11] The number of citations of this particular quotation together with their tone suggest that Porphyry's was a fairly uncontroversial point of view.

II. Origen and Gregory of Nyssa: The Body, the Past and the Transfigured Body

In this section I offer my own interpretation of one theme in Origen's hermeneutics. I do not claim that my approach solves all of the difficulties previous scholars have raised. In particular, it does not iron out the tensions between Origen's description of his exegetical method and the way his exegesis proceeds in practice.[12] Nor does it address in detail the question of how Origen's exegesis of the Hebrew Bible dealt with Israel and Jews.[13] Rather, my approach is to investigate what I believe to be a fruitful, albeit not unproblematic, idea in Origen's scriptural hermeneutics and then to ask whether it might profitably be applied to present-day readings of the church fathers. My reason for doing this is that Origen was undoubtedly a well-trained, sophisticated and thoughtful exegete, who was well aware of the problems associated with reading ambiguous texts, particularly those from cultures temporally and culturally distant from the reader. I hope that my interpretation captures something of the spirit of Origen's hermeneutics, especially by recovering its eschatological emphasis, which has perhaps been lost in some recent discussions.

Much debate has centred on the question of whether Origen's method overrides or even obliterates the material (the body) in favour of the spiritual. This very question seems to assume a crude opposition between the 'body' and the 'spirit' in Origen's thought, which makes it difficult to locate the third aspect of the text – the 'soul' – in Origen's hermeneutics. (If the 'spirit' of a text is defined as a meaning which points to the immaterial, in what way can it differ from the 'soul' of the text?) In what follows, I will argue that a more fruitful way to read Origen's notion of the body, soul and spirit of a text, might be to see them not in terms of material versus immaterial referents, but in terms of different temporal perspectives on a text.

As a preliminary, I suggest that it is useful to draw a distinction in Origen's theology between the *meaning* of a text and a *method of reading* a text. It is confusing to talk about 'literal meaning' and 'allegorical meaning' (even if Origen is himself sometimes guilty of doing so). Instead it is helpful to distinguish the *levels of meaning* in a text from the *ways of reading* a text. When Origen asserts that 'just as a person consists of body, mind and spirit, so in the same way does the scripture', he also suggests that each aspect has a distinctive purpose:

> . . . the simple man may be edified by what we may call the flesh of the
> scripture, this name being given to the obvious interpretation; while the man

who has made some progress may be edified by its soul, as it were; and the man who is 'perfect' and like those mentioned by the apostle . . . this man may be edified by the spiritual law, which has a 'shadow of the good things to come'.[14]

He usually assumes that someone reads the text of Scripture 'according to the letter'[15] in order to access the bodily meaning, and that one can use a variety of other methods of readings, including typology and allegory, to access the soul-ish and spiritual meanings.[16] However, a literal reading is not the same thing as the bodily meaning. This becomes evident from Origen's contention that 'with regard to the whole of divine scripture . . . it all has a spiritual meaning, but not all a bodily meaning, for the bodily meaning is often proved to be an impossibility'.[17] It would be absurd to assume that this means that not all of Scripture could be read literally, for it is clear from Origen's explanation that one *must* read *all* of Scripture literally (κατὰ τὴν λέξιν – 'according to the letter').[18] Indeed, this is the first thing one must do, precisely in order to work out what parts are 'impossible' (ἀδύνατον) and 'did not happen' (μὴ γεγενημένοις) and which parts are 'not impossible but historically true' (οὐκ ἀδυνάτοις ἀλλὰ καὶ ἀληθέσι κατὰ τὴν ἱστορίαν).[19]

This passage also gives us a clue as to what lies at the heart of the bodily meaning for Origen: it is a meaning which is fundamentally tied to the past. Origen divides Scripture as a whole into two genres, history and law – a distinction he applies to both the Old and New Testaments. The bodily meaning in relation to history is what truly happened; the bodily meaning of a law indicates its relevance or normativity in the past. Thus, while arguing that Christians need not be bound by the laws of the Pentateuch, Origen assumes that these are historical records of genuine laws applied to the people of Israel as their tutor (*paidagōgos*) before the arrival of Christ.[20] Because of the twofold way in which the body of the text refers both to past events and laws which were previously normative, one cannot summarize this meaning as referring to 'what really happened'. For this reason, I cautiously suggest that the bodily meaning of Scripture is for Origen a 'historical' meaning – although I am well aware of the dangers of reading modern notions of historicity back into the fathers.[21]

Origen argues that in those cases in which a literal reading renders a bodily meaning which is 'impossible', the literal reading acts as a 'stumbling block', which should encourage the reader to search deeper for the soul-ish and spiritual meanings.[22] This is done by reading the text allegorically or typologically, and so forth. Mostly, however, Origen is concerned with preserving or defending the historical meaning of the Biblical text[23] – a fact that has sometimes been denied or ignored, but which has been vigorously defended by many scholars, perhaps most famously by Henri de Lubac in his *Histoire et Esprit*.[24] De Lubac pointed out that Origen goes to great lengths to explain the more improbable episodes in the Old Testament and passionately defends the occurrence of miracles in the New.[25] When Origen describes history as astonishing (as frequently in *Against Celsus*), he does not mean that it did not happen; rather, it is astonishing precisely because it did happen! Since Origen was defending the truth of the Christian message about salvation history against the arguments of pagan critics, such as Celsus, and Valentinian gnostics, it was crucial for him that the Old Testament recorded things – the very events, not just their description – that actually pointed towards the Incarnation, death and resurrection of Jesus Christ.[26]

One strand of comment on Origen's spiritual meaning has suggested that the visible/material events of history (the 'body') point towards the invisible/immaterial plane of salvation history (the 'spirit').[27] As we shall see, there is undeniably a current in Origen's thought that draws an opposition between the visible and the intellectual; however, I would like to suggest that, on the whole, Origen views the 'pointing' function of the history recorded in Scripture rather differently: it points not to an abstract atemporality but to present and future meanings of the text. The past events of the history of salvation point to the believer's present experience of salvation, and the future consummation of that salvation. So, just as the 'bodily' meaning of the Biblical text is rooted in the past, the 'soul' meaning is rooted in the present and the 'spiritual' meaning is rooted in the future.

This interpretation is suggested by passages such as this extract from Origen's homilies on Leviticus:

> [Scripture] consists of a body, namely, the visible letter, and of a soul which is the meaning found within it, and of a spirit, by which it also has something of the heavenly in it, as the Apostle says: 'They serve as a copy and shadow of the heavenly sanctuary' (Heb. 8.5). Since, this is so, calling upon God who made the soul and body and the spirit of Scripture – the body for those who came before us, the soul for us and the spirit for those who 'in the age to come will receive the inheritance of eternal life' (Luke 18.18, 31) by which they will come to the heavenly things and the truth of the law – let us seek out not the letter but the soul.[28]

In another passage, Origen says that the bodily meaning of a certain passage refers to the law of the past (circumcision and sacrifice), the soul-ish meaning to the ethics of the present (abstinence from food and the chastisement of the body) and the spiritual meaning to the nourishment of the saints 'not only in the present life, but in the future'.[29] Furthermore, in his *Commentary on John*, Origen argues that prescriptions about the Passover lamb, which once applied validly in the past, now refer to the keeping of a 'second Passover'. Specifically, they apply to the treatment of Scripture that is interpreted as the body of Christ who was sacrificed for humanity. Christians 'must approach the whole of Scripture as one body, [they] must not lacerate nor break through the strong and well-knit connections which exist in the harmony of its whole composition'.[30] As for the third, eschatological meaning of keeping the Passover, Origen is circumspect: 'It is not necessary that our discourse should now ascend to that third Passover which is to be celebrated with myriads of angels in the most perfect and most blessed exodus; we have already spoken of these things to a greater extent than the passage demands'.[31]

Several sentences earlier, Origen makes his oft-quoted remark that 'we ought not to suppose that historical things (τὰ ἱστορικα) are types of historical things, and bodily things (τὰ σωματικὰ) of bodily, but that bodily things are typical of spiritual things (πνευματικῶν), and historical things of intellectual (νοητῶν)'.[32] When τὰ σωματικὰ is translated 'material things' (as it is in Allan Menzies' translation for the Ante-Nicene Fathers series), this does suggest that Origen's prime concern is with an opposition between the visible/material and the invisible/immaterial. But the comment that 'bodily things are typical of spiritual things' in fact simply states there is a logical relationship between the 'body' and the 'spirit' of Scripture – although it does not identify what the body or spirit are. Even the claim that historical things are types of intellectual things is not obviously a statement about materiality as such. Instead of assuming that the quotation indicates the relationship between a temporal material- ity and a timeless, perhaps abstract, immateriality (a relationship which is assumed to be Platonic), perhaps one should attend to Young's argument that '*historia* in the first place has to do with enquiry, the knowledge acquired by investigation'.[33] Could Origen then be concerned, not with materiality and abstraction, but with two ways of knowing, one proceeding by investigation (such as the investigation of events recorded as having happened in the past) and the other 'noetic' knowledge provided to the reader by faith and the inspiration of the Spirit?

In any case, this much-cited extract should be glossed by a statement Origen makes some lines earlier, which reiterates the idea that the body of the text points to the spirit that has to do with the future: 'not only such things as food and drink and new moons and sabbaths, but the festivals also, are a shadow *of the things to come*'.[34] Such passages as these seem to suggest that Origen did not view the spiritual meaning as a timeless abstraction from history, but rather as a future meaning indicated by the bodily – that is, the historical – meaning of the text. In other words, we could read Origen's contrast between historical and spiritual as being not between temporal and atemporal, but between past and future. This way of reading Origen allows one to connect his belief in the spiritual progression of the individual with the reading of Scripture, and it emphasises the eschatological nature of the spiritual meaning of Scripture.[35]

A further advantage is that it also solves a few difficulties with the usual categorizations of Origen's three meanings. Often, scholars draw a contrast between the 'soul-ish' meaning as moral or ethical and the 'spiritual' meaning as theological or mystical. But frequently the distinction which Origen makes between the two is not clear.[36] Conventional analyses frequently view the three meanings as pointing to three different referents: for example, the bride in the Song of Songs, the individual soul, and the church. I am suggesting that perhaps Origen's three meanings are better viewed not with regard to their referents but with regard to their contexts. This would explain why the referents of the soul-ish and spiritual meanings are often the same (e.g. the believer's soul), but treated in a slightly different way. This interpretation is supported by De Lubac's comment that when Origen treats the individual soul as referent of the third meaning, 'the point of view has changed': 'it is now a question of . . . the soul "tending towards perfection"'.[37] De Lubac describes this as 'the soul in the church'[38] – it might better be called 'the soul viewed eschatologically'.

Another example of how the past–present–future model is more satisfactory than the usual history–ethics–mystery model can be seen in Origen's commentary on 1 Corinthians. In this work, Origen gives both ethical and 'mystical' instruction and, as Judith Kovacs points out, he 'explains that there are different levels of *both* ethical teaching and mystical theology'.[39] For example, there are ethical commands which are given as concessions to the weaker members of the flock, and others – such as 'perfect purity . . . virginity or chastity' – which are given to the stronger.[40] While it is clear that Origen did think some Christians could be chaste in their lifetime, he – like other church fathers – saw 'perfect purity . . . virginity or chastity' as an *eschatological* ethic: a mode of life which one could begin on earth, but which was an anticipation of the kingdom of God and could only be truly perfected eschatologically. Similarly, Origen offers a twofold interpretation of the 'mystical' or theological truths, the first part of which seems to refer to the present and the second part of which certainly refers to salvation history.[41]

A further reason for thinking that Origen held that the text of Scripture could refer to past, present and future can be found by reference to classical understandings of texts. We have seen already that the conception of works as having a 'body' and 'soul' was not uncommon. But one also finds in rhetoric the notion that different texts might have different temporal reference. So, for example, Aristotle distinguishes three kinds of rhetoric, by analysing them in terms of their temporal reference: *forensic* rhetoric seeks to persuade an audience with regard to the truth (or falsity) of events which happened in the past; *epideictic* rhetoric praises its subjects for qualities they possess at the present time; finally, *deliberative* rhetoric seeks to persuade people about what they should do in the future.[42] Each type of rhetoric also has a different audience: jurors, the general public, political decision-makers. There is no direct evidence that Aristotle (or other writers on rhetoric) influenced Origen on this specific point, but the convergence is suggestive.[43] In rhetoric, one has three kinds of speech, each with its particular audience and techniques of composition. In Scripture, Origen suggests there are three kinds of meaning, again each with its particular audience and, I have suggested, appropriate methods of exegesis. Origen squeezes the three kinds of discourse into one text, as if claiming that God, the divine orator, could manage all at once.

In sum, I am here making three suggestions about Origen's hermeneutics of Scripture: first, that one can make a distinction between meaning and method of interpretation in Origen's work (bodily, soul-ish and spiritual *meanings*; literal, allegorical, typological and other *methods*); secondly, that the bodily meaning is rooted in the past; and thirdly, that the soul-ish and spiritual meanings are rooted in the present and the future, respectively. Origen seems to assume that the bodily/historical meaning points to the other meanings by virtue of the qualities of the Biblical text in itself – its marvellous fecundity.

It seems to me that the advantage of Origen's method is that he acknowledges that it is possible, useful and in fact necessary to read one text in different ways: the bodily, soul-ish and spiritual meanings can all be truthful. If he thinks that the latter two reveal a deeper or more profound truth, it is due to Origen's notion of salvation history, which is moving towards fulfilment in the eschaton, and not to a crude opposition between the material and immaterial. It is true that Origen sometimes rejects the bodily meaning, but he claims that this should be done in exceptional cases when that meaning is impossible; in general, he assumes that the bodily, soul-ish and spiritual meanings should be kept together.[44] This sense of belonging together is suggested not only by the analogue of human nature itself but also by previous and contemporary literary usage which, as we have seen, often implied that the 'body' of a text should serve and be perfectly adapted to its 'soul' or core truth. One can imagine Origen agreeing with the opinion that only the badly educated 'separate words from thoughts as one might sever body from mind'.[45] In accordance with his literary training, Origen shows a fascination with the body of the text – including its precise vocabulary and inflexions – and advises a deep respect for it, for example (as we saw above), by warning his readers not to 'lacerate' or 'break' the body of Scripture (that is, not to read isolated passages out of context).

I think that Origen's approach could be fruitful for reflecting on how one reads early Christian writers today. His method could enable a reader to read a religious text in several different ways, allowing one to take the historical context and sense of the text seriously and see the other meanings as informed, but not enslaved by, the historical meaning. It should free the reader from the burden of having to negotiate between the historical and other possible meanings as if they were direct competitors: it liberates the reader from the elusive search for one 'real' meaning. It raises the possibility that one can read the fathers in the acknowledgement that there are meanings of different kinds, meanings reached by different audiences by applying different methods of reading and critique – meanings which are closely interrelated, but not ultimately commensurable. Thus, for example, one could draw a distinction between what a text meant in the past (e.g. a father's well-intentioned advice to a young woman beginning an ascetic life) and what the text could mean in the present (evidence of the thoroughgoing presence of patriarchy). One kind of 'historical meaning' would be that which is accessed by the historico-critical method and would approximate to 'what Origen/Gregory/Augustine really meant'.[46] However, the techniques of reception history could also be used to identify other meanings the text had for different readers or communities in the past (and especially, the influence of earlier interpretations on later ones).[47]

Importantly, however, by maintaining the distinction between levels of meaning and different ways of reading a text (discussed above), one can free Origen's soul-ish and spiritual meanings from a necessary connection with allegory, especially allegory as narrowly conceived. In other words, by acknowledging that present meanings of the text are different from its historical meaning, one would not be committed to saying that present meanings of the text can only be derived by methods such as allegory or typology. These days, other kinds of theological reflection or philosophical argument are much more likely to come to the fore. Origen's method also opens up possibilities for acknowledging the role of the spiritual/future meaning of the text. While Origen sometimes cannot resist speculating about what that meaning is, he declares restraint perhaps more often than one might suspect (e.g. declaring that 'it is not necessary that our discourse should now ascend' that far[48]). The awareness that a future meaning of a text might transcend all current understandings of it is a useful curb against either historical or theological over-confidence.[49]

Finally – and developing Origen's thought somewhat – I also emphasize the idea that the present and future meanings are generated by the continuing interpretational history of the text. In other words, it is the interaction between the text, its readers and the ever-changing context in which it is read that brings about the new meanings (a viewpoint which to a certain extent reflects Origen's own emphasis on the dynamic interaction between the Spirit-inspired reader and the Spirit-inspired Biblical text).

However, there is a problem with the past–present–future idea as a reading strategy. In Origen's description of his hermeneutics, he often seems to create a very clear distinction between each type of meaning. But are the bodily, soul-ish and spiritual meanings (that is, the past, present and future meanings) able to be so clearly isolated from one another? More specifically, there are two problematic tendencies in Origen's exegesis which might arise from too careful a separation of the meanings from one another. First, as critics of Origen have pointed out, he does sometimes seem to dispose of the bodily meaning in favour of the other two (despite his contention that one should keep them together).[50] One might easily connect this move with Origen's other infamous alleged error – that is, his supposed ambivalence towards the reality of the resurrected body. Is it surprising, one might ask, that the man who argued that some bodily/historical readings of Scripture are impossible, was the one who also asserted that it would be impossible for the resurrected body to be the same body that one had during one's earthly life? The problem of the overthrow of the bodily sense is not protected, but only exacerbated, by my suggested interpretation of his hermeneutics in a temporal dimension: surely the past is, by definition, to be left behind in the light of the present (and soon, the future)? Daniel Boyarin's critique of Origen, for example, rests on the observation that while Origen believes in the real existence and history of Jews before Christ, he is seemingly unable to acknowledge their real continued existence beyond Christ's death and resurrection.[51]

A second problem is that Origen's way of identifying three discrete possible meanings in a text often leads him, paradoxically, to over-emphasize the importance of the bodily meaning. This is sometimes evident in the way in which he asserts that every letter of the text has significance; if there is an apparent grammatical error in the text, he claims that this too must count for something, for there is nothing useless in the Biblical text. Most defenders of Origen's hermeneutics appeal to his detailed attention to the bodily meaning and his treatment of the whole Biblical text (even every letter) as sacred, but seen from another perspective, might Origen be taking things too far? Might he in fact be guilty of paying too much attention to the bodily meaning, an attention which causes him, ironically, to reject it when he finds it 'impossible'? To put it another way, does Origen idolize the bodily meaning and let it obstruct that to which it points?

There are also potential difficulties with developing the past–present–future idea as a model for our reading of the fathers today: if one draws too strong a distinction between each kind of meaning, might this encourage an ever deeper divide between 'historical' and 'theological' (or 'philosophical'[52]) readings – and readers – of a text? While some scholars might be happy to let the historical/bodily meaning of an ancient text be overridden by a present theological interpretation, they might not be aware of how past historico-critical readings have deeply influenced theological interpretations. Conversely, historians with a focus on the authorial intention of a text are sometimes less aware than they could be of the way in which theological trends have affected historical readings of a text: fears or hopes about what a text might 'mean for the church today' often have an important, but undetected, effect on the direction of historical scholarship.[53]

Interestingly, there are indications that Origen may have been aware of the potential problems arising from drawing too blunt a distinction between the bodily, soul-ish and spiritual meanings. As many commentators have pointed out, his exegesis in practice often does not seem to follow the rules he sets out when he describes it: not infrequently, for example, only two meanings seem to emerge from his reading of a text. In this and other respects, his actual exegesis sometimes reflects an awareness of the fluidity and interpenetration of the three levels of meaning (an awareness which is obscured in his own analysis of his hermeneutical method when subtlety is sacrificed for clarity).

An interesting example is Origen's interpretation of the commands about the Passover lamb. As we have already noted above, he thinks that the soul-ish/present meaning of the command not to break up the lamb's body refers to the manner in which Christians should read Scripture. But he also offers an exegesis of the Law's injunction not to eat the meat uncooked:

> We are not, however, to eat the flesh of the Lamb raw, as those do who are slaves of the letter, like irrational animals, and those who are enraged at men truly reasonable, because they desire to understand spiritual things; truly,

they share the nature of savage beasts. But we must strive to convert (μεταλαμβάνοντι) the rawness of Scripture into well-cooked food, not letting what is written grow (μεταλαμβάνειν) flabby and wet and thin.[54]

This analogy suggests the idea that the different levels of meaning in Scripture are not discrete, but that – with the appropriate work or preparation from the reader – the lower meanings can be 'converted' or transformed into the higher ones. Exactly the same point arises from a passage in the prologue to Gregory of Nyssa's *Commentary on the Song of Songs*.

> Having gathered up a myriad of examples from the rest of prophecy in addition to these, one can show the necessity of a *theoria* (θεωρία) according to the meaning of the words (τῆς κατὰ διάνοιαν τῶν ῥητῶν θεωρίας). When the *theoria* is rejected – as it pleases some – this situation seems to me to be similar to someone setting cereals on the table as human food without threshing the stems, without separating the seeds from the chaff by winnowing, without refining the grain into meal, without preparing (κατασκευάσας) dough in the usual way for bread-making. So, just as unprepared (ἀκατέργαστον) produce is food for the herds and not for humans, so someone might say that those divinely-inspired words which are not prepared (κατεργασθέντα) through the refining of *theoria* are food for irrational rather than rational beings. This applies not just to the words of the Old Testament, but to many from the teaching of the Gospels.[55]

Just as Origen asserted that only savage beasts eat raw meat, Gregory argues that no one sets before humans grain which has not been winnowed, ground and cooked – that kind of food goes only to animals. Both Origen and Gregory use the idea that only untrained and irrational (i.e. 'bestial') Christians read the words of Scripture without close preparation and examination. It is important to note here that Gregory does *not* draw the main conclusion that the 'kernel' of Scripture should be separated from the chaff – that is, that the spiritual sense should be *removed* from the bodily. The idea of winnowing forms only part of his analogy (and its presence is explained by the fact that Gregory proceeds to offer an exegesis of the Gospels' reference to a winnowing fork[56]). The main point of the analogy seems to be the idea of 'working at' a text in order to transform it (cooking the grain, for example, changes it without taking anything away). Here, Gregory plays on various meanings of the verb κατεργάζομαι: in its basic sense it means 'work on' or 'achieve by labour', but it had already been applied in its negative form both to food (e.g. uncooked bread or indigestible food) and texts which have not been properly 'worked up'.[57] Further on in his *Commentary on the Song of Songs*, Gregory uses a slightly different image: just as one needs to 'work on' – that is, to chew – a dense hunk of bread before swallowing it, so Paul the Apostle takes a dense morsel of Scripture and turns the 'unworked bread' (ὁ ἀκατέργαστος ἄρτος) into something softer, and more spiritual.[58] Like Paul, the church (indicated in the *Song* by the bride's teeth) must chew Scripture to render it edifying. (The point to note here, though, is that Gregory seems to imply that it is the church's job first to produce the spiritual meaning, then to communicate it to *all* its members.)

At a general level, Gregory and Origen are making the same point: one needs to work at reading Scripture. If the reader does this, they suggest, those passages which, when read only literally, appeared indigestible become transformed into nourishing spiritual food. From this perspective, it is not so much that one meaning replaces another, but that the text is transfigured. Or, to put it another way, inner possibilities and potentialities are drawn out of the text. It is no accident that Gregory's *Commentary* begins with a reference to the transfiguration of Christ. In Gregory's theology, Christ's body was not replaced (either at the transfiguration or at the resurrection or ascension), but it was transformed. The transfiguration also could be said to reveal the 'inner possibility' of the incarnation, by pointing forwards towards Christ's resurrection and ascension. This draws our attention to the Christological significance of each of the metaphors: for Origen, the Passover lamb signifies both Scripture and Christ; in the two texts from Gregory it is reasonable to assume that he intended a more indirect and tentative resonance between the nourishing spiritual bread and Jesus the 'bread of life'.[59] However, there is also an interesting difference between Origen's and Gregory's metaphors. By using the analogy of an animal's carcass, explicitly comparing it with the embodied Jesus Christ, Origen brings the notion of bodiliness or fleshliness to the fore; on the other hand, by focusing on wheat (which we recognize as material, but much less regularly think of as having a 'body') Gregory keeps the notion of bodiliness firmly in the background. Why?

The answer may perhaps lie in a difference in how the two theologians reflect on and perform their respective hermeneutical methods. As we have seen, Origen uses the body–soul–spirit character of human nature as an analogy for Scripture. Gregory, on the other hand, does use the notion of 'spiritual' (*pneumatikos*) interpretation, but more often uses the term *theoria*. He very rarely uses the term *bodily* in a hermeneutical context.[60] In his defence of allegory in his *Commentary on the Song of Songs*, for example, Gregory studiously avoids referring to the historical meaning of the text as bodily, instead referring to it as the 'plain' (προχείρος) meaning.[61]

Why does Gregory avoid the term σωματικός for one of the meanings of Scripture? It is evident from the defensive tone of, for example, the

prologue to Gregory's *Commentary* that he was well aware of the controversies surrounding Origen's exegesis.[62] It is also clear that Gregory knew
that Origen's doctrine of the resurrection had met with strong criticism.
Even though Gregory thought Origen's theology was broadly defensible
on both counts, he took steps to make sure he could not be accused of the
same errors. His eschatology can certainly be interpreted as (among other
things) an attempt to develop and nuance Origen's ideas in a way which
made them more sound.[63] It is reasonable, I think, to interpret Gregory's
hermeneutics in a similar way. But these two areas of Origen's influence on
Gregory are not unconnected: as I have already noted, Origen was guilty,
in his opponents' eyes, of underestimating the value of the body, whether
the bodily aspect of human nature or the bodily meaning of Scripture.
Gregory's general disinclination to describe one level of meaning in Scripture as a body may therefore be read in the context of his staunch defence
of the resurrection of the body (most importantly, in his treatise *On the
Soul and the Resurrection*): they are both connected to his concern that his
opponents not paint him as an Origenist. In one case, his method is to
strongly defend the continued existence of the human body in the eschaton:
interpreting Paul's notion of a 'spiritual body', Gregory assumes that
however 'spiritual' one's transformed body will be, it will nevertheless be
a body – indeed, one's own earthly body. In his hermeneutics, however,
Gregory pursues a different strategy. The transformation of the plain or
historical meaning of Scripture into the spiritual meaning or *theoria* is so
radical that perhaps Gregory feared he would be held a hostage to fortune
if he wrote of the transformation of the *bodily* into the spiritual meaning:
opponents of Origen so frequently accused users of allegory of leaving
the bodily meaning completely behind that Gregory chose to alter the
terminology of the debate altogether. Gregory's decision to do so is all
the more striking given the history of body and soul language in both
philosophical and rhetorical traditions.

III. Conclusion

In the exegeses of both Origen and Gregory of Nyssa, there is an assumption
that the Scriptural text has different levels of meaning. The two analogies
that we have studied here suggest that both writers think that the various
meanings, rather than being utterly discrete and unconnected, can be transformed one into the other by being 'changed', 'worked on' or 'prepared' by
the reader of the text. This notion of transformation fits with the dynamic
aspect of Origen's exegesis, evident in the way that he associates the bodily

meaning of Scripture with the past, the soul-ish meaning with the present and the spiritual meaning with the future. However, I contend that there is a shift of emphasis in Gregory's exegesis, which retains the notion of transformation but largely sets aside the categories of body, soul and spirit. As many scholars have already noted, fluidity is key in Gregory's exegesis: meanings are transformed, metaphors have shifting referents, characters change one way and then back again (even apparently changing their gender). The fruitfulness of this bold use of language and imaginative approach to the Bible has already been the subject of much discussion.[64]

I am generally very sympathetic to Gregory's literary approach. In particular, I think the way in which he chose to highlight the notion of transformation of meaning – which he found in Origen's work but elaborated on much more fully – marked an important development in Christian hermeneutics. It seems to me that his fluid approach captures something important about the way different readings of a text interpenetrate and influence each other and cannot be regarded as sealed units (e.g. the way in which the present and future meanings are generated by the continuing interpretational history of the text). In his strong emphasis on eschatology, Gregory retains the dynamism of Origen's approach– indeed, he emphasizes the apophatic aspect of Biblical exegesis even more firmly than his predecessor, continually stressing the idea that the spiritual journey is a never-ending progress into the knowledge and love of God (both of which are stimulated by the regular reading of the Bible, among other things). As other chapters in this book note, Gregory's method here resonates with much more recent hermeneutical approaches.

Nevertheless, it remains to be asked whether something was lost in Gregory's rejection of Origen's tripartite body–soul–spirit characterization of the Biblical text. In other words, since I have used Gregory to critique Origen, does anything constructive emerge from using Origen to critique Gregory? I will close this chapter by making two tentative suggestions.

First, although it might sometimes appear to be drawn with too much clarity, Origen's distinction between the body, soul and spirit of a text does have the merit of suggesting that sometimes different readings of a text are not only different readings, but *different kinds* of reading. That is, what a text (the Bible, a father's theological treatise or sermon) meant to the author might differ from what it means for a reader today – or tomorrow. This idea is reinforced in Origen's work by the idea that different kinds of meaning are often accessed by different kinds of reading (and by different kinds of readers). Without being committed to allegorical interpretation per se, the modern systematic theologian can see that he or she is reading an ancient Christian text in a different way from a historian. The methods used by historians and theologians might overlap (as might the meanings they attribute to the text), but too much emphasis on fluidity can sometimes obscure the distinctions and lead to the sense that somehow historians and theologians are competing for only one kind of reading.

Secondly, one of Origen's great strengths is that he is very aware of the sheer 'textiness' of the Biblical text. Much more so than Gregory, he is attentive to vocabulary, spelling, syntax, possible mistakes and so on. These features often seem to form part of what Origen means by the 'body' of Scripture. That is, he seems to bring together under the one heading of the 'body' the linguistic features of the text and the meaning derived from reading the text literally – elements which historico-critical methods tend to separate. The form of the body of the text has great significance in Origen's exegesis: the question of the relationship between the beauty of a text and its truth becomes a very real one. For example, in *Against Celsus* Origen reflects on whether the gospels' relatively informal literary style reflects a vulgar subject matter? Far from overemphasizing the structure and form of the text, then, perhaps Origen's concern for it – and his use of the body–soul analogy to express its relation to the meanings of the text – resonates with debates about form and content among philosophers and literary critics, both ancient and modern.[65] Finally, Origen's insistence that one takes even difficult elements of the text seriously fits in well with the key themes of this volume. Far from being mere spring-boards from which he launches irresponsible leaps of fantasy, the stumbling-blocks in the text are for Origen a reminder that it is precisely the most difficult texts that are the most productive. While others might think that he uses such features of the text in a fashion which is irresponsible, for him it would be irresponsible to smooth them over.

Notes

1 ὥσπερ γὰρ ὁ ἄνθρωπος συνέστηκεν ἐκ σώματος καὶ ψυχῆς καὶ πνεύματος, τὸν αὐτὸν τρόπον καὶ ἡ οἰκονομηθεῖσα ὑπὸ θεοῦ εἰς ἀνθρώπων σωτηρίαν δοθῆναι γραφή. Origen, *De Principiis* [henceforth *DP*], in *Origenes, Vier Bücher von den Prinzipien* (Herwig Görgemanns and Heinrich Karpp (eds); Texte zur Forschung, 24 Darmstadt: Wissenschaftliche Buchgesellschaft, 1976) IV.2.4; Origen, *On First Principles*, (G. W. Butterworth (trans.); London: SPCK, 1936), 276.

2 For example, Gregory of Nyssa's prologue to his *Commentary on the Song of Songs* defends the use of allegory and mentions Origen by name as an illustrious applier of that method to the Song. Gregory of Nyssa, *In Canticum Canticorum* (H. Langerbeck (ed.); Gregorii Nysseni Opera [henceforth *GNO*] VI; Leiden: Brill, 1986), 3–13, especially 13; Gregory of Nyssa, *Commentary*

on the Song of Songs [henceforth *Comm. Song*] (Casimir McCambley (trans.);
Brookline, Mass.: Hellenic College Press, 1987), 35–40, especially 39. Basil of
Caesarea's *Hexameron* IX ostensibly rejects allegory in the face of criticism:
Basil of Caesarea, *Homélies sur l'Hexaéméron* (Stanislas Giet (trans.); Sources
Chrétiennes, 26 bis; 2nd edn; Paris: Les Editions du Cerf, 1968). English
translation: *Homilies on the Hexameron* (B. Jackson (trans.); Nicene and Post-
Nicene Fathers, series 2, 8; Edinburgh: T & T Clark, 1894). For important
scholars of Origen who were associated with the *ressourcement* movement
and who argued that his theology needed to be reassessed, see Jean Daniélou,
Origène (Paris: La Table Ronde, 1948); Henri De Lubac, *Histoire et Esprit:
l'intelligence de l'Écriture d'après Origène* (Paris: Aubier, 1950); Henri Crouzel,
Origène et la philosophie (Paris: Aubier, 1962).

3 My comments here are necessarily very sketchy reflections on a complex
and much-debated field. For a survey of the questions and an introductory
bibliography, see Charles Griswold, 'Plato on Rhetoric and Poetry' in *Stanford
Encyclopedia of Philosophy* (article first published 22 Dec. 2003, substantive
revision 12 Nov. 2008), http://plato.stanford.edu/entries/plato-rhetoric/,
accessed 8 Sept. 2009.

4 Plato, *Republic* (Paul Shorey (trans.); Loeb Classical Library, 237, 276;
Cambridge, Mass.: Harvard University Press, 1930–5); *Phaedrus* (Harold
North Fowler (trans.); Loeb Classical Library, 36; Cambridge, Mass.: Harvard
University Press, 1930–5).

5 C. J. Rowe argues that one must take seriously Plato's critique of texts through
the mouth of Socrates, while at the same time understanding Plato's works as
a persuasive presentation of philosophical dialectic in action which he intended
to be the next best thing to dialectic itself: *Plato and the Art of Philosophical
Writing* (Cambridge: Cambridge University Press, 2007), introduction and
chapter 1.

6 On the connection of texts with pleasure, see Griswold, 'Plato on Rhetoric and
Poetry', *Stanford Encyclopedia of Philosophy* (2008), http://plato.stanford.
edu/entries/plato-rhetoric/.

7 Aristotle, *Art of Rhetoric* III.14.8 (J. H. Freese (trans.); Loeb Classical Library,
193; (Cambridge, Mass.: Harvard University Press, 1926).

8 Aristotle, *Poetica* 1450a38 – although the plot is elsewhere also compared to a
body! (see 1451a3). *Poetics, Aristotle. On the sublime, Longinus. On style,
Demetrius.* (Stephen Halliwell et al. (trans.); Loeb Classical Library, 199;
Cambridge, Mass.: Harvard University Press, 1995).

9 [Cicero], *Rhetorica ad Herennium*, III.v.19 (Harry Caplan (trans.);
Loeb Classical Library, 403; Cambridge, Mass.: Harvard University Press,
1954).

10 Quintilian, *Institutio Oratoria* (Donald Russell (trans.) Cambridge, Mass.;
London: Harvard University Press, 2001), 2.10.1.

11 τοῦ γὰρ λόγου ψυχὴν δοκοῦντος ἔχειν καὶ σῶμα ἡ μὲν τῶν νοημάτων εὕρησις
δικαίως ἂν ψυχὴ τοῦ λόγου νομίζοιτο, ἡ δὲ ἑρμηνεία σῶμα. Porphyry,
fragment group 4, edited and translated by Malcolm Heath in ibid.,
'Porphyry's rhetoric, texts and translation', *Leeds International Classical
Studies* 1.5 (2002), www.leeds.ac.uk/classics/lics/2002/200205.pdf, accessed
3 Nov. 2010.

12 This problem is a theme in two recent studies of Origen's exegesis. See Karen Jo Torjesen, *Hermeneutical Procedure and Theological Method in Origen's Exegesis* (Berlin; New York: de Gruyter, 1986) and Elizabeth Dively Lauro, *The Soul and Spirit of Scripture within Origen's Exegesis* (Boston: Brill, 2005).

13 See, especially, Daniel Boyarin, *A Radical Jew: Paul and the Politics of Identity* (Berkeley; London: University of California Press, 1994) and a response by David Dawson, *Christian Figural Reading and the Fashioning of Identity* (Berkeley; London: University of California Press, 2002), especially 50, discussed in Morwenna Ludlow, 'Spirit and Letter in Origen and Augustine' in *Spirit and Letter; Letter and Spirit* (Günter Bader and Paul Fiddes (eds); Edinburgh: T & T Clark, forthcoming).

14 Origen, *DP*, IV:2:4 (cf. 1 Cor. 2.6–7 and Heb. 10.1): ἵνα ὁ μὲν ἁπλούστερος οἰκοδομῆται ἀπὸ τῆς οἱονεὶ σαρκὸς τῆς γραφῆς, οὕτως ὀνομαζόντων ἡμῶν τὴν πρόχειρον ἐκδοχήν, ὁ δὲ ἐπὶ ποσὸν ἀναβεβηκὼς ἀπὸ τῆς ὡσπερεὶ ψυχῆς αὐτῆς, ὁ δὲ τέλειος καὶ ὅμοιος τοῖς παρὰ τῷ ἀποστόλῳ λεγομένοις... ἀπὸ τοῦ πνευματικοῦ νόμου, σκιὰν περιέχοντος τῶν μελλόντων ἀγαθῶν.

15 For example, *DP*, IV.3.5.

16 Ibid.

17 *DP*, IV.3.5: διακείμεθα γὰρ ἡμεῖς περὶ πάσης τῆς θείας γραφῆς, ὅτι πᾶσα μὲν ἔχει τὸ πνευματικόν, οὐ πᾶσα δὲ τὸ σωματικόν· πολλαχοῦ γὰρ ἐλέγχεται ἀδύνατον ὂν τὸ σωματικόν.

18 Ibid.

19 *DP*, IV.3.5: ἐπεὶ τοίνυν, ὡς σαφὲς ἔσται τοῖς ἐντυγχάνουσιν, ἀδύνατος μὲν ὁ ὡς πρὸς τὸ ῥητὸν εἱρμός, οὐκ ἀδύνατος δὲ ἀλλὰ καὶ ἀληθὴς ὁ προηγούμενος, ὅλον τὸν νοῦν φιλοτιμητέον καταλαμβάνειν, συνείροντα τὸν περὶ τῶν κατὰ τὴν λέξιν ἀδυνάτων λόγον νοητῶς τοῖς οὐ μόνον οὐκ ἀδυνάτοις ἀλλὰ καὶ ἀληθέσι κατὰ τὴν ἱστορίαν, συναλληγορουμένοις τοῖς ὅσον ἐπὶ τῇ λέξει μὴ γεγενημένοις.

20 Origen, *Commentary on John* [henceforth *Comm. John*] X.85 (C Cécile Blanc (ed. and trans.); Sources Chrétiennes, 120, 157; Paris: Éditions du Cerf, 1964): ὑπὸ τὸν ἀληθῆ πρότερον παιδαγωγούμενοι νόμον παρὰ ἐπιτρόποις καὶ οἰκονόμοις ἕως τὸ ἐκεῖ πλήρωμα τοῦ χρόνου; *Comm. John* X.15 (Allan Menzies (trans.); Ante-Nicene Fathers Series, IX; Edinburgh: T & T Clark, 1897), 389: 'those who have been trained by tutors and governors under the true law'. cf. Gal. 3.24 and 4.2. Note: the division into sections in the Greek edition and English translations is different.

21 Frances Young advises caution on this question throughout her *Biblical Exegesis and the Formation of Christian Culture* (Cambridge: Cambridge University Press, 1997), especially 78–81. At the same time, however, she points out that while Origen's method was once criticized for its lack of attention to the 'historical', what 'historical' meant in relation to the Bible was then very much determined by the dominant historico-critical approach to Biblical criticism. Now that the historico-critical approach is itself coming under criticism, she suggests that the time is ripe for a reassessment of Origen's approach (see, for example, ibid., 3).

22 Origen, *DP*, IV.2.9: 'Consequently, the Word of God has arranged for certain stumbling-blocks, as it were, and hindrances and impossibilities to be inserted

in the midst of the law and the history' (ᾠκονόμησέ τινα οἱονεὶ σκάνδαλα καὶ προσκόμματα καὶ ἀδύνατα διὰ μέσου ἐγκαταταχθῆναι τῷ νόμῳ καὶ τῇ ἱστορίᾳ ὁ τοῦ θεοῦ λόγος); see also, IV.2.5 and IV.3.

23 See, for example, Origen, *DP*, IV.3.4

24 De Lubac, *Histoire et Esprit*. For more recent defenders, see, for example, Mark Edwards, *Origen against Plato* (Aldershot: Ashgate, 2002), chapter 4 and Young, *Biblical Exegesis*, for example, 87.

25 De Lubac, *Histoire et Esprit*, 103–18.

26 This is a point emphasised by Torjesen, *Hermeneutical Procedure*, 52–3.

27 For example, a strain found in Daniélou, *Origène* and (much more critically) R. P. C. Hanson, *Allegory and Event* (Richmond: John Knox Press, 1959).

28 ἐπεὶ οὖν συνέστηκεν ἡ Γραφὴ καὶ αὐτὴ οἱονεὶ ἐκ σώματος μὲν τοῦ βλεπομένου, ψυχῆς δὲ τῆς ἐν αὐτῷ νοουμένης καὶ καταλαμβανομένης καὶ πνεύματος τοῦ κατὰ τὰ ὑποδείγματα καὶ σκιὰν τῶν ἐπουρανίων· φέρε, ἐπικαλεσάμενοι τὸν ποιήσαντα τῇ Γραφῇ σῶμα καὶ ψυχὴν καὶ πνεῦμα, σῶμα μὲν τοῖς πρὸ ἡμῶν, ψυχὴν δὲ ἡμῖν, πνεῦμα δὲ τοῖς ἐν τῷ μέλλοντι αἰῶνι κληρονομήσουσι ζωὴν αἰώνιον καὶ μέλλουσιν ἥκειν ἐπὶ τὰ ἐπουράνια καὶ ἀληθινὰ τοῦ νόμου, ἐρευνήσωμεν οὐ τὸ γράμμα, ἀλλὰ τὴν ψυχὴν ἐπὶ τοῦ παρόντος. See Origen, *Homiliae in Leviticum* [*Homilies on Leviticus*] in *Origenes Werke*, vol. 6 (W. A. Baehrens (ed.); *Die griechischen christlichen Schriftsteller*, 29; Leipzig: Teubner, 1920), 333–4. English translation in Hans Urs von Balthasar (ed.), *Origen, Spirit and Fire – Origen: A Thematic Anthology of his Writings* (Robert Daly (trans.); Edinburgh: T & T Clark, 2001). Cf. Mark Edwards, *Origen against Plato*, 134–5.

29 Origen, *Homilies on Numbers 9.7*, extract 210 in von Balthasar, *Origen, Spirit and Fire*.

30 Origen, *Comm. John* X:107: Ὡς ἑνὶ δὲ σώματι τῇ ἁπάσῃ προσελθετέον γραφῇ, καὶ τὰς ἐν τῇ ἁρμονίᾳ τῆς πάσης συνθέσεως αὐτῆς εὐτονωτάτας καὶ στερροτάτας συνοχὰς οὐ συντριπτέον οὐδὲ διακοπτέον. English translation: *Comm. John* X:13 Ante-Nicene Fathers, IX, 390.

31 Origen, *Comm. John* X:111 (Ante-Nicene Fathers, IX, *Comm. John* X:13). The threefold exegesis is dependent on an assumed typology between the Passover lamb and Christ, supported by 1 Cor. 5.7: 'For our paschal lamb, Christ, has been sacrificed' (NRSV); 'Christ our passover is sacrificed for us' (AV). However, the object of Origen's discussion here is the law concerning keeping the Passover, not the narrative in Exodus.

32 Origen, *Comm. John* X:110 (Ante-Nicene Fathers, IX, *Comm. John* X:13, tr. altered).

33 Young, *Biblical Exegesis and the Formation of Christian Culture*, 79.

34 Origen, *Comm. John* X:110 (Ante-Nicene Fathers, IX, *Comm. John* X:13), quoting Col. 2.16–17: 'Therefore do not let anyone condemn you in matters of food and drink or of observing festivals, new moons, or sabbaths. These are only a shadow of what is to come, but the substance belongs to Christ'. See also, Origen, *DP* IV.2.6: 'It is a spiritual explanation when one is able to show of what kind of "heavenly things" the Jews "after the flesh" served as a copy or a shadow, *and of what* "good things to come" *the law has a* "shadow"' (my emphasis), alluding perhaps both to Col. 2.16–17 and Heb. 10.1 ('Since the law has only a shadow of the good things to come and not the true form of

these realities, it can never, by the same sacrifices that are continually offered year after year, make perfect those who approach'.)

35 See Torjesen, *Hermeneutical Procedure*; Lauro, *The Soul and Spirit of Scripture*.

36 De Lubac, *Histoire et Esprit*, 160–2.

37 Ibid., 163–4.

38 Ibid., 164; cf. Edwards, *Origen against Plato*, 136.

39 Judith Kovacs, 'Servant of Christ and Steward of the Mysteries of God' in *In Dominico Eloquio. In Lordly Eloquence. Essays on Patristic Exegesis in honour of Robert Louis Wilken* (Paul M. Blowers, et al. (eds); Grand Rapids: Eerdmans, 2002), 163, my emphasis.

40 Kovacs, 'Servant of Christ', 163, quoting Origen, *Commentary on 1 Corinthians* [henceforth *Comm in 1 Cor.*], XII.12–17.

41 Kovacs, 'Servant of Christ', 164, citing Origen, *Comm in 1 Cor.* XII.17–31.

42 Aristotle, *Art of Rhetoric* I:3.

43 For a rather different attempt to read Origen through the lens of ancient rhetoric, see Karen Jo Torjesen, 'Influence of rhetoric on Origen's Old Testament homilies' in *Origeniana Sexta. Origène et la Bible / Origen and the Bible. Actes du Colloquium Origenianum Sextum Chantilly, 30 août– 3 septembre 1993* (Gilles Dorival and Alain Le Boulluec, et al. (eds); Bibliotheca Ephemeridum Theologicarum Lovaniensium, 118; Leuven: University Press/Uitgeverij Peeters, 1995) and eadem., 'The rhetoric of the literal sense. Changing strategies of persuasion from Origen to Jerome' in *Origeniana Septima. Origenes in den Auseinandersetzungen des 4. Jahrhunderts.* (W.A. Bienert and U. Kühneweg (eds); Bibliotheca Ephemeridum Theologicarum Lovaniensium, 137; Leuven: University Press/Uitgeverij Peeters, 1999).

44 See *DP* IV:2.5 (the water pots at the wedding at Cana *contain* two or three firkins).

45 [Cicero], *Rhetorica ad Herennium* III.v.19 (Guy Achard (trans.); Paris: Belles Lettres, 1989).

46 I stress 'approximate'. As Matthieu Cassin notes in his essay, 'I do not claim I have reached a neutral and exhaustive reading of Nyssen's texts, nor a reading that would enable us to reach the original book, freed from the layers of successive interpretations. Such a hope would only lead to a new fabric as artificial as the former' (this volume, 111).

47 As noted by Johannes Zachhuber, Chapter 1 of this volume.

48 Origen, *Comm. John* X:111 (Ante-Nicene Fathers, IX, *Comm. John* X:13).

49 On this theme, see Morwenna Ludlow, '"The task of theology is never finished." John Macquarrie and Karl Rahner on the challenges and limits of doing theology' in Robert Morgan (ed.) *In Search of Humanity and Deity* (London: SCM, 2006).

50 This is theme in the critiques of Hanson, *Allegory and Event* and Boyarin, *A Radical Jew*.

51 Boyarin, *A Radical Jew*, 95.

52 Merely for the purposes of what follows, I am not assuming a sharp distinction between 'theological' and 'philosophical' readings of the Fathers, although I acknowledge that there is a difference in other respects (e.g. in confessional commitment, reference to the Bible and tradition, etc.).

53 These two points are major themes running through my *Gregory of Nyssa, Ancient and (Post)modern* (Oxford: Oxford University Press, 2007).

54 Origen, *Comm. John.* X:103–4.

55 Gregory of Nyssa, *Comm. Song* Prologue, GNO VI.12.1–14; my translation; cf. *Commentary on the Song of Songs* (Casimir McCambley (trans.); Brookline: Holy Cross Press, 1987), 39. I have chosen to leave *theoria* untranslated: the term, literally meaning 'viewing', seems to be used by Gregory here in an almost technical sense to mean the kind of interpretation he is defining and other translations (e.g. speculation, contemplation) seem to impose one particular interpretation or another on the word.

56 Matthew 3.9–12; Luke 3.8–9, 17.

57 See Liddell and Scott, *Greek English Lexicon* (Oxford: Clarendon Press, 1996 edn), 924; on the literary sense, see, for example, Longinus, *On the Sublime* 15.5 in *Poetics, Aristotle. On the sublime, Longinus. On style, Demetrius.* (Stephen Halliwell, et al. (trans); Loeb Classical Library, 199; Cambridge, Mass.: Harvard University Press, 1995).

58 Gregory of Nyssa, *Comm. Song*, GNO VI.225.21–228.3, especially 226.10–11.

59 John 6.35, 48. The bread of life theme is also strongly present in Origen's *Commentary on John*.

60 A search of the online *Thesaurus Lingua Graecae* revealed that most uses of the term were Christological, especially in the *Antirrhetikos against Apollinarius*, in which Gregory defends the fully human bodiliness of Christ.

61 GNO VI.3.5, 5.2, 6.16, 13.2. πρόχειρος is a term also used by Origen. When Gregory does use the term σωματικωτέρας, it is in conjunction with σαρκωδεστέρας meaning a *sinful* interpretation of the obvious meaning (GNO VI.6.19). By using πρόχειρος not σωματικός Gregory avoids the *automatic* association of the obvious meaning with fallenness.

62 See note 2.

63 See Ludlow, *Universal Salvation. Eschatology in the Thought of Gregory of Nyssa and Karl Rahner* (Oxford: Oxford University Press, 2000), 64–73.

64 The fluidity of Gregory's exegesis and its fruitfulness for modern theology has already been discussed in this volume by Tamsin Jones in Chapter 4.

65 For example, it resonates with the themes raised by Scot Douglass, in Chapter 5 of this volume.

Afterword:
Conversations about Reading

Framing the Conversation

Backwards, sideways and forward – it has always been the nature of texts to slip and spill beyond their borders. Plato clearly understood this and proclaimed, therefore, that all texts were orphans. Knowing he must abandon his textual children without paternal protection to a dangerous world of readers, he attempted to keep his ideas alive via the employment of a dialogical method, by casting his conclusions within a stylized version of the very process by which he claimed they had dynamically emerged. That is, in calling them orphans, Plato was always saying much more about texts as texts than simply what a shame it was that he could not be present at every reading to guarantee their correctness – although that would certainly have been helpful. But helpful ultimately for what? For Plato, it would have served his larger hope of the ongoing dialogue, the ongoing pursuit of the particular truth in question – to facilitate the next step in the conversation. His dialogues invited dialogue; they were designed to spill forward to unknown readers in such a way that their thoughts, questions and commitments would spill backwards to his text and sideways to other texts, while always spilling forward to future thoughts, decisions and the production of new texts. Plato's strange initial framing of the *Symposium* put all of this in play: Apollodorus retells Glaucon what he had heard from Aristodemus (and recently confirmed by Socrates) about speeches delivered decades ago at Agathon's house – a textually constructed non-linear chain of backwards, sideways and forward that spilled beyond itself the moment Plato orphaned it, in order to begin a new chain outside his authorial control that has continued its multidirectional dissemination through the Renaissance to today. All of which to say, textual spillage, as old as textuality itself, is very complicated. All would agree, though, that at the very least such spillage includes a text's relationship to its sources (backwards); its historical context, language, and mode of production (sideways); and its reception and influence (forward) – understanding as well that none of these gestures, even in themselves, can ever be isolated from each other in the messiness of their practice.

Much of this, of course, can be addressed via the practices of the traditional historico-critical method, but just as Heidegger inserted the problem of time into the question of Being, part of the reason we gathered outside of Boulder for our own symposium was to wrestle with the insertion of time into the question of reading ancient texts. Not unexpectedly, we found that the question became more complicated the closer we examined both it and each other's thoughts about it. In reading ancient texts from our viewpoint in the twenty-first century, we are not only dealing with very old orphans who were abandoned in a world largely inaccessible to us, but also with a multimillennial history of other readers who had entered the multidirectional conversation. In particular, we were always also engaging (explicitly and implicitly) a certain type of reader, the scholar, who had not only entered the conversation, but had also engaged the history of the conversation as well as the conversation about the conversation – and, to the degree they were good at it, had transformed all subsequent conversations. That is, depending upon who those readers were and to what historical dialogues they belonged, the dialogue itself had radically changed. It was these very questions of the ongoing dialogues between text and reader, between text and other texts, between present and past, between present and future, between thinkers and the ideas they were thinking, and between one reading and other readings that animated our gathering in Boulder and organized our thinking around the question of what constitutes a responsible reading. What is it? Who decides? How possible is it to leap back to the text – back to its own backwards and sideways motion? Are we reduced to talking about trade-offs between different approaches to reading? These questions are further complicated by considerations of the goals of reading, current (and past) normative standards of reading and the role of reading texts in the production of new texts. When, as is the case here, the ancient texts in view happen to be written by Church Fathers, then we also have to take into account claims that these texts belong to living discourses, frequently having the status of authoritative sources with some connection to the divine. That is, to appreciate the question of how we are reading, we have to take into account who is reading what and why.

To better get at all of this, it might be helpful to take our own brief step sideways. Over the past decade and a half, there has been a renewed interdisciplinary interest in the reading of early Christian thought by a strange variety of highly influential "secular" philosophers/literary theorists: Jacques Derrida, Slavoj Žižek, Alain Badiou, Giorgio Agamben and Gianni Vattimo, to name a few. As a result, there has been a blurring of the line between the secular and the religious to such an extent that it has become commonplace in national conferences such as the American Comparative Literature Association to speak of the 'return of religion' and having entered a 'post-secular' epoch. At the same time, contemporary theologians and religious scholars conversant in the phenomenological tradition and postmodern thinking have also turned to early Christian documents to enrich, validate, contextualize and illustrate their own thinking (e.g. Jean-Luc Marion, John Caputo, John Milbank). At yet the same time, there has been an intense study of the relevance of contemporary thinkers to theological thinking and the reading of Christian texts as part of the scholarship of modern theology. These larger projects, by both philosophers and theologians, have required re-reading these ancient texts outside the bounds of traditional interpretations established by those hitherto thought to have some proprietary concern in their reading (i.e. Patristics scholars). Or perhaps, to put it another way, it was only a matter of time until the incredibly diverse and rich writings of the Fathers gained the attention of the much wider scholarly community (a community asking questions distinct from doctrinal concerns) *and* only a matter of a little more time until the implications of all of this became part of the 'in-house' discussion of Patristics scholars.

Somewhere close to the centre of this 'in-house' conversation are multiple questions concerning the risks and rewards of applying any method to the study of early Christian texts: how does one negotiate/justify/theorize the chronological gap; what sense of reading must one have to read simultaneously in a chronological register; what competing criteria are in play with different methods; how do the various goals of scholars (the theologian, the philosopher, the historian) impact the larger question; can one employ particular aspects of a method without embracing all the conclusions and presuppositions of that method; and so on. This debate transcends the question of the history of ideas (the chronological appraisal of ideas in terms of their sources, influences and trajectories) to include the more complex question of the two-way interaction between contemporary and ancient thought. That is, how does one theorize the reading of pre-secular texts in the context of the post-secular? Although this is something particular to our twenty-first-century context, such questions would have been equally valid in the midst of the Enlightenment or during the nineteenth- and twentieth-century emergence of the scientific–philological method. That is, every reading involves methods that are historically conditioned and, therefore, subject to an interrogation of not only what is gained and lost in its application, but how the very method (including the scientific) is a product of its own place in time.

The issue of time, though, did not primarily enter our discussion in terms of the gap between reader and text – although this is clearly an important issue – but in respect to a more subtle analysis of the constant impact of time upon modes of thinking and reading. That is, what does it mean that we can never escape reading from within time, from within our own time? How do we negotiate the transition from time-bound words to fluid thoughts? Yet another implication about which we spoke concerned a very subtle aspect of textual spillage: texts always say more than they can say – that is, they engage ideas, questions and themes that cannot be rhetorically or noetically exhausted. So what type of access can a reader have to the surplus or excess of meaning not contained by the text? Or, more to one of the temporal implications of this, what do we do when a future thinker engages a problem of a past thinker and, in light of the concerns of his/her own time, is able to name some of the latent excess of the earlier text? How do we read backwards with that type of reading at our disposal? Is it possible, as seems to happen quite frequently in normal conversations with friends, that Rosenzweig, for example, understands something in what Augustine is saying better than Augustine did?

As already stated in the Forward, the scholars who assembled for our symposium, while all sharing a deep knowledge of early Christian texts, answer these questions in very different ways. Our purpose was to establish an explicit discourse that debated these differences. The following 'conversations' can be read forward, sideways or backwards with the accompanying essays in this volume. The questions being asked are rooted in the essays but concern the larger methodological implications of the essays. The particular questions, although presented in what follows anonymously as a single voice, reflect actual lines of inquiry first pursued in Boulder, as well as a year's worth of subsequent discussions that took place between all of us online and during chance encounters at conferences. Like all complex questions that must be answered publicly in a few minutes, the following answers were never meant to be exhaustive nor as precise as they might have been if developed in ten times the space. What they are meant to be is a slightly more theoretical frame for the methodology that each of the essays has attempted to enact – a series of now orphaned conversations designed, like those of Plato, to provoke reflection and further conversations.

Morwenna Ludlow and Scot Douglass

A Conversation with Tamsin Jones (Harvard University)

Question: In your paper, you mention something of a personal motivation for reading Gregory of Nyssa and Levinas together: 'both . . . have something to teach me about reading' (p. 82). You go on to say that this lesson takes the form of learning that 'the creative paradox in which the polysemic and necessarily interpretive aspect of reading texts, especially normative texts, lies in the very excessiveness of the divine imprint found therein' (p. 82). As you point out, this excessiveness for both Gregory and Levinas has two implications regarding the goals of reading: a hermeneutical one resulting in the endless task of interpretation and an ethical one recognizing the demand upon the reader to respond to the other. What is the relationship between being responsive and being responsible as a reader? Is a non-responsive reading, therefore, regardless of the method, ultimately irresponsible in the sense that a text containing an excessive divine imprint and thus calling for responsiveness can only be understood from within the attempt to respond? Could you say more from a theoretical perspective about the connection between these two aspects of excessiveness?

Tamsin Jones: Responsible reading requires our response; it requires that we respond to texts – biblical or not – of which we cannot fully capture or contain the meaning. So yes, a non-responsive reading – one which doesn't take seriously the fact that we are in fact subjectively responding to a text and thus interpreting it for ourselves – is likewise irresponsible. The implicit polemic of this essay is to provide a defence of ahistorical readings of thinkers such as Gregory of Nyssa and Levinas. Nevertheless, a synchronic and systematic comparison does not mean that one pays no attention to the two historical contexts of the thinkers involved. Lack of attention to what makes the words Levinas uses *different* from those of Gregory risks simply reducing the reading to the ideas of the one reading and comparing the two – making the 'responsive reader' somewhat irresponsible! The 'practice of discipleship', or submitting oneself to the material in the texts (as Virginia Burrus spoke of in our web discussion), provides the necessary corrective. If the text is the 'other' to which one responds, one must first hear what it has to say, one must first listen closely. In other words, *responsive* readings need also be *responsible*.

One of the things I find most intriguing about both Levinas and Gregory of Nyssa is their intuition that the way we read, and what we read, is constitutive of who we are. Thus there is an ethics of reading. What is the relationship between hermeneutical and ethical implications of responsive reading? Any hermeneutic contains or implies a particular ethic – as for instance, the hermeneutic approaches of 'generosity' and of 'suspicion' imply. The hermeneutical ethic of responsiveness, I would argue, assumes an attitude of open wonder or curiosity as well as a stance of hospitality that is eager to encounter previously un-met visitors: an openness to welcome the unexpected, and a curiosity to find out as much as possible about it.

Question: Right after saying you are providing a 'defence of ahistorical readings of thinkers like Gregory and Levinas', you 'nevertheless' speak of the importance of historical sensitivity to the contexts of each thinker. Can you say more about how this relationship works itself out?

Tamsin Jones: Absolutely! It is perhaps easiest to do so with reference to my essay on Levinas and Gregory of Nyssa. That essay approaches a comparison between the two systematically, on such loci as the relation between God and creation, revelation, the understanding of human subjectivity and of the role of desire. Thus far, the essay would seem to proceed ahistorically in an abstract sphere of ideas and concepts. But this is, of course, never the case. To discuss such loci as they present themselves in either thinker, in Gregory and in Levinas, requires a close, careful and historically sensitive reading of both thinkers within their own historical contexts. What are the questions and issues of the day? Who are the contemporaries of either thinker? Who are they reading, engaging and debating? How do those debates inform their thinking and, especially, the expression of their ideas? One needs to know and consider the thought of not only Eunomius, but also Origen (as well as later Origenist controversies), to begin to understand Gregory's approach to the interpretation of Scripture. Similarly, one must be able to locate Levinas in relation to Heidegger and Buber to understand his phenomenology of alterity and its reflection in Levinas's interpretation of Scripture.

The ahistorical comparison is second-order work, in other words; it comes after historical readings. Furthermore, the ahistorical comparison is improved by the quality of historical investigation. But one need be careful here. I am not saying that to be a systematic thinker, one must first be a philologist or historian, as though there was still one fundamental historical test one must pass in order to be given entry to talk about these texts of thinkers. Rather, I am saying that a responsible reading, which would include attention to historical context, inevitably improves the quality of the ahistorical comparison and guards against the danger of the comparison, doing no more than reflecting the thoughts and ideas of the 'comparer'.

How might one decide whether the ahistorical comparison relies on a historical-enough foundation? That simply comes down to a debate. If someone is allergic to such an ahistorical comparison as that between Gregory and Levinas, then a debate could be had over the readings of each individual being compared. In this case, a phenomenologist might challenge me on my reading of Levinas, or a historian or philologist might query a translation of a term on Gregory. In such a case, both

I and my challenger could sit down and read the text or author together, to decide whether my reading is fair and responsible within its own context and prior to comparison. This would be a textual debate. As someone interested in a systematic or philosophical approach to comparative readings, I can only welcome such debates as opportunities to improve the sharpness and full complexity of the comparison. But the possibility and benefit of debating at this level does not declare judgement upon the appropriateness and constructive value of ahistorical comparison per se, just upon the relative strength or weakness of particular comparisons.

Finally, even if, as I said earlier, the implicit polemic of this essay is to provide a defence of ahistorical readings of thinkers such as Gregory of Nyssa and Levinas, the argument *proceeds* from a responsible reading of either author. For instance, I argue that reading Gregory of Nyssa carefully and historically, one finds within Gregory justification for the necessity of *interpreting* his words and personally *responding* to them. I am not (here) making the further claim that *all* reading is interpretative, or that there is no one single meaning to a text. Rather, I am making the smaller claim that Gregory himself advocates for a kind of reading that 'contemporizes' and translates the text into one's own context. Furthermore, from Gregory one learns that the more authority a text or collection of texts has, the more they *cannot* be reduced to a single meaning or interpretation, or, to put it another way, ought not be 'logocentric'.

Question: The second motivation you claim for reading Levinas and Gregory together is an apologetic one: 'a desire to rescue Gregory as at least one example from the Christian tradition that ought not be included within this overly broad critique' [that Christian exegesis is a violent, logocentric mastery of truth that has attempted to silence the polysemic hermeneutic of Jewish Midrashic exegesis]. This motivation seems, on the surface, to be more traditionally responsible, a setting straight of an inaccurate application to Gregory of a generally true scholarly critique of Christian logocentrism. At the same time, this rescue performs a deeper critique of logocentrism itself and the concept of the nature of revelation. If this is the case, what general theory of responsible reading is implied for any and all texts that contain an excessive divine imprint? Put in another way, does your normative claim that Gregory and Levinas have something to teach you about reading result in a larger and apologetic normative claim about the nature of reading (revelation) in general?

Tamsin Jones: The apologetic aim to 'rescue' Gregory from the overly broad application of a critique of Christian logocentric readings of Scripture does *not* challenge the basic parameters of the critique of logocentrism. On one level it is an attempt to be traditionally respons-ible by setting straight an inaccurate inclusion of Gregory within a critique of Christian logocentrism. And simply on this level, Gregory is surely not the only Christian writer/reader deserving of rescue – one thinks of Origen at the very least. However, I am not challenging the need for such a critique. In fact, the way I read Gregory and Levinas involves making a normative claim about how one ought to read authoritative texts in general (whether authoritative because 'word of God' or authoritative because part of, and representative of, a tradition/discourse in which one places oneself), namely, with a *lecture infinie*.[1]

There is a lot at stake in intervening in this debate on a number of levels. Most basically the accusation of a logocentric tendency of Christian readers of Scripture by Jewish readers of Scripture serves as a valuable and necessary corrective. It guards against a too-simple and too-univocal Christian identification with the signification of all the scriptural texts and Christ – as the founding 'Logos'. Thus it is a necessary intervention into a history of hermeneutical violence.

However, on another level, it is important to guard against an unhelpful binary which enables the dismissal of the writings of the early Christians as simply 'logocentric'. These texts, especially in the case of one like Gregory, cannot be reduced to simplistic equivocations of all words with the 'Word'. They are more complex, and more *diverse*, than such a binary presupposes.

A Conversation with Matthieu Cassin (Sorbonne University)

Question: Are you saying that previous conceptions of what has constituted a 'historical' reading have been too narrow? Or are you trying to criticize the very notion of a 'historical' reading?

Matthieu Cassin: I surely say here that some previous conceptions of 'historical reading' are too narrow if they are only concerned with reconstructing the *historical* and *theological* context of a book – perhaps even editing the best text we can now reconstruct – without also taking great care to be attentive to the literary form of the writing. This is true in so far as the text is seen mainly as a theological work whose interest to the modern reader is as a testimony to past theology.

Because the theological writings from the Patristic era have not been written for the most part in the same scientific way as modern theological writings, a reading that does not take into account the specific literary form and tools of such works seems too narrow. I'm trying here to widen reading from inside *historical reading* by adding a literary perspective that is not a simple gimmick in order to criticize other readings, but rather the introduction of a real twist to our reading perspective. That is, because the very nature of literature is to be not enclosed in the past but to go through subsequent eras, such a literary reading should open up new vistas, even theological.

Question: Is a literary reading, therefore, of a text like the *Contra Eunomium* III *necessary* or just *better* than the usual historical reading? In many ways, your analysis is very concerned with the 'how' of Gregory's theological production – bringing a more historical light on his choice of allusions, intertwining of genres, etc. What do you think are the implications for moving from a more sophisticated rhetorical understanding of *how* to a more sophisticated understanding of *what* he is saying? In particular, does your distinction between the literary and the theological aspects of Gregory's writing risk losing the content of what Gregory is saying? Are the literary aspects content neutral?

Matthieu Cassin: I think that a literary reading of *Contra Eunomium* III – and of many other Patristic writings – is necessary because of the very nature of the text: literature (to say it briefly) is part of the refutation *and* part of the theological elaboration, as M. Ludlow has also shown.[2] The literary aspects are not neutral and they have direct influence on the *what*, on the theological elaboration. To understand this influence, therefore, an investigation of the *how* is needed. To take two brief examples, Gregory of Nyssa's images are of vivid concern both for understanding the refutation of his adversaries and for understanding his own theological investigations. To explain his exegetical method about Pr 8, 22 (*CE* III.1), Gregory uses the image of the peacock's tail. At first look, this image is just an illustration of his theoretical explanation about the right way to read Scripture. But a second look should show that this image is richer than the theory: the beauty of the upper side of the tail mirrors the beauty of Scripture *when it is properly read* and the aesthetic pleasure that one experiences when looking at the upper side of the tail mirrors the spiritual pleasure of the true reader of Scripture, etc. Another example: a closer look at the literary structure of the *Contra Eunomium* will help [one] to understand how Gregory builds up his refutation of Eunomius's text. Such an investigation allows us to see which part of Nyssen's books is directly addressed against Eunomius, which is turned against other adversaries, which is not directly concerned with refutation.

A literary investigation, therefore, allows the reader to discover some elements that are not immediately visible, but that are of real importance not only to understand a Patristic text, but also to interpret it in a modern context.

Question: If the context or the paratext is important, how do we know where to stop? (How much context do we need to read in order for our reading to be 'responsible'? Or to be a 'good' reading?)

Matthieu Cassin: This is a difficult question: I should say that we need as much context as we may be able to find and how deep our reading might go is, in fact, dependent upon this. 'No context' or 'minimal context' is not enough. Truly though, to unfold the whole context for a reasonably long text – historical, theological, literary context and so on – a whole life would not be enough. So, from a practical point of view, one should not go too deep and should proportion his investigation to his duty or goals. But a reading that just takes a Patristic work at face value and pretends to read it with fresh eyes and modern glasses would at least miss some important aspects of the text, and at worst introduce some major misinterpretations. Due to the historical, cultural and linguistic distance, a responsible reading of a Patristic text requires some investigations around the text.

Question: Clearly, many people think that the doctrinal aspects of the CE are translatable into the present (they read the CE as evidence for cogent arguments about the nature of God, of the limits of human language, etc.) But what about the reception of the other aspect of the CE: its invective? Can modern-day readers read this with pleasure? Two issues are raised here: (1) Has the cultural context which makes the text *pleasurable* been lost? (2) Do we now have ethical scruples about reading such invective with pleasure – especially if, for example, Gregory accuses Eunomius of being 'Jewish'?

Matthieu Cassin: I think that the cultural context that makes the text pleasurable has been partially lost. As a result, the standard modern reader, without any historical explanation, is not able to place the text back in its literary frame, making a more accessible process that makes it more enjoyable like we experience in the reading of a modern literary text. The intertextual frame of the ancient text – its simultaneous process of integration and distance from literary genre and conventions, and so on – is no longer self-evident to a modern reader. But a scholarly reading can reconstruct at least part of this background, and give it back to the 'simple' reader. A good explanation wouldn't place the modern reader in exactly the same reading posture as a fourth-century reader, of course, but may help him to find some pleasure in Nyssen's text – not only pleasure caused by an understanding of the non-evident meaning, but also literary pleasure in the same way that an informed reader discovers in a medieval novel or of Rabelais that would, in large part, be missed by the uninformed reader. To expand a bit upon the example of Rabelais, if you do not know the literary conventions that preceded him and that he indirectly criticized, if you do not understand the allusions and ironical references, you will miss a great part of the pleasure a sixteenth-century reader would experience while reading Rabelais's novels. In the same way, if a reader does not know the literary conventions and references Gregory was playing with in his refutation of Eunomius, a good part of the potential literary pleasure of reading him will be lost.

A non-contextualized reading of Nyssen's invectives against Eunomius would produce ethical concerns, especially when Gregory accuses him of being Jewish, but I think that a contextualized reading should not, or at least should induce less scruples, because of the distance such a reading establishes. We may not ask fourth-century writers – even Christian writers – to behave in the same way or according to the same contextual standards as present writers, Christians or not. When Gregory is accusing Eunomius of being Jewish, he does not talk of any racial inferiority, but only of a religious attitude as the New Testament's authors do when they speak collectively of 'the Jews' or 'the Pharisees' or 'the priests'. 'Jew, here, is not a racial indication, but a spiritual one, as Nyssen himself reminded the reader: a 'Jew' is not the person from Judea or even someone taking part at the cult in Nyssa's synagogue (if there were ever to be a synagogue in Nyssa), but the man who read the Bible like the Jews in the New Testament. So, again, a non-contextualized reading of Gregory's invectives is clearly misleading if we were to understand such invectives as we should read them in a twentieth-century anti-Semitic (Semite, not Jew . . .) text. If we do so, we miss the purpose of Gregory. As a result, our ethical concerns will have arisen from our own preconceptions, not from the text itself. If we want to properly understand these attacks, we must take into account the meaning they had in the context in which they have been written.

Question: A reading which focuses on the dogma can either be historical or theological-philosophical: that is, it can 'remain' in the past, or seek to carry over something from the past into the future. But to what extent can a literary reading transcend the past?

Matthieu Cassin: Literature, unlike dogma, is not strongly attached to an era, because concepts are not its central topic. Literature may become distant and strange, but this gap can be bridged (at least partially) with investigation. Literature does not need to be carried over from the past to the future because literature (I do not say cultural references of a particular book) isn't part of the past but rather the present. It is the very nature of Literature to be transhistorical: even if one were not to read Euripides' plays exactly in the same way in the twentieth century as when they had been written, they still do not need to be transposed to the present time. That is, you should prefer a production that makes Oedipus an apparent orphan from the Chechen war rather than a traditional production that reconstructs ancient Greece, while not changing anything to the text itself. You may need some linguistic help to understand Rabelais's French, but not any rewriting, not any conceptual translation and adaptation. So literature needs scholarship insofar as the past is distant from the present – and past culture from present culture – but needs no actualization except via reading. When dealing with dogma, on the contrary, we need a conceptual transposition and adaptation from a past intellectual context to the present one. If you just repeat ancient formulations, you should be true to your faith, but would not be able to explain it to your contemporaries, nor discuss it with anyone else. Literature is not inserted in the history of humanity in the same way: it needs contextualization, not adaptation.

A Conversation with Johannes Zachhuber *(Trinity College, Oxford University)*

Question: In your genealogical tracing of Jean Luc Marion's reading of Dionysius back to Schelling via Heidegger and Balthasar, you identify something of a fork in the reception history of Dionysius and apophaticism: the positive Schelling-Heidegger trajectory (that 'negation ultimately produces true positivity', p. 17) and the negative Kant-Nietzsche-early-Barth-Levinas-Derrida arc. This backward tracing, in theory, would eventually return to Dionysius and beyond to his antecedents, including numerous branches like the one you developed that represent key interpretive decisions that determined the canonical direction of reading Dionysius. Could you speak more broadly to the following statements/questions. To what degree does Marion's positive reading represent, therefore, something of a recovery of one option of thought 'actually' potential in Dionysius but suppressed by the dominance of one branch over another in its reception history?

Johannes Zachhuber: In my view, Marion represents something of a halfway house between these two trajectories. This makes him liable to being criticized from both sides, but it is also what makes him in a way original and interesting. Those scholars who feel strongly about the 'positive' interpretation (e.g. Denys Turner) would say he gives in too much to the 'negative' side. I think that historically and exegetically they have a point, but that Marion still makes a valuable point to the extent that he insists on an element, which I believe is vital for the Judeo-Christian tradition. In this sense I agree that he 'uncovers' a potential in Dionysius, which is perhaps not even fully actualized in his (i.e. Dionysius's) own writing.

There is a broader issue involved as well. This is the question of how far dominant readings of historical texts determine our own readings of them, and how far they ought to dominate them. Historical-critical scholarship has been driven by an effective denial of the latter; today it is sometimes accused of this as well as of naivety with regard to the former. I think it is right to acknowledge our debt to traditional readings; no one today who reads the writings of Pseudo-Dionysius is unaffected by the history of his interpretations. However, this acknowledgement must be coupled with a willingness to detect novel elements in those texts, including such elements that pose a serious challenge to traditionally accepted interpretations. I find it therefore important that reception history has this dual emphasis of understanding our own position as the result of past developments on the one hand, while also allowing genuinely new departures to happen.

Question: Although reception history obviously emerges in a forward chronological movement, its study moves both forward and backwards – perhaps primarily backwards. Does the identification of these clear moments of choice not only open the productive possibility of the movement of reading backwards, but necessitate an always already both/and reading forward and backwards?

Johannes Zachhuber: There are several issues here. As I said before, I very much consider it a specific strength of reception history that it combines the 'determinist' perspective of historicism, which sees us merely as products of our past, and the 'productive' perspective of postmodernism. It thus moves beyond both of those. When we understand ourselves as the results of past events, we do so as beings seeking to shape the world we inhabit. At the same time, whichever 'projects' we undertake in forming our future, we cannot but see them as an extension of our histories.

The other issue is methodological. First of all, we ought to acknowledge that all our reading moves primarily 'backwards'; the texts we interact with are remnants and traces of past writing. As such they are separated by some distance from us individually but also more generally from the world we inhabit. The ineluctable result of historicism is this sense of alienation between reader and text, which Schleiermacher classically expressed by saying that misunderstanding someone else's text should be seen as the default result of reading. And yet, while recognizing the full extent of this alienation, we must also seek to comprehend how we as readers are part of an ongoing story which was begun with the first writing of that text. Paradoxically, this latter insight does not only serve to mitigate our sense of separation; methodologically it may even sharpen it. Realizing how strongly we are still entangled in traditional patterns of reading and understanding a text may actually increase our critical edge towards those exegetical and hermeneutical premises we initially took for granted. However, as it becomes ever more apparent that there is a real possibility in our culture of simply losing much of what has always been cherished in our heritage, it is crucial to acknowledge to ourselves and to others how much the 'forward element', the continuity between the text and ourselves, informs, motivates and underlies any serious attempt at 'backwards' reading. Ultimately, backwards and forward reading are not two separate methods that can be applied subsequently, but they should mutually enforce one another.

Question: In other words, does the possibility of tracing backwards the Dionysian tree of reception history not end up at some Dionysian root?

Johannes Zachhuber: Radical versions of reception history would deny that a text exists apart from its 'being received' by its readers. Perhaps, with my own commitment to historical scholarship, I would not go that far, but I certainly do not think that there is an 'objectifiable' root that could be uncovered once and for all with the help of any kind of method. That said, I would not deny that somehow any serious exegetical 'archaeology' leads us back to some origin. However, it is very difficult to understand how the relationship between this origin and subsequent developments can be conceptualized. Perhaps one way might be to appropriate the organic metaphor of the seed, which in antiquity was so popular (and has more recently been tried by Newman in his exposition of the history of doctrine). The point in the traditional use of this metaphor (and I suspect in Newman this is still the case) was that the seed turns into the full plant merely by actualizing its potential. However, we now know just how crucial the impact of all sorts of extraneous factors is on this biological development and how contingent this makes it. Perhaps the reception of an ancient text can be compared to the growth of a seed in the latter sense, that is by allowing that it is determined by more than its internal potential (though this is not irrelevant), and that new circumstances could always give this development a new and unexpected turn. 'Tracing back the Dionysian tree', as you put it, would indeed lead us back to some 'root', but we must resist the temptation of seeing this as the reconstruction of a pre-determined process, which subsequently permits us to 'know' what the text or indeed its author really 'wanted' to say.

Question: In the end, are you mapping out a method (the close reading of reception history) for a responsible a/chronological engagement of ancient texts?

Johannes Zachhuber: This would be an overly ambitious claim to make about such a limited exercise as I have offered here. However, it would be legitimate to say that my engagement with Marion and Dionysius rests on methodological and hermeneutical considerations that could and, in my view, should be applied more generally. Or perhaps I ought to say, they should be tried out – given so little work of this kind exists, it might be more honest to call for some exploratory work, which would help us see clearer about potential gains and pitfalls. Dionysius would perhaps be an ideal candidate for such a pilot given the almost unique way he has informed theological and philosophical reflection in a variety of areas for so long. At the same time, his readings have varied greatly between East and West, but even just within his Western reception they have been far from uniform. An added benefit might even be the notorious elusiveness of the original author of the corpus – in a sense we never have Dionysius without his readers! Some great work in this area already exists, but it would surely be fascinating to apply the backwards-and-forward strategy systematically to at least some of his many readers through the centuries.

Question: It seems that part of what goes hand-in-hand with reception history is the continual development of certain aspects of thought as a function of historical contingencies, concerns and questions. This is perhaps most clear in the history of doctrine and the development, for example, of Nicene Trinitarianism and Chalcedonian Christology. In these theological cases, there is a clear reading backwards (both then and now) through the Fathers to the source texts of Scripture and the discovery there the very inspiration for this future development. In what sense does this also function theologically/philosophically? That is, is it possible that the historical contingencies that produced the Schelling-Heidegger-Balthasar trajectory, for example, allow for a certain development in doing fundamental thinking about apophaticism that re-opens certain latent texts in Dionysius whose implications remained undeveloped due to different historical pressures? Perhaps put more provocatively, does any attempt to deny this constant bidirectional reading process (Barth's claim, for example, that his reading of Paul was atemporal and independent of the impact of the Great War) or the doing of a purely historical reading result in the naïve disavowal of doing the same thing?

Johannes Zachhuber: I think the latter is definitely the case. In a sense then all 'readings' are both products and parts of reception history in the sense I wish to give to it. The difference is whether this is acknowledged or not. The further question then is whether (or how) the fact that this becomes itself reflective (i.e. that I see my own 'reading' in this way) influences such a reading. If one wished to be provocative with regard to my own argument in my chapter, one could say that while it is true that Barth was (in a sense) naïve about his reading, this spared him a kind of self-consciousness that might otherwise have prevented him from writing the very book he wrote without necessarily enabling him to write a better one. This isn't just a hypothetical question. An interesting character, a generation above Barth and Heidegger, was Wilhelm Dilthey who, both as an intellectual historian and a philosopher, personified the perfectly scrupulous scholar who (therefore?) in spite of his immense learning and considerable ingenuity left behind a vast torso of unfinished works.

A Conversation with David Newheiser (University of Chicago)

Question: One of the interesting things about your paper is that you reverse the way the problem of time to interpretation is normally discussed: instead of talking about the backwards impossible gap between the modern reader and the ancient author/text (which, of course, you also acknowledge), you turn to both Dionysius and Derrida to explore the forward impossible gap between any historical moment and the future eschaton, the unknowable and unforeseeable future event. That is, the two 'present' moments of Dionysius and his modern reader are more homogenous than either of these moments of presence and the unattainable future event (an event within which, if it ever were to come, an unimaginable responsible reading would take place). In doing so, you are critical of three modern readers, each with something of an unidentified theological motive (disavowal, appropriation, recuperation), who are able to arrive at three different definitive readings of Dionysius because they do not attend to the alterity of discontinuance future time. As a result, it seems that Dionysius and Derrida share a great structural affinity that somehow precedes any specific theological orientation to their disparate content and motivations. Could you say more about how responsible reading must be rooted in (or at least pay attention to) these deeper structures of the alterity of time? Part of what is at play here is the amazing atheistic claim of Derrida that eschatology haunts all discourse.

David Newheiser: This question highlights a link between the two parts of my argument that my paper leaves largely implicit. I do think the gap between the reader and the text is momentously important; in fact, my treatment of modern readings of Dionysius is meant to suggest that this gap cannot be crossed by hypotheses concerning the author's context, for in each of the cases I discuss the appeal to history serves to sanctify the interpreter's own prejudices. Derrida's reading is valuable in its own right because his admission that there are 'a number of voices' at play in Dionysius's texts precludes such collapse between the text's past and the interpreter's present; it finds further support in the fact that, where some theologically motivated interpreters neglect Dionysius's critique of present practice in light of the unforeseeable future, Derrida's account allows the tension to stand. My first point, then, is that Derrida reads Dionysius well, but a second point follows from my reading of the two authors together: the gap between present and future casts light on the gap between present and past, for an irreducible distance pertains in both cases.

To answer your question directly, my argument is meant to suggest that responsibility in reading is never present (and rather is always to come) precisely because the meaning of the text is never present (and rather is irreducibly past). The upshot of this eschatological approach is that responsible reading is a task to be continually renewed, and this refusal of complacent completion opens the joy of repeated re-reading in the realization that there is always more to be found. Responsible reading should be rooted in the alterity of time by recognizing that it is not yet responsible and by refusing to take root, which is to say, the distance of past and future keeps our present in constant motion, straining towards something better. To speak less abstractly, I take this to exclude the assertion that the reconstruction of a text's context makes its meaning transparently available, for hypotheses concerning history cannot make the past present, and I surmise from this that reading may be oriented primarily by an ethic of attention. In fact, it is such an ethic that my discussion of the implicit affinities between Derrida and Dionysius is meant to model.

This is not to say that the content and motivation of their respective texts is irrelevant to my reading (which your question might imply); rather, my point is that texts limit and guide the practice of reading in their own right, prior to historical speculation. Do I then rely upon deeper structures that somehow precede the particularities of time? I'm fascinated and perplexed by the suggestion and unsure how to answer, but it occurs to me that the claim to have identified a structure that is not historically situated may be legitimate as long as the identification itself is acknowledged to be conditioned by time. (Thus, although Derrida and Dionysius do suggest that the alterity of time possesses a priority such that it forms the condition of responsibility and reflection, both of them could acknowledge that this judgement might itself be mistaken.) In fact, this latter historicity exemplifies the gap between past and present that I suggest is always in play, even in the reading of 'contemporary' texts: since interpretation always follows what it interprets in time, quantitative differences in the distance of time do nothing to alter the gulf that divides every text from every interpreter.

Question: A quick follow-up question to the last part of your answer. In talking about reading Dionysius, whether by Derrida or modern theologians, the historical gap involved is quite huge. Your last sentence takes this structure of the irreducible past-future gap from the macro-gap to the micro-gap, to the irretrievable present of the very moment of writing, itself. That is, every act of writing, given that the resultant text is by definition for a future reader (even if this gap is only a week) and that future reader's future acts, enacts the same tension. Can you speak more generally of the significance of this?

David Newheiser: I mean to suggest that the 'particular difficulty' with which my paper begins applies in all cases – it is simply more starkly apparent in the case of ancient texts (and with Dionysius in particular). Because every text occupies the past in relation to every reader, there is no such thing as a contemporaneous reading; even the act of reading one's own writing, even something one wrote just minutes ago, confronts one with an author who is no longer present. Although I may reconstruct what I was thinking with more or less certainty, I cannot determine how my own writing must be read, for I cannot be certain that my reconstruction is correct, not least because one is never completely transparent to oneself, not even in the moment of writing. Because reading one's recent self might seem like the easiest task, I take it that the point applies *a fortiori* in all cases.

This illustrates that the difficulty in reading ancient texts is not merely quantitative, as if a text that is 50 years old were more accessible than one that is 1,450 years older. Of course, the difference in distance matters to a reading that aims at the greatest possible understanding of the author's context; however, my point in this paper is that, because the distance is (from another perspective) absolute in every case, a historical reading cannot determine the terms of other possible readings. Because the gap between the past and the present is never bridged, not even in part, this ethic of attention need not be subordinated to questionable historical reconstructions. All of which is to say, the upshot of my attempt to generalize the gap between past and present is that responsibility is ever endless, even in a reading under apparently optimal conditions.

Question: Which do you think is more accessible: the not-yet-future or the distant past? Is the gap to the past simply structurally impossible, never bridgeable, whereas the gap to the future is also unbridgeable, but in practice is productive in the present to seek?

David Newheiser: This question is intriguing. I'll continue to reflect upon it, but I'm inclined to insist on an extensive parallel between past and future. Neither can be said to be more accessible than the other, for both are inaccessible in an absolute sense; crucially, because the futurity I have in mind will not simply be present later on (as if it lay on a continuous timeline), it is no easier to reach the future than it is to recover the past. Although it remains necessary to distinguish the future and the past, I'm not sure at this point how best to do it.

I wonder, for instance, whether the past requires a category analogous to the future's 'to come'. Contra your suggestion, I think it may be productive to seek both the past and the future, but I'm not sure how to articulate arrival in the case of the past. I think the past and future share the characteristic of impending within and alongside the present, albeit in a way that they cannot be grasped or identified, but there is nonetheless an important difference between them. Perhaps there is a story to be told about the obscure heritage of tradition, which runs within our present without our being able to distinguish what is old from what is innovation, and about the mysterious potentialities in the midst of which we live without understanding them. But perhaps the future here is simply a figure for heterogeneity, in which case one could conclude that the past has the character of futurity, of being in a certain sense still 'to come'. (In fact, I think both stories should be told, nor need they be mutually exclusive.)

This begins to answer the question about backwards reaching, which is very suggestive. Problematically, our straining towards the future always operates on the basis of some present expectation of the shape of responsibility, democracy, hospitality, etc. (ideals that are, for Derrida, all constitutively 'to come'). Similarly, the very language of Dionysius's 'negative theology' is formed by the 'scripture and hierarchical traditions' that represent, for him, our understanding 'in the best way we can', but on his own terms neither these materials for reflection nor his interpretation of them be ultimate. So, although we inevitably seek responsibility, etc. from some 'where', we ought to realize that that 'where' may itself be revised, for we are not yet 'there'.

In the terms of your question, I wouldn't say that backwards reaching is necessary to responsibly reach forward; instead, I think that reaching backwards may be a form of reaching forward, for the past has the character of being to come. But I would also say that a sort of reaching backwards can help illuminate the 'where' where we are by non-exhaustively clarifying the ambiguous heritage that continues to shape us. (With Foucault, I think that a sort of archaeology may in fact relativize our 'where' by showing the way in which it is contingent, though I think historical dependence is but one form of this contingency.) But perhaps the two stories intersect here insofar as reaching backwards may propel us onward through unprecedented possibilities that were somehow already among us.

Question: In your opening paragraph you use the phrase 'Derrida's Dionysius' (uttered by Derrida's critics). To what degree do you think that this locution is hidden in every scholarly utterance? That is, when even a historically grounded exegete says something like 'What Origen means here', what they are really saying is 'My Origen means here . . .' In other words, does John Jones's desire to 'interpret a text "in its own right"' (which you quote in footnote 5) ultimately take the word 'interpret' in a very unsophisticated way? Put slightly differently (and perhaps asking a different question), it seems that one of your implicit claims about responsible reading ends up being very traditional: Derrida as the unbiased, theologically indifferent, rightly passing as an atheist reader is able to read the theological text of Dionysius more cleanly because he lacks the theologically motivated bias of the theologians you cite? Derrida, of course, is attracted to Dionysius because of the structural similarities they share that both he and his critics saw. You say in your introduction that attending to the tension created by the alterity of the discontinuance future can speak to the posited alterity between historical-critical and theoretical-constructive readings. Can you expand on what your thinking, in light of any or all of these comments/questions, suggests about a more general theory of responsible reading?

David Newheiser: It is because I think every reading operates within this spacing that I attend to the ways in which *both* Derrida and Dionysius have been badly read. If thinking is always historically conditioned and if the present is constantly slipping into an unattainable past, then every reading can speak only of 'my Derrida', 'my Dionysius', etc. There is thus a sense in which John Jones's assertion that texts should be interpreted in their own right is right, and there is a sense in which it is wrong. On the one hand, I have argued for the legitimacy of reading a text 'in its own right', without reference to hypotheses concerning the author's context and intentions; on the other hand, my argument entails that even the most attentive reading involves a mediation between past and present such that we have no access to the text 'in its own right', unaccompanied by the residue of the present. Insofar as Jones's statement neglects the necessary imperfection of such mediation, I do think his claims about interpretation call for complication.

As your comments suggest, my criticism of attempts made to assimilate Derrida and Dionysius to an alien scheme aims to defend the first sort of reading 'in its own right' against the second. A reading that claims to access the denuded text constrains readings that attend to the complex dynamics at work in the text itself, and in fact the supposed transparency of historical-critical interpretation simply provides cover for the interpreter's own prejudice. Derrida's virtue as an interpreter is neither that he is unbiased nor that he lacks theological motivations; in fact, his initial reservations concerning 'negative theology' display a problematic (and theological) bias that does obscure his vision. Instead, Derrida is a good reader because his recognition that his reading is limited allows his reading to develop significantly between 1964 and 1992 – namely, by attending more carefully to the texts in question – and it is this commitment to corrigible attention that I think lies at the heart of our responsibility as readers.

My claim about responsibility in this paper is actually quite limited: responsibility is a demand that, because it is endless, requires readers to remain open to continual revision. However, the temporal dynamics I describe furthermore imply that historical critical and theoretical constructive readings, rather than representing competitive alternatives, are equally at play in each other. For one thing, since reading always involves the projection of the present upon the past, there is a constructive and theoretical dimension to every interpretation, and even the most circumspect scholarship deploys the texts it treats in the service of its own goals. For another thing, since even a reading that expressly serves a constructive theoretical project is conditioned by history, it cannot be totally unmoored from historical critical concerns. I emphasize the former point in the paper because the latter point is often taken to constrain constructive appropriations, but I think it is important to see these two styles of interpretation as inseparable. In fact, although I think interpretations may be legitimate which take minimal or maximal account of the results of philology, archaeology, etc., in each case responsibility is best evaluated in relation to how well the reading in question attends to the text itself, and I believe such attention is best preserved when it is predicated upon its inevitable imperfection.

Question: In your paper and your answers here, you keep returning to words related to 'attending' (your last sentence uses both 'attends to' and 'attention' and you speak above of an 'ethics of attention'). Can you expand on what you mean by this word and, therefore, what it means to 'attend well to the text'?

David Newheiser: The short answer is 'no'. Because I have in mind a practice rather than a method, it would be inappropriate to fill out its content. Attention includes various ways of being with the text, reading the text, reflecting with it, living with it, and returning. Attention is improvised, and so its course cannot be plotted beforehand – it requires the possibility of surprise, after all. In this paper, then, 'attention' serves as the placeholder for an improvised practice that has for its condition the refusal of totalizing interpretation in the conviction that it is always possible to attend more closely.[3]

Of course, in particular cases it is possible to distinguish between more and less attentive readings, but such questions operate on a different level than that of my argument here. Although it is important to be as attentive as one can, one's understanding of that in which attention consists remains subject to revision insofar as attention as such is never achieved. A longer answer, then: 'I could, but I won't – because to do so might distract from my point in this paper'.

A Conversation with Virginia Burrus (Drew University)

Question: Your paper explores the complex temporality of reading by placing your own reading of Augustine in the middle of complex reading projects by Rosenzweig and Wolfson – in which Augustine figures prominently as both a witness and a thinker. In doing so, one of the claims you make is that Rosenzweig's Star of Redemption is perhaps unsurpassed as 'an elusive and creative interpretation of Augustine's theory of time and eternity' (p. 61). As you point out, Rosenzweig initially conceived his project "in the form of a biblical commentary" but then wrote "under erasure of the text," editing out his sources in the hope of renewing his sources (including Augustine) as 'living speech'. As you conclude: "Interpretation thus becomes a dialogical (re)voicing of what is latent in writing's silent repose: 'What was mute becomes audible, the secret manifest, what was closed opens up, that which as thought had been complete inverts as word into a new beginning . . .'" (*SR*, 119). Foundational to the dialogue your paper performs, it seems, is your situating yourself, Augustine, Rosenzweig and Wolfson as thinkers thinking with each other. Could you speak more broadly about the engagement of texts as 'living speech'?

Virginia Burrus: Engaging the writings of the "church fathers" on their own terms is an impossible goal, as David Newheiser, among others in this volume, has emphasized. Its impossibility renders it no less alluring for the historical theologian, however. . . . Paradoxically, perhaps, I feel I can approach closest to this goal by intensifying the performative character of interpretation – by giving body to a reading that is always taking place *in the moment*. A performative reading brings out the rhetoricity, the materiality of the patristic texts, and I agree with Matthieu Cassin that taking their literary character seriously is crucial and indispensible – and all too often neglected by theologians, philosophers, and historians alike. (Burcht Pranger's recent work on Augustine is a brilliant exception.) However, the literary medium and the doctrinal message are not separable, it seems to me: such a reading also revives moribund doctrine, restoring its vigor as on-going thinking. Here is where Rosenzweig's notion of *Sprachdenken*, or speech-thought, naming the dialogical aspect of language and thought, seems very powerfully apt. (It is obviously resonant too with the Platonic tradition of dialogism invoked by Morwenna Ludlow and Scot Douglass in their remarks in 'Framing the Conversation.') The point is not to contrast writing and speaking – on the contrary. Rather, from this perspective, interpretation becomes a revoicing of a written text, and as such an act of both memory and anticipation, repetition and innovation, response and call. The *moment* of reading is thus complex, fractured, and ultimately elusive. It speaks with many tongues. If I give the text voice, I also steal its voice, and I am never reading only one text at once, nor am I ever the only one reading the text in the moment of my reading – as Johannes Zachhuber's rethinking of reception history makes clear.

There are many ways, rhetorically as well as theoretically, to try to bring out this dialogism, this hybridity and density of thought. What I try to do in my essay, in a very, very simplified way, is to perform a back-tracking, nonlinear path of reading that takes me from Rosenzweig to Augustine, from Wolfson to Rosenzweig, and back to Augustine again. . . . Of course, in a way it is just silly for me to say that Rosenzweig is 'perhaps unsurpassed' as an interpreter of Augustine's theory of temporality, as if one could make such a judgement. But the fact is that something like this was my experience: reading Augustine drew me to read other philosophers of time, and in particular reading Wolfson on time sent me to Rosenzweig, where I stayed quite a while before returning to Augustine, feeling I could now read him differently and better; and I could only do this because Wolfson had helped me read Rosenzweig differently and better, so that really my Augustine is as Wolfsonian as he is Rosenzweigian. . . . It seemed to me especially felicitous that I was able to engage three thinkers who have (on my reading) profoundly nonlinear theories of time and non-dualistic understandings of time and eternity, as I attempted *both* to embody textually a nonlinear temporality of reading *and* to explore the implications of this kind of thinking of time for eschatology and for our understanding of the relation of the divine to bodies generally.

I will say too that I am very struck by the complex ways in which the dialogic of *Sprachdenken* (as Rosenzweig names it) configures and reconfigures Jewish and Christian thinking as such: there is tension and also a kind of vitality in the shifting play of identification and alienation – to frame the matter very broadly indeed. Tamsin Jones explores this in her reading of Gregory of Nyssa and Levinas. Readers of Augustine are a particularly interesting case. Augustine is part of the curriculum for Jewish as well as Christian thinkers in early twentieth-century Germany, for example, and there is an interesting chapter in the history of reception to be recounted here, including students of Heidegger such as Jonas and Arendt, younger contemporaries of Rosenzweig. The point, for me, is not merely to recount the history, of course, but also, yes, to renew these 'sources' as 'living speech', as mindful as possible of the ways that they are always already speaking to each other, intersecting along paths that run backwards, sideways, and forward all at once.

Question: It seems that, in reality, every reading performs a nonlinear path of reading – if for no other reason than that is how we all have learned, think and ultimately write. Part of what makes your performance so rich is not only your choice of additional voices, but your awareness of the particular bends and intersections of the various paths. As a result you can acknowledge that every attempt to give a text voice simultaneously steals that voice. Since theft of one sort is inevitable, can you speak to what constitutes responsible theft?

Virginia Burrus: Rosenzweig is an interesting case here: in the line you cite, he speaks of wanting to write the *Star* in the form of 'commentary' on a text that has been placed 'under erasure'. He mentions biblical commentary, but of course the scope of his engagement is much, much greater. Yet there are no annotations and very few writers are even named. He makes only a handful of explicit references to Augustine, in fact, though it seems clear that his debts to Augustine are profound. Is that irresponsible theft? Not to my mind, because the thinking is so engaged and responsive, and the assumption is that thinking is always done in the company of others: what I write is not simply "mine," it is "ours," and who knows how vast the community of readers and thinkers might be?

I suppose that for me, responsible reading is responsive, open, humble, even submissive to the text, but the extremes of submissiveness can also entail a kind of arrogance or ambition. Certainly one senses that with both Augustine and Rosenzweig! If I want to submit to a text, is this so that I can master it? As soon as I have mustered the boldness to interpret a text, to claim its voice, I must also give it back again, humble myself, return to uncertainty, to a kind of muteness.

Question: Part of your intriguing treatment of miracle in Augustine, Rosenzweig and Wolfson has to do with the necessary relationality of revelation – revelation as a type of miracle – in which there is an 'irreducible relationality and thus temporality of divinity, cosmos and humanity' (p. 60). As a result, you remark: 'If time is opened up and not closed by miracle, it is because its finitude is riven by infinitude, its temporality by eternity. This is the site of revelation – eternity irrupting within time's ever-becoming' (p. 61). What does this all mean to a practice of reading? Of reading as engaging/becoming part of the relationality of revelation? What type of site do you want the reading of your reading to become?

Virginia Burrus: I cannot possibly do justice to these challenging questions, but I will give it a try nonetheless. A more deterministic, less open theory of time would correspond with the notion that a single, true, unchanging meaning is harbored in the ancient writings and that we have only to uncover it – whatever that might mean. Such an expectation obviously weighs particularly heavily on biblical or patristic texts that are imbued with the authority of revelation. However, as Augustine argues, revelation inheres in the reading as much as in the writing of a text – or, rather, it necessarily encompasses both. (This is the basis of his affirmation of the authority of the Septuagint alongside the Hebrew "original" of the Bible, as Jerome construes it.) Augustine and Rosenzweig would agree that writing does not signify until it has been read, translated, responded to. The text then becomes a kind of prophecy or promise, its interpretation a miracle of revelatory signification, legible across the weave of time. Both would also agree that interpretation is communal and dialogical – so, yes, relational. The relational moment of reading is intensely temporal not only because it looks backward to the promise secreted in writing, but also because it opens itself to novelty, moving forward, as it were – or perhaps better, moving *beyond*, where what lies beyond is also what lies before, but our sense of that *before* is now transformed. *Eternity* might be a way to point toward the plenitude of such temporalized readings of a text, of all readings of all texts – the excess that ever exceeds our reach.

We can all hope that our best readings open up something new for the reader, while also confirming a promise that was somehow already there in the texts being read; we can hope that our readings become, in some perhaps very modest way, not only the fulfillments of promises but also promises to be fulfilled . . . .It is a lot to hope for, audacious really, but I think it is what we do hope when we venture to read and to write and to think together.

Notes

1 This is a term from David Banon's book, *La lecture infinie. Les voies de l'interprétation midrachique* (Paris: Seuil, 1987). Banon, a French scholar of Midrash, was very influenced by Levinas.

2 See her forthcoming paper in the Proceedings of the 12th International Gregory
   of Nyssa's colloquium, to be published in the *Vigiliae christianae Supplements*,
   Brill. The comparison, at the end of the whole *Contra Eunomium*, of Eunomius
   with Demosthenes is not only a literary joke and a personal attack, but is also a
   final touch to the theological portrait of Eunomius's errors and pretentions, that
   is, an indirectly theological conclusion to the whole refutation.

Bibliography

Anon., *Vita Aesopi Westermanniana*, in *Aesopica. A Series of Texts Relating to Aesop or Ascribed to Him or Closely Connected with the Literary Tradition that Bears his Name. Collected and Critically Edited, in Part Translated from Oriental Languages, with a Commentary and Historical Essay* (B. E. Perry (ed.); Urbana: University of Illinois Press, 1952).

Aristides, Aelius, *Works* (C. A. Behr (trans.); Loeb Classical Library, 458–61; Cambridge, Mass.: Harvard University Press, 1973).

Aristophanes, *Nubes* [Clouds] in *Aristophanes Volume II: Clouds. Wasps. Peace.* (Jeffrey Henderson (trans.); Loeb Classical Library, 488; Cambridge, Mass.: Harvard University Press, 1998).

Aristotle, *Poetica* in *Poetics, Aristotle. On the Sublime, Longinus. On Style, Demetrius.* (Stephen Halliwell, Donald Russell, Doreen C. Innes and W. R. Roberts (trans); Loeb Classical Library, 199; Cambridge, Mass.: Harvard University Press, 1995).

—, *Art of Rhetoric* (J. H. Freese (trans.); Loeb Classical Library, 193; Cambridge, Mass.: Harvard University Press, 1926).

—, *Rhetorica* in *The Rhetoric of Aristotle* (Edward Meredith Cope and John Edwin Sandys (eds); Cambridge: Cambridge University Press, 1877).

Augustine, *Confessions* (James Joseph O'Donnell (ed.); Oxford, New York: Clarendon Press, Oxford University Press, 1992).

—, *Sancti Aurelii Augustini De Civitate Dei Libri I-X* (Corpus Christianorum. Series Latina, 47, 48; Turnhout: Brepols, 1955).

Balthasar, Hans Urs von, *Origen, Spirit and Fire: A Thematic Anthology of His Writings* (Robert J. Daly (trans.); Edinburgh: T & T Clark, 2001).

—, *Presence and Thought: An Essay on the Religious Philosophy of Gregory of Nyssa* (Mark Sebanc (trans.); San Francisco: Ignatius Press, 1995).

—, *Présence et pensée: Essai sur la philosophie religieuse de Grégoire de Nysse* (Paris: Beauchesne, 1988).

—, *The Glory of the Lord: A Theological Aesthetics, 2: Studies in Theological Style: Clerical Styles* (Andrew Louth, Francis McDonagh and Brian McNeil (trans); John Riches (ed.); Edinburgh: T & T Clark, 1985).

Banon, David, *La lecture infinie. Les voies de l'interpretation midrachique* (Paris: Seuil, 1987).

Barth, Karl, *The Epistle to the Romans* (Edwyn C. Hoskyns (trans.); London: Oxford University Press, 1968).

Basil of Caesarea, *Contre Eunome: Suivi de Eunome Apologie / Basile de Césarée* (Bernard Sesboüé, Georges-Matthieu de Durand and Louis Doutreleau (eds); Bernard Sesboüé (trans.); Sources Chrétiennes, 299, 305; Paris: Les Éditions du Cerf, 1982–3).

—, *Homélies sur l'Hexaéméron* (Stanislas Giet (trans.); Sources Chrétiennes, 26 bis; 2nd edn; Paris: Les Éditions du Cerf, 1968).

—, *Saint Basile, Lettres* (Yves Courtonne (ed. and trans.); Paris: Les Belles Lettres, 1957).

—, *Homilia in martyrem Julittam* [Homily on the Martyr Julitta], Patrologia Graeca, 31, 238–262.

—, *Homilies on the Hexameron* (B. Jackson (trans.); Nicene and Post-Nicene Fathers, Series 2, 8; Edinburgh: T & T Clark, 1894).

Bergjan, Silke-Petra, 'Die Beschäftigung mit der alten Kirche an deutschen Universitäten in den Umbrüchen der Aufklärung', in *Zwischen Altertumswissenschaft und Theologie: zur Relevanz der Patristik in Geschichte und Gegenwart* (Christoph Markschies and Johannes van Oort (eds); Leuven: Peeters, 2002).

Bion of Borysthenes, *Bion of Borysthenes: A Collection of the Fragments with Introduction and Commentary* (Jan Fredrik Kindstrand (ed.); Acta Universitatis Upsaliensis, Studia Graeca Upsaliensia, 11; Stockholm: Almqvist and Wiksell International, 1976).

Bombart, Mathilde, *Guez de Balzac et la querelle des Lettres : écriture, polémique et critique dans la France du premier XVIIe siècle* (Lumière Classique, 76; Paris: Honoré Champion, 2007).

Bonhoeffer, Dietrich, *Works*, vol. 12: *Berlin: 1932–1933* (L. Rasmussen (ed.); Minneapolis: Augsburg Fortress Press, 2009), 300.

—, *Act and Being: Transcendental Philosophy and Ontology in Systematic Theology* (Wayne Whitson Floyd Jr. and Hans-Richard Reuter (eds); Martin Lukens-Rumscheidt (trans.); Works, 2; Minneapolis: Augsburg Fortress, 1996).

Boulluec, Alain Le, *La Notion d'hérésie dans la littérature grecque 2e-3e siècles* (Études Augustiniennes, Série Antiquité, 110–111; Paris: Institut d'études Augustiniennes, 1985).

Bowie, Andrew, *Schelling and Modern European Philosophy: An Introduction* (London, New York: Routledge, 1993).

Boyarin, Daniel, 'Midrash', in *Handbook of Postmodern Biblical Interpretation* (A. K. M. Adam (ed.); St Louis: Chalice Press, 2000).

—, *A Radical Jew: Paul and the Politics of Identity* (Contraversions; Berkeley: University of California Press, 1994).

—, *Intertextuality and the Reading of Midrash* (Indiana Studies in Biblical Literature; Bloomington: Indiana University Press, 1990).

Bruaire, Claude, *Le droit de Dieu* (Paris: Aubier-Montaigne, 1974).

—, *Schelling ou la quête du secret de l'être* (Paris: Seghers, 1970).

Budick, S., and Hartman, Geoffrey H., *Midrash and Literature* (New Haven: Yale University Press, 1986).

Burrus, Virginia, 'Augustine and Rosenzweig on the Possibility of Experiencing Miracles', in *Material Spirit* (Carl Good, Manuel Asensi and Gregory Stallings (eds); forthcoming).

—, 'Nothing is Not One: Revisiting the Ex Nihilo', in *Polydoxy: Theology of Multiplicity and Relation* (Laurel Schneider and Catherine Keller (eds); Drew Transdisciplinary Theology Colloquium at Drew Theological School, 2009; New York: Routledge, 2010).

—, 'Carnal excess: flesh at the limits of imagination', *Journal of Early Christian Studies*, 17/2 (2009), 247–65.

Burrus, Virginia, Jordan, Mark D., and MacKendrick, Karmen, *Seducing Augustine: Bodies, Desires, Confessions* (New York: Fordham, 2010).

Caputo, John D., 'Apostles of the Impossible: On God and the Gift in Derrida and Marion', in *God, The Gift, and Postmodernism* (John D. Caputo and Michael J. Scanlon (eds); Bloomington: Indiana University Press, 1999), 185–222.

—, *The Prayers and Tears of Jacques Derrida: Religion without Religion* (Indiana Series in the Philosophy of Religion; Bloomington: Indiana University Press, 1997).

Caputo, John D., and Scanlon, Michael J., *God, The Gift, and Postmodernism* (The Indiana Series in the Philosophy of Religion; Bloomington: Indiana University Press, 1999).Carlson, Thomas A., 'Translator's Introduction', in *The Idol and Distance: Five Studies* (Jean-Luc Marion (ed.); Thomas A. Carlson (trans.); New York: Fordham University Press, 2001).

Cassin, Matthieu, 'L'écriture de la polémique à la fin du IVe siècle : Grégoire de Nysse, *Contre Eunome III*' (Thèse de doctorat; Université Paris IV – Sorbonne, 2009).

—, '"Plumer Isocrate": usage polémique du vocabulaire comique chez Grégoire de Nysse', *Revue des études grecques,* 121 (2008), 783–96.

Choricius of Gaza, *Choricii Gazaei Opera* (Richard Foerster and Eberhard Richtsteig (eds); Bibliteca Scriptorum Graecorum et Romanorum Teubneriana; Stuttgart: Teubner, 1972).

[Cicero], *Rhetorica ad Herennium* [*Rhétorique à Herennius*] (Guy Achard (trans.); Paris: Belles Lettres, 1989).

—, *Rhetorica ad Herennium* (Harry Caplan (trans.); Loeb Classical Library, 403; Cambridge, Mass.: Harvard University Press, 1954).

Cicero, *De Natura Deorum* in *Cicero Volume XIX: On the Nature of the Gods, Academics* (H. Rackham (trans.); Loeb Classical Library, 268; Cambridge, Mass.: Harvard University Press, 1933).

—, *De Legibus* in *Cicero Volume XVI: On the Republic. On the Laws.* (Clinton W. Keyes (trans.); Loeb Classical Library, 213; Cambridge, Mass.: Harvard University Press, 1928).

Ciglia, Francesco Paulo, 'Auf der Spur Augustins: *Confessiones* und *De Civitate Dei* als Quellen des Stern der Erlösung', in *Rosenzweig als Leser: kontextuelle Kommentare zum "Stern der Erlösung"* (Martin Brasser (ed.); Tübingen: Max Niemeyer Verlag, 2004).

—, 'Der gordische Knoten der Zeit: Aspekte des Dialogs zwischen Rosenzweig und Augustin', in *Franz Rosenzweigs "neues Denken": internationaler Kongreß, Kassel 2004* Band I: Selbstbegrenzendes Denken – in philosophos (Wolfdietrich Schmied Kowarzik (ed.); Freiburg, Munich: Karl Alber Verlag, 2004), 323–45.

Clement of Alexandria, *Stromata* [Les Stromates] (Alain Le Boulluec and Marcel Caster (eds); Alain Le Boulluec, Marcel Caster and Pierre Voulet (trans.); Sources Chrétiennes, 30, 38, 278, 279, 428, 446, 463; Paris: Les Éditions du Cerf, 1951–).

—, *Protrepticus* in *The Exhortation to the Greeks. The Rich Man's Salvation. To the Newly Baptized* (G. W. Butterworth (trans.); Loeb Classical Library, 92; Cambridge, Mass.: Harvard University Press, 1919).

Coakley, Sarah, 'Introduction: re-thinking Dionysius the Areopagite', in *Re-Thinking Dionysius the Areopagite* (Sarah Coakley and Charles M. Stang (eds); Oxford: Wiley-Blackwell, 2009), 1-25.

—, 'Does Kenosis Rest on a Mistake? Three Kenotic Models in Patristic Exegesis', in *Exploring Kenotic Christology: The Self-emptying of God* (C. Stephen Evans (ed.); Oxford: Oxford University Press, 2006).

Crouzel, Henri, *Origène et la philosophie* (Paris: Aubier, 1962).

Cunningham, Conor, *Genealogy of Nihilism: Philosophies of Nothing and the Difference of Theology* (Radical Orthodoxy Series; London, New York: Routledge, 2002).

Cupitt, Don, 'Kant and the Negative Theology', in *Is Nothing Sacred? The Non-Realist Philosophy of Religion: Selected Essays* (New York: Fordham University Press, 2002).

Daniélou, Jean, *Origène* (Paris: La Table Ronde, 1948).

Dawson, David, *Christian Figural Reading and the Fashioning of Identity* (Berkeley, London: University of California Press, 2002).

Demosthenes, *Philippics* in *Demosthenes Orations, Volume I* (J. H. Vince (trans.); Loeb Classical Library, 238; Cambridge, Mass.: Harvard University Press, 1930).

Derrida, Jacques, *De quoi demain: dialogue* (Histoire de la Pensée; Paris: Fayard, Galilée, 2001).

—, *Adieu: To Emmanuel Levinas* (Stanford: Stanford University Press, 1999).

—, 'Derrida's Response to Jean-Luc Marion', in *God, the Gift, and Postmodernism* (John. D. Caputo and Michael J. Scanlon (eds.); The Indiana series in the Philosophy of Religion; Bloomington: Indiana University Press, 1999), 42–53.

—, 'Passions', in *On the Name* (Thomas Dutoit (ed.); David Wood (trans.); Stanford: Stanford University Press, 1995), 3–31.

—, 'Sauf le nom (Post-Scriptum)', in *On the Name* (Thomas Dutoit (ed.); John P. Leavey (trans.); Stanford: Stanford University Press, 1995), 35–85.

—, *Aporias: Dying – Awaiting (One Another at) the 'Limits of Truth'* [Mourir – s'attendre aux "limites de la vérité"] (Thomas Dutoit (trans.); Stanford: Stanford University Press, 1993).

—, 'Of an Apocalyptic Tone Newly Adopted in Philosophy', in *Derrida and Negative Theology* (Harold Coward and Toby Foshay (eds); Albany: State University of New York Press, 1992), 25–72.

—, 'How to Avoid Speaking: Denials', in *Derrida and Negative Theology* (Harold Coward and Toby Foshay (eds); Albany: State University of New York Press, 1992), 73–142.

—, 'Différance', *Margins of Philosophy* (Chicago: University of Chicago Press, 1982), 3–27.

—, 'Letter to John P. Leavey', *Semeia* 23 (1982), 61–2.

—, 'From Restricted to General Economy: A Hegelianism without reserve', in *Writing and Difference* [L'écriture et la différence] (Alan Bass (trans.); Chicago: Chicago University Press, 1978), 317–50.

—, 'Violence and Metaphysics: An Essay on the Thought of Emmanuel Levinas', in *Writing and Difference* [L'écriture et la différence] (Alan Bass (ed.); Chicago: Chicago University Press, 1978), 97–192.

Derrida, Jacques and Elisabeth Roudinesco, *For What Tomorrow: A Dialogue* [De quoi demain] (Jeff Fort (trans.); Stanford: Stanford University Press, 2004).

Diekamp, F., 'Literargeschichtliches zu der Eunomianischen Kontroverse', *Byzantinische Zeitschrift* 18 (1909), 1–13.

Dionysius the Areopagite, Pseudo-, *Corpus Dionysiacum, 2: De Coelesti Hierarchia, De Ecclesiastica Hierarchia, De Mystica Theologia, Epistulae* (Adolf Martin Ritter and Günter Heil (eds); Patristische Texte und Studien; Berlin: Walter de Gruyter, 1991).

—, *The Celestial Hierarchy* [De Caelesti Hierarchia] in *Pseudo-Dionysius: The Complete Works* (Colm Luibheid and Paul Rorem (trans); The Classics of Western Spirituality; Mahwah, NJ; London: Paulist Press; SPCK, 1987).

—, *The Divine Names* [De Divinis Nominibus] in *Pseudo-Dionysius: The Complete Works* (Colm Luibheid and Paul Rorem (trans); The Classics of Western Spirituality; Mahwah, NJ; London: Paulist Press; SPCK, 1987).

—, *The Ecclesiastical Hierarchy* [De Ecclesiastica Hierarchia] in *Pseudo-Dionysius: The Complete Works* (Colm Luibheid and Paul Rorem (trans); The Classics of Western Spirituality; Mahwah, NJ; London: Paulist Press; SPCK, 1987).

—, *The Letters* [Epistulae] in *Pseudo-Dionysius: The Complete Works* (Colm Luibheid and Paul Rorem (trans); The Classics of Western Spirituality; Mahwah, NJ; London: Paulist Press; SPCK, 1987).

—, *The Mystical Theology* [De Mystica Theologia] in *Pseudo-Dionysius: The Complete Works* (Colm Luibheid and Paul Rorem (trans); The Classics of Western Spirituality; Mahwah, NJ; London: Paulist Press; SPCK, 1987.

—, *Pseudo-Dionysius: The Complete Works* (Colm Luibheid and Paul Rorem (trans); The Classics of Western Spirituality; Mahwah, NJ; London: Paulist Press; SPCK, 1987).

Douglass, Scot, 'Heidegger and Gregory of Nyssa's *Ad Ablabium: Quod non sint Tres Dei*', in *Gregory of Nyssa's* Opera Minora. *Proceedings of the 11th International Colloquium on Gregory of Nyssa (Tübingen and Freiburg, September, 2008)* (Supplements to Vigiliae Christianae; Leiden, Boston: Brill, forthcoming).

—, *Theology of the Gap: Cappadocian Language Theory and the Trinitarian Controversy* (Theology and Religion; New York: Peter Lang AG, 2005).

Dubarle, Dominique, *Dieu avec l'être: de Parménide à Saint Thomas: essai d'ontologie théologale* (Paris: Beauchesne, 1986).

Edwards, Mark Julian, *Origen against Plato* (Aldershot: Ashgate, 2002).

Eunomius of Cyzicus, and Pottier, Bernard, *Dieu et le Christ selon Grégoire de Nysse: Étude systématique du contre Eunome avec traduction inédite das extraits d'Eunome* (Ouvertures; Namur, Belgium: Culture et Vérité, 1994).

Eunomius, *The Extant Works* (R. P. Vaggione (ed. and trans.); Oxford Early Christian Texts; Oxford: Clarendon Press, 1987).

Fackenheim, Emil L., 'Franz Rosenzweig, his Life and Thought, by Nahum N Glatzer', *Judaism*, 2/4 (1953), 367–72.

Fackenheim, Emil L., and Burbridge, John W., *The God Within: Kant, Schelling and Historicity* (Toronto: University of Toronto Press, 1996).

Failler, A., 'Origine et authenticité des titres dans l'Histoire de Georges Pachymérès', *Revue des études byzantines* 66 (2008), 95–123.

Ford, David F., 'Apophasis and the Shoah: Where was Jesus Christ at Auschwitz?', in *Silence and the Word* (Oliver Davies and Denys Turner (eds); Cambridge: Cambridge University Press, 2002), 185–200.

Frank, Manfred, *Der unendliche Mangel an Sein: Schellings Hegelkritik und die Anfänge der Marxschen Dialektik* (Munich: W. Fink, 1992).

Fredriksen, Paula, 'Secundum Carnem: History and Israel in the Theology of St. Augustine', in *The Limits of Ancient Christianity: Essays on Late Antique Thought in Honor of R. A. Markus* (William E. Klingshirn and Mark Vessey (eds); Ann Arbor: University of Michigan Press, 1999), 26–41.

Fuhrmans, H., *Schellings letzte Philosophie. Die negative und positive Philosophie im Einsatz des Spätidealismus* (Berlin: Junker und Dünnhaupt, 1940).

Funkenstein, Amos, *Perceptions of Jewish History* (Berkeley: University of California Press, 1993).

Gadamer, Hans Georg, *Truth and Method* (2nd rev. edn; Joel Weinsheimer and Donald G. Marshall (eds); London: Sheed & Ward, 1989).

Genette, Gérard, *Seuils* (Paris: Seuil, 1987).

—, *Palimpsestes: la littérature au second degré* (Paris: Seuil, 1982).

Glatzer, Nahum N., *Franz Rosenzweig: His Life and Thought* (Indianapolis: Hackett Publishing Co., 1998).

Golitzin, Alexander, 'Dionysius Areopagita: a Christian mysticism?', *Pro Ecclesia*, 12/2 (03/01/Spring 2003), 161–212.

—, '"A contemplative and a liturgist": Father Georges Florovsky on the Corpus Dionysiacum', *St Vladimir's Theological Quarterly*, 43/2 (1999), 131–61.

—, 'Hierarchy versus anarchy: Dionysius Areopagita, Symeon the New Theologian, and Nicetas Stethatos', *St Vladimir's Theological Quarterly*, 38/2 (1996): 131–79. Republished in *New Perspectives on Historical Theology: Essays in Memory of John Meyendorff* (Bradley Nassif (ed.); Grand Rapids: Eerdmans, 1996), 250–76.

—, *Et Introibo ad Altare Dei: The Mystagogy of Dionysius Areopagita, with Special Reference to its Predecessors in the Eastern Christian Rradition* (Analekta Vlatadôn, 59; Thessalonike: Patriarchikon Hidryma Paterikôn Meletôn, 1994).

—, 'The Mysticism of Dionysius Areopagita: Platonist or Christian?', *Mystics Quarterly*, 19/3 (1993), 98–114.

Gregory of Nyssa, *On the Making of Humankind* (H. A. Wilson (trans.); Nicene and Post-Nicene Fathers Series, 2, V:386–427; Edinburgh: T & T Clark).

—, in *Gregory of Nyssa: Contra Eunomium II: An English Version with Supporting Studies, Proceedings of the 10th International Colloquium on Gregory of Nyssa, (Olomouc, September 15–18, 2004)* (Lenka Karfiková, Scot Doublass and Johannes Zachhuber (eds); S. G. Hall (trans.); Supplements to Vigiliae Christianae; Leiden; Boston: Brill, 2007).

—, *Gregory of Nyssa: The Letters: Introduction, Translation, and Commentary* (Anna Silvas (ed. and trans.); Supplements to Vigiliae Christianae, 83; Boston: Brill, 2007).

—, *Epistulae* in *Opera Ascetica et Epistulae, Volume 2 Epistulae* (Giorgio Pasquali (ed.); Gregorii Nysseni Opera, 8; Leiden: Brill, 1998).

—, *De Deitate Filii et Spiritus Sancti et in Abraham* in *Sermones, Volume 2, Pars III* (Ernestus Rhein and Friedhelm Mann (eds.); Gregorii Nysseni Opera, X/2; Leiden: Brill, 1996).

—, *Homélies sur l'Ecclésiaste / Grégoire de Nysse* (P. Alexander (ed.); Françoise Vinel (trans.); Sources Chrétiennes, 416; Paris: Les Éditions du Cerf, 1996).

—, *Oratio Catechetica* (Ekkehard Mühlenberg (ed.); Gregorii Nysseni Opera, III/4; Leiden: Brill, 1996).

—, *Contra Eunomium I,l-146* (Jürgen-André Röder (trans.); Patrologia, 2; Frankfurt am Main: Peter Lang, 1993).

—, *On Soul and the Resurrection* (Catherine P. Roth (trans.); Crestwood, N.Y.: St Vladimir's Seminary Press, 1993).

—, *De Oratione Dominica* in *Opera Exegetica In Exodum et Novum Testamentum, Volume 2 De Oratione Dominica, De Beatitudinibus* (Johannes F. Callahan (ed.); Gregorii Nysseni Opera, VII/2; Leiden: Brill, 1992).

—, *De vita Moysis* (H. Musurillo (ed.); Gregorii Nysseni Opera, VII:1; Leiden: Brill, 1991).

—, *Lettres. Grégoire de Nysse* (Pierre Maraval (ed. and trans.); Sources Chrétiennes, 363; Paris: Les Éditions du Cerf, 1990).

—, *Contra Eunomium I* (W. Moore (trans.); Nicene and Post-Nicene Fathers, series 2, V; Edinburgh: T & T Clark, 1988).

—, *Contra Eunomium I* (Lucas F. Mateo-Seco and Juan L. Bastero (eds); S. G. Hall (trans.); Colección Teológica, 59; Pamplona: Ediciones Universidad de Navarra, 1988).

—, *Commentary on the Song of Songs* (Casimir McCambley (trans.); Brookline: Holy Cross Press, 1987).

—, *In Canticum Canticorum* (H. Langerbeck (ed.); Gregorii Nysseni Opera, VI; Leiden: Brill, 1986).

—, *On the Three-day Period of the Resurrection of our Lord Jesus Christ* in *The Easter Sermons of Gregory of Nyssa* (Andreas Spira and Christoph Klock (eds); S. G. Hall (trans.); Patristic Monograph Series, 9; Philadelphia: Philadelphia Patristic Foundation, 1981).

—, *The Life of Moses* (Abraham Malherbe and Everett Ferguson (trans); The Classics of Western Spirituality; New York: Paulist Press, 1978).

—, *Ascetical Works* (Virginia Woods Callahan (trans.); Fathers of the Church, 58; Washington, D.C.: Catholic University of America Press, 1967).

—, *Contra Usurarios* in *Sermones, Pars 1* (E. Gebhardt (ed.); Gregorii Nysseni Opera, IX; Leiden: Brill, 1967).

—, *De Tridui Spatio* in *Sermones Pars I* (G. Heil et al. (eds); Gregorii Nysseni Opera, IX; Leiden: Brill, 1967).

—, *In Ecclesiasten Homiliae* in *In Inscriptiones Psalmorum; In Sextum Psalmum; In Ecclesiasten Homiliae* (J. McDonough and P. Alexander (eds); Gregorii Nysseni Opera, V; Leiden: Brill, 1962).

—, *Contra Eunomium I and II* (Werner Jaeger (ed.); Gregorii Nysseni Opera, I; Leiden: Brill, 1960).

—, *Contra Eunomium Libri Pars Altera* (Werner Jaeger (ed.); Gregorii Nysseni Opera, II; Leiden: Brill, 1960).

—, *Contra Eunomium Libri Pars Prior* (Werner Jaeger (ed.); Gregorii Nysseni Opera, I; Leiden: Brill, 1960).

—, *Refutatio Confessionis Eunomii* in *Contra Eunomium Libri Pars Altera* (Werner Jaeger (ed.); Gregorii Nysseni Opera, II; Leiden: Brill, 1960).

—, *The Lord's Prayer, The Beatitudes* (Hilda Graef (trans.); Ancient Christian Writers, 18; Westminster, Md.: Newman Press, 1954).

—, *De Instituto Christiano* in *Opera Ascetica* (W. Jaeger, J. P. Cavarnos and V. W. Callahan (eds); Gregorii Nysseni Opera, VIII/1; Leiden: Brill, 1952).

—, *De Virginitate* in *Opera Ascetica* (W. Jaeger, J. P. Cavarnos and V. W. Callahan (eds.); Gregorii Nysseni Opera, VIII/1; Leiden: Brill, 1952).

—, *De Hominis Opificio* (Patrologia Graeca, 44:125–256).

Griswold, Charles, 'Plato on Rhetoric and Poetry', *Stanford Encyclopedia of Philosophy*, 2008, http://plato.stanford.edu/entries/plato-rhetoric/.

Hadot, Ilsetraut (ed.), *Simplicius, sa vie, son oeuvre, sa survie : actes du colloque international de Paris*, 28 Sept.–1 Oct. 1985 (Peripatoi, 15; Berlin, New York: de Gruyter, 1987).

Handelman, Susan A., *Fragments of Redemption: Jewish Thought and Literary Theory in Benjamin, Scholem and Levinas* (Jewish Literature and Culture; Bloomington: Indiana University Press, 1991).

Hanson, Richard P. C., *Allegory and Event: A Study of the Sources and Significance of Origen's Interpretation of Scripture* (Richmond: John Knox Press, 1959).

Hart, David B., *The Beauty of the Infinite: The Aesthetics of Christian Truth* (Grand Rapids: Eerdmans, 2004).

Heath, Malcolm, 'Porphyry's rhetoric, texts and translation', *Leeds International Classical Studies,* 1/5 (2002), www.leeds.ac.uk/classics/lics/2002/200205.pdf.

Heidegger, Martin, *Kant and the Problem of Metaphysics* (5th edn; Richard Taft (trans.); Bloomington: Indiana University Press, 1997).

—, 'The Origin of the Work of Art (Der Ursprung des Kunstwerkes)', in *Poetry, Language, Thought* (Albert Hofstadter (trans.); New York: Harper Row, 1994).

—, 'Der Ursprung des Kunstwerkes', in *Holzwege* (Gesamtausgabe; Frankfurt am Main: Klostermann, 1994).

—, *Kant und das Problem der Metaphysik* (Gesamtausgabe 3, Klostermann, Frankfurt, 1991).

Hemmerle, Klaus, *Gott und das Denken nach Schellings Spätphilosophie* (Freiburg: Herder, 1968).

Herodotus, *The Histories* (Carolyn Dewald (ed.); Robin Waterfield (trans.); Oxford World's Classics; Oxford: Oxford University Press, 2008).

—, *Historiae* (Haiim B. Rosén (ed.); Bibliotheca Scriptorum Graecorum et Romanorum Teubneriana; Leipzig: Teubner, 1987–1997).

Hoffmann, Philippe, 'Sur quelques aspects de la polémique de Simplicius contre Jean Philopon : de l'invective à la réaffirmation de la transcendance du ciel', in *Simplicius, sa vie, son œuvre, sa survie : actes du colloque international de Paris*, 28 Sept.–1er Oct. 1985 (Ilsetraut Hadot (ed.); Berlin, New York: de Gruyter, 1987), 183–221.

Homer, *Odyssey* (A. T. Murray and George Dimock (trans); Loeb Classical Library, 104–5; Cambridge, Mass.: Harvard University Press, 1919).

Horner, Robyn, *Jean-Luc Marion: A Theo-logical Introduction* (Aldershot: Ashgate, 2005).

Janicaud, D., 'The Theological Turn of French Phenomenology', in *Phenomenology and the 'Theological Turn'. The French Debate* (id. et al. (eds); B. G. Prusak (trans.); New York: Fordham University Press, 2000), 16–103.

John of Scythopolis, 'Scholia', in *John of Scythopolis and the Dionysian Corpus: Annotating the Areopagite* (Paul Rorem and John C. Lamoreaux (eds and trans); Oxford Early Christian Studies; Oxford: Clarendon Press, 1998).

Jones, John N., 'Sculpting God: The Logic of Dionysian Negative Theology', *Harvard Theological Review,* 89/4 (1996), 355–71.

Jones, Tamsin, *A Genealogy of Marion's Philosophy of Religion: Apparent Darkness* (Indiana Series in the Philosophy of Religion; Bloomington: Indiana University Press, 2011).

—, 'Dionysius in Hans Urs von Balthasar and Jean-Luc Marion', in *Re-thinking Dionysius the Areopagite* (S. Coakley and Charles M. Stang (eds); Oxford: Wiley-Blackwell, 2009), 213–24.

— [Tamsin Jones Farmer], 'Revealing the invisible: Gregory of Nyssa on the gift of revelation', *Modern Theology,* 21/1 (2005), 67–85.

Kierkegaard, Søren, *Fear and Trembling* (C. Stephen Evans and Sylvia Walsh (eds); Sylvia Walsh (trans.); Cambridge: Cambridge University Press, 2006).

Kovacs, Judith, 'Servant of Christ and Steward of the Mysteries of God: The Purpose of a Pauline Letter according to Origen's Homilies on 1 Corinthians', in *In Dominico Eloquio. In Lordly Eloquence. Essays on Patristic Exegesis in Honor of Robert Louis Wilken* (Paul M. Blowers et al. (eds); Grand Rapids: Eerdmans, 2002), 157–65.

Lauro, Elizabeth Dively, *The Soul and Spirit of Scripture within Origen's Exegesis* (Boston: Brill, 2005).

Levinas, Emmanuel, *God, Death, and Time* (Bettina Bergo (trans.); Meridian Crossing Aesthetics; Stanford: Stanford University Press, 2000).

—, 'God and Philosophy', in *The Levinas Reader* (Emmanuel Levinas (ed.); Oxford: Basil Blackwell, 1989).

—, *The Levinas Reader* (Sean Hand (trans.); Oxford: Basil Blackwell, 1989).

—, 'Revelation in the Jewish Tradition', in *The Levinas Reader* (Emmanuel Levinas (ed.); Oxford: Basil Blackwell, 1989).

—, *L'au Delà du verset: Lectures et discours talmudiques* (Paris: Éditions de Minuit, 1982).

—, *Révélation* (Bruxelles: Éditions des Facultés Universitaires Saint-Louis, 1977).

—, *Autrement qu'être ou au-delà de l'essence* (The Hague: Nijhoff, 1974).

—, *Totality and Infinity. An Essay in Exteriority* (Alphonso Lingis (trans.); Pittsburgh: Duquesne University Press, 1969).

Libanius, *Orations (Discours)* (Jean Martin (ed.); Paul Petit (trans.); Paris: Les Belles Lettres, 1979).

—, *Progymnasmata* (Richard Foerster (ed.); Libanii Opera, 8; Bibliotheca Scriptorum Graecorum et Romanorum Teubneriana; Leipzig: Teubner, 1903–27).

Liddell, H. G. and R. Scott, *Greek English Lexicon* (Oxford: Clarendon Press, 1996).

Longinus, *De Sublimitate* in *Poetics, Aristotle. On the Sublime, Longinus. On Style, Demetrius.* (Stephen Halliwell, Donald Russell, Doreen C. Innes and W. R. Roberts (trans); Loeb Classical Library, 199; Cambridge, Mass.: Harvard University Press, 1995).

López, Antonio, *Spirit's Gift: The Metaphysical Insight of Claude Bruaire* (Washington, D.C.: Catholic University of America Press, 2006).

Louth, Andrew, *Denys the Areopagite* (Outstanding Christian Thinkers Series; London: Continuum, 2002).

—, *The Origins of the Christian Mystical Tradition* (Oxford: Oxford University Press, 1981).

Lubac, Henri de, *Histoire et Esprit: L'intelligence de l'Écriture d'après Origène* (Paris: Aubier, 1950).

Lucian, *Necyomancia sive Menippus* in *Luciani Opera* (M. D. MacLeod (ed.); Oxford: Clarendon Press, 1972).

Ludlow, Morwenna, 'Spirit and Letter in Origen and Augustine', in *Spirit and Letter; Letter and Spirit* (Günter Bader and Paul Fiddes (eds); Edinburgh: T & T Clark, forthcoming).

—, 'Divine Infinity and Eschatology: The Limits and Dynamics of Human Knowledge according to Gregory of Nyssa (CE II:67–170)', in *Gregory of Nyssa: Contra Eunomium II: An English Version with Supporting Studies, Proceedings of the 10th International Colloquium on Gregory of Nyssa, (Olomouc, September 15-18, 2004)* (Karfíková, et. al (eds); Supplements to Vigiliae Christianae; Leiden; Boston: Brill, 2007), 217–37.

—, *Gregory of Nyssa, Ancient and (Post)modern* (Oxford: Oxford University Press, 2007).

—, 'The Task of Theology is Never Finished': John Macquarrie and Karl Rahner on the Challenges and Limits of Doing Theology', in *In Search of Humanity and Deity* (London: SCM, 2006), 117–26.

—, 'Theology and allegory: Origen and Gregory of Nyssa on the unity and diversity of Scripture', *International Journal of Systematic Theology*, 4/1 (2002), 45–66.

—, *Universal Salvation: Eschatology in the Thought of Gregory of Nyssa and Karl Rahner* (Oxford: Clarendon Press, 2000).

Luther, Martin, *Lectures on Genesis* in *Martin Luthers Werke: Kritische Gesamtausgabe* (WA) (Weimar: H. Böhlaus Nachfolger, 1883–), vol. 43; English Translation: *Luther's Works* (J. Pelikan et al. (eds); St Louis, Mo.: Concordia Publishing House, 1955–1986), vol. 4.

—, 'The Babylonian Captivity', in *Luther's Works*, vol.36: *Word and Sacrament II* (Abdel Ross Wentz (ed.); Philadelphia: Fortress Press, 1959).

Macarios of Magnesia, *Le Monogénès. Macarios de Magnésie* (Richard Goulet (ed. and trans.); Textes et Traditions, 383, 444; Paris: J. Vrin, 2003).

Marion, Jean-Luc, *The Crossing of the Visible* [La croisée du visible] (James K. A. Smith (trans.); Stanford: Stanford University Press, 2004).

—, *Being Given: Towards a Phenomenology of Givenness* (Jeffrey L. Kosky (trans.); Palo Alto: Stanford University Press, 2002).

—, *In excess: Studies of Saturated Phenomena* (Robyn Horner and Vincent Berraud (trans); Perspectives in Continental Philosophy; New York: Fordham University Press, 2002).

—, *The Idol and Distance: Five Studies* (Thomas A. Carlson (trans.); New York: Fordham University Press, 2001).

—, 'In the Name: How to Avoid Speaking of "Negative Theology"', in *God, the Gift, and Postmodernism* (John D. Caputo and Michael J. Scanlon (eds); Bloomington: Indiana University Press, 1999), 20–53.

—, *Reduction and Givenness: Investigations of Husserl, Heidegger, and Phenomenology* (Northwestern University Studies in Phenomenology and Existential Philosophy; Evanston, Ill.: Northwestern University Press, 1998).

—, *God Without Being: Hors-texte* (Thomas A. Carlson (trans.); Studies in Religion and Postmodernism; Chicago: University of Chicago Press, 1991).

—, *La croisée du visible* (Paris: La Différence, 1991).

McGinn, Bernard, 'Vere tu es Deus Absconditus: The Hidden God in Luther and Some Mystics', in *Silence and the Word* (Oliver Davies and Denys Turner (eds); Cambridge: Cambridge University Press, 2002), 94–114.

Merkelbach, R., 'Der neue Euphranor in Bargylia und Euphranor, der Admiral von Caesars rhodischem Geschwader', *Epigraphica Anatolica* 1(1981), 29–32.

Mooney, T., 'Hubris und Humility: Husserl's Reduction and Givenness', in *Givenness and God: Questions of Jean-Luc Marion* (Ian Leask and Eoin Cassidy (eds); New York: Fordham University Press, 2005).

Mühlenberg, Ekkehard, *Die Unendlichkeit Gottes bei Gregor von Nysse: Gregors Kritik am Gottesbegriff der klassischen Metaphysik* (Göttingen: Vanderhoek & Ruprecht, 1966).

Newheiser, David, 'Ambivalence in Dionysius the Areopagite: The Limitations of a Liturgical Reading', in *Studia Patristica* XVLIII (Jane Baun, Averil Cameron and Mark Julian Edwards (eds); Leuven: Peeters, 2010), 211–16.

Nicephor Gregoras, *Antirrhetika I* (Hans V. Beyer (ed. and trans.); Wiener Byzantinische Studien, 12; Vienna: Österreichischen Akademie der Wissenschaften, 1976).

Nicetas of Heraclea, *Synagôgê Paterôn eis to kata Loukan Euangelion* (Christou Th. Krikônê (ed.); Vyzantina keimena kai meletai, 9; Thessalonike: Kentron Vyzantinou Ereunôn, 1973).

Noble, Ivana, 'The Apophatic Way in Gregory of Nyssa', in *Philosophical Hermeneutics and Biblical Exegesis* (Petr Pokorny (ed.); Tübingen: Mohr Siebeck, 2002).

Nygren, Anders, *Agape and Eros* (London: SPCK, 1983).

Oakes, Edward T., *Pattern of Redemption: the Theology of Hans Urs von Balthasar* (New York: Continuum, 1994).

Ojell, Ari, 'Service or Master? "Theology" in Gregory of Nyssa's Contra Eunomium II', in *Gregory of Nyssa: Contra Eunomium II: An English version With Supporting Studies, Proceedings of the 10th International Colloquium on Gregory of Nyssa (Olomouc, September 15–18, 2004)* (Leiden, Boston: Brill, 2007), 473–84.

Origen, *Vier Bücher von den Prinzipien / Origenes* [*De Principiis*, German and Latin with Greek fragments] (Herwig Görgemanns and Heinrich Karpp (eds); Texte zur Forschung, 24; Darmstadt: Wissenschaftliche Buchgesellschaft, 1976).

—, *Commentarius in Evangelium Ioannis (Commentaire sur Saint Jean par Origène)* (Cécile Blanc (ed. and trans.); Sources Chrétiennes, 120, 157; Paris: Les Éditions du Cerf, 1964).

—, *On First Principles* [De Principiis] (G.W. Butterworth (trans.); London: SPCK, 1936).

—, *Homiliae in Leviticum* [Homilies on Leviticus] in *Origenes Werke*, vol. 6 (W. A. Baehrens (ed.); *Die Griechischen Christlichen Schriftsteller*, 29; Leipzig: Teubner, 1920).

—, *Commentary on John* (Allan Menzies (trans.); Ante-Nicene Fathers, IX; Edinburgh: T & T Clark, 1897).

Ovid, *Metamorphoses* (Frank Justus Miller and G. P. Goold (trans); Loeb Classical Library, 42–3; Cambridge, Mass.: Harvard University Press, 1916).

Papavasileiou, A. N., *Euthymios-Iōannēs Zygadenōs: Vios, Syngraphai* (Leukōsia: Papavasileiou, 1979).

Pasquali, Giorgio, 'Le lettere di Gregorio di Nissa', *Studi italiani di filologia classica*, n.s. 3 (1923), 75–136.

Pelikan, Jaroslav, 'The Odyssey of Dionysian Spirituality', in *Pseudo-Dionysius: The Complete Works* (Colm Luibheid and Paul Rorem (eds); The Classics of Western Spirituality; Mahwah, N.J., London: Paulist Press, SPCK, 1987), 11–32.

Peter of Callinicus, Patriarch of Antioch, *Petri Callinicensis Patriarchae Antiocheni Tractatus contra Damianum II–III* (Rifaat Y. Ebied, Lionel R. Wickham and Albert van Roey (eds); Corpus Christianorum Series Graeca, 29, 32, 35, 54; Belgium, Brepols, Leuven: Leuven University Press, 1994–2003).

Petrarch, *Selections from the Canzoniere and Other Works* (Oxford World's Classics; Oxford: Oxford University Press, 1985).

Philostratus, *Vitae Sophistarum (Lives of the Sophists) / Flavius Philostratus* (C. L. Kayser (ed.); Hildesheim, N.Y.: G. Olms, 1971).

—, *Vitae Sophistarum (Lives of the Sophists)* in *Philostratus Volume IV: Lives of the Sophists. Eunapius: Lives of the Philosophers and Sophists* (Wilmer C. Wright (trans.); Loeb Classical Library, 134; Cambridge, Mass.: Harvard University Press, 1921).

Plato, *Phaedrus* (Harold North Fowler (trans.); Loeb Classical Library, 36; Cambridge, Mass.: Harvard University Press, 1930–5).

—, *Republic* (Paul Shorey (trans.); Loeb Classical Library, 237, 276; Cambridge, Mass.: Harvard University Press, 1930–5).

—, *Timaeus* in *Timaeus. Critias. Cleitophon. Menexenus. Epistles.* (R. G. Bury (trans.); Loeb Classical Library, 234; Cambridge, Mass.: Harvard University Press, 1929).

—, *Leges* [Laws] (R. G. Bury (trans.); Loeb Classical Library, 187, 192; Cambridge, Mass.: Harvard University Press, 1926).

—, *Symposium* (W. R. M. Lamb (trans.); Loeb Classical Library, 166; Cambridge, Mass.: Harvard University Press, 1925).

—, *Apologia Socratis* in *Plato Volume I: Euthyphro. Apology. Crito. Phaedo. Phaedrus.* (Harold North Fowler (trans.); Loeb Classical Library, 36; Cambridge, Mass.: Harvard University Press, 1914).

Plutarch, *Adversus Colotem* [Reply to Colotes in Defence of the Other Philosophers] in *Moralia, Volume XIV* (Benedict Einarson and Phillip H. De Lacy (trans); Loeb Classical Library, 428; Cambridge, Mass.: Harvard University Press, 1967).

—, *Amatorius* [Dialogue on Love] in *Plutarch Moralia, Volume IX: Table-Talk, Books 7–9. Dialogue on Love* (Edwin L. Minar Jr., F. H. Sandbach and W. C. Helmbold (trans); Loeb Classical Library, 425; Cambridge, Mass.: Harvard University Press, 1965).

—, *De Vitioso Pudore* [On compliancy] in *Plutarch Moralia, Volume VII* (Phillip H. de Lacy and Benedict Einarson (trans); Loeb Classical Library; Cambridge, Mass.: Harvard University Press, 1959).

—, *Quaestiones Convivales VII* in *Plutarch Moralia, Volume IX: Table-Talk, Books 7–9, Dialogue on Love* (Edwin L. Minar Jr., F. H. Sandbach and W. C. Helmbold (trans); Loeb Classical Library, 425; Cambridge, Mass.: Harvard University Press, 1959).

—, *De Garrulitate* [On Talkativeness] in *Plutarch Moralia, Volume VI* (W. C. Helmbold (trans.); Loeb Classical Library, 337; Cambridge, Mass.: Harvard University Press, 1939).

—, *De Pythiae Oraculis* [The Oracles at Delphi No Longer Given in Verse] in *Plutarch Moralia, Volume V* (Frank Cole Babbitt (trans.); Loeb Classical Library, 306; Cambridge, Mass.: Harvard University Press, 1936).

—, *De Tuenda Sanitate Praecepta* [Advice on Keeping Well] in *Plutarch Moralia, Volume II* (F. C. Babbitt (trans.); Loeb Classical Library, 222; Cambridge, Mass.: Harvard University Press, 1928).

Pottier, Bernard, *Dieu et le Christ selon Grégoire de Nysse: Étude systématique du contre Eunome avec traduction inédite das extraits d'Eunome* (Ouvertures; Namur, Belgium: Culture et Vérité, 1994).

Proclus, *In Platonis Parmenidem* in *Procli Philosophi Platonici Opera Inedita* (Victor Cousin (ed.); Frankfurt am Main: Minerva, 1962 [Paris, 1864]).

Quintilian, *Institutio Oratoria* [The Orator's Education] (Donald Russell (trans.) Cambridge, Mass.; London: Harvard University Press, 2001).

Rensch, B., 'Theologie, Negative', in *Historisches Wörterbuch der Philosophie* Volume 10 (Joachim Ritter et al. (eds); Basel: Schwabe, 1998), 1102–5.

Ricœur, Paul, 'Le symbole donne à penser', *Esprit* 27/7-8 (1959).

—, *Philosophie de la volonté* Volume 2 (Paris: Aubier, [1949]–1960).

Robert, Louis, 'Une épigramme satirique d'Automédon et Athènes au début de l'empire', *Revue des études grecques*, 94 (1981), 338–61.

Rorem, Paul, *Pseudo-Dionysius: A Commentary on the Texts and an Introduction to their Influence* (New York: Oxford University Press, 1993).

Rosenzweig, Franz, *The Star of Redemption* (Barbara E. Galli (trans.); Madison: University of Wisconsin Press, 2005).

—, *The New Thinking* (Alan Udoff and Barbara E. Galli (trans); Syracuse, N.Y.: Syracuse University Press, 1999).

—, *Der Stern der Erlösung* (3rd edn; Heidelberg: Lambert Schneider, 1954).

—, *Briefe* (Edith Rosenzweig (trans. and ed.); Berlin: Schocken Verlag, 1935).

Rowe, C. J., *Plato and the Art of Philosophical Writing* (Cambridge, UK; New York: Cambridge University Press, 2007).

Rubenstein, Mary-Jane, 'Dionysius, Derrida, and the critique of "ontotheology"', *Modern Theology*, 24/4 (2008), 725–41.

Saenger, Paul, *Space between Words: The Origins of Silent Reading* (Stanford: Stanford University Press, 1997).

Saffrey, Henri-Dominique, 'New Objective Links between the Pseudo-Dionysius and Proclus', in *Neoplatonism and Christian Thought* (Dominic J. O'Meara (ed.); Albany: State University of New York Press, 1982), 64–74.

—, 'Homo Bulla: une image épicurienne chez Grégoire de Nysse', *Epektasis. Mélanges patristiques offerts au cardinal Jean Daniélou* (Jacques Fontaine and Charles Kannengiesser (eds); Paris: Beauchesne, 1972), 533–44.

Samuelson, Norbert Max, 'Halevi and Rosenzweig on Miracles', in *Approaches to Judaism in Medieval Times* (David R. Blumenthal (ed.); Chico, Calif: Scholars Press, 1984), 157–73.

Santner, Eric L., 'Miracles Happen: Benjamin, Rosenzweig, Freud and the Matter of the Neighbor', in *The Neighbor: Three Inquiries in Political Theology* (Slavoj Žižek, Eric L. Santner and Kenneth Reinhard (eds); Chicago: Chicago University Press, 2005).

Schelling, Friedrich Wilhelm Joseph, 'Die Weltalter (1814?)', in *Friedrich Wilhelm Joseph von Schellings sämmtliche Werke* Volume 13 (Karl Friedrich August Schelling (ed.); Stuttgart: J. G. Cotta, 1856–1861).

—, 'Philosophie der Mythologie', in *Friedrich Wilhelm Joseph von Schellings sämmtliche Werke* (Karl Friedrich August Schelling (ed.); Stuttgart: J. G. Cotta, 1856–1861).

Schleiermacher, Friedrich, *Hermeneutics and Criticism: And Other Writings* (Andrew Bowie (trans. and ed.); Cambridge: Cambridge University Press, 2008).

Stern, David H., *Midrash and Theory: Ancient Jewish Exegesis and Contemporary Literary Studies* (Rethinking Theory; Evanston, Ill.: Northwestern University Press, 1996).

Theodore Dexios, *Theodori Dexii Opera Omnia* (Ioannis D. Polemis (ed.); Corpus Christianorum Series Graeca, 55; Turnhout; Leuven: Brepols; Leuven University Press, 2003).

Tilliette, Xavier, *Schelling: une philosophie en devenir* (Paris: J. Vrij, 1970).

Torjesen, Karen Jo, 'The Rhetoric of the Literal Sense. Changing Strategies of Persuasion from Origen to Jerome', in *Origeniana Septima. Origenes in den Auseinandersetzungen des 4. Jahrhunderts* (W. A. Bienert and U. Kühneweg (eds); Bibliotheca Ephemeridum Theologicarum Lovaniensium, 137; Leuven: University Press/Uitgeverij Peeters, 1999).

—, 'Influence of Rhetoric on Origen's Old Testament Homilies', in *Origeniana Sexta. Origène et la Bible / Origen and the Bible. Actes du Colloquium Origenianum Sextum Chantilly, 30 août - 3 septembre 1993* (Gilles Dorival and Alain Le Boulluec et al. (eds); Bibliotheca Ephemeridum Theologicarum Lovaniensium, 118; Leuven: University Press/Uitgeverij Peeters, 1995).

—, *Hermeneutical Procedure and Theological Method in Origen's Exegesis* (Patristische Texte und Studien; Berlin: Walter de Gruyter, 1986).

Turner, Denys, 'How to read the Pseudo-Denys today?', *International Journal of Systematic Theology*, 7/4 (2005), 428–40.

—, *The Darkness of God: Negativity in Christian Mysticism* (Cambridge: Cambridge University Press, 1995).

Vanneste, Jan, 'Is the mysticism of Pseudo-Dionysius genuine?', *International Philosophical Quarterly*, 3/2 (May 1963), 286–306.

Wallraff, M., 'Il "Sinodo de tutte le eresie" a Costantinopoli (383)', in *Vescovi e pastori in epoca teodosiana: in occasione del 16 centenario de la consecrazione episcopale di S Agostino, 396–1996: 25 incontro di studiosi dell 'antichità cristiana, Roma, 8–11 maggio 1996, vol.2* (Studia Ephemeridis Augustinianum, 58; Roma, 1998): 271–9.

Wickert, Jacob, 'Die Panoplia dogmatica des Euthymios Zygabenos. Untersuchung ihrer Anlage und ihrer Quellen, ihres Inhaltes und ihrer Bedeutung', *Oriens Christianus*, 8 (1908), 278–388.

Wolfson, Elliot R., 'Light Does not Talk but Shines: Apophasis and Vision in Rosenzweig's Theopoetic Temporality', in *New Directions in Jewish Philosophy* (Elliot R. Wolfson and Aaron W. Hughes (eds); Bloomington: Indiana University Press, 2010), 87–148.

—, *Open Secret: Postmessianic Messianism and the Mystical Revision of Menaḥem Mendel Schneerson* (New York: Columbia University Press, 2009).

—, *Alef, Mem, Tau: Kabbalistic Musings on Time, Truth, and Death* (The Taubman Lectures in Jewish Studies; Berkeley: University of California Press, 2006).

—, *Venturing Beyond: Law and Morality in Kabbalistic Mysticism* (Oxford: Oxford University Press, 2006).

—, 'Introduction to Barbara Galli's Translation of Rosenzweig's Star', *The Star of Redemption* (Madison: University of Wisconsin Press, 2005), xvii–xx.

—, *Language, Eros, Being: Kabbalistic Hermeneutics and Poetic Imagination* (New York: Fordham University Press, 2005).

—, 'Facing the effaced: mystical eschatology and the idealistic orientation in the thought of Franz Rosenzweig', *Zeitschrift für neuere Theologiegeschichte*, 4/1 (1997), 39–81.

Xenophon, *Memorabilia* in *Xenophon Volume IV: Memorabilia. Oeconomicus. Symposium. Apology.* (E. C. Marchant and O. J. Todd (trans); Loeb Classical Library, 168; Cambridge, Mass.: Harvard University Press, 1923).

Young, Frances, *Biblical Exegesis and the Formation of Christian Culture* (Cambridge: Cambridge University Press, 1997).

Zenobius in *Paroemiographi Graeci* (E. L. Leutsch and F. G. Schneidewin (eds); Göttingen: Vandenhoeck et Ruprecht, 1839–1851).

INDEX